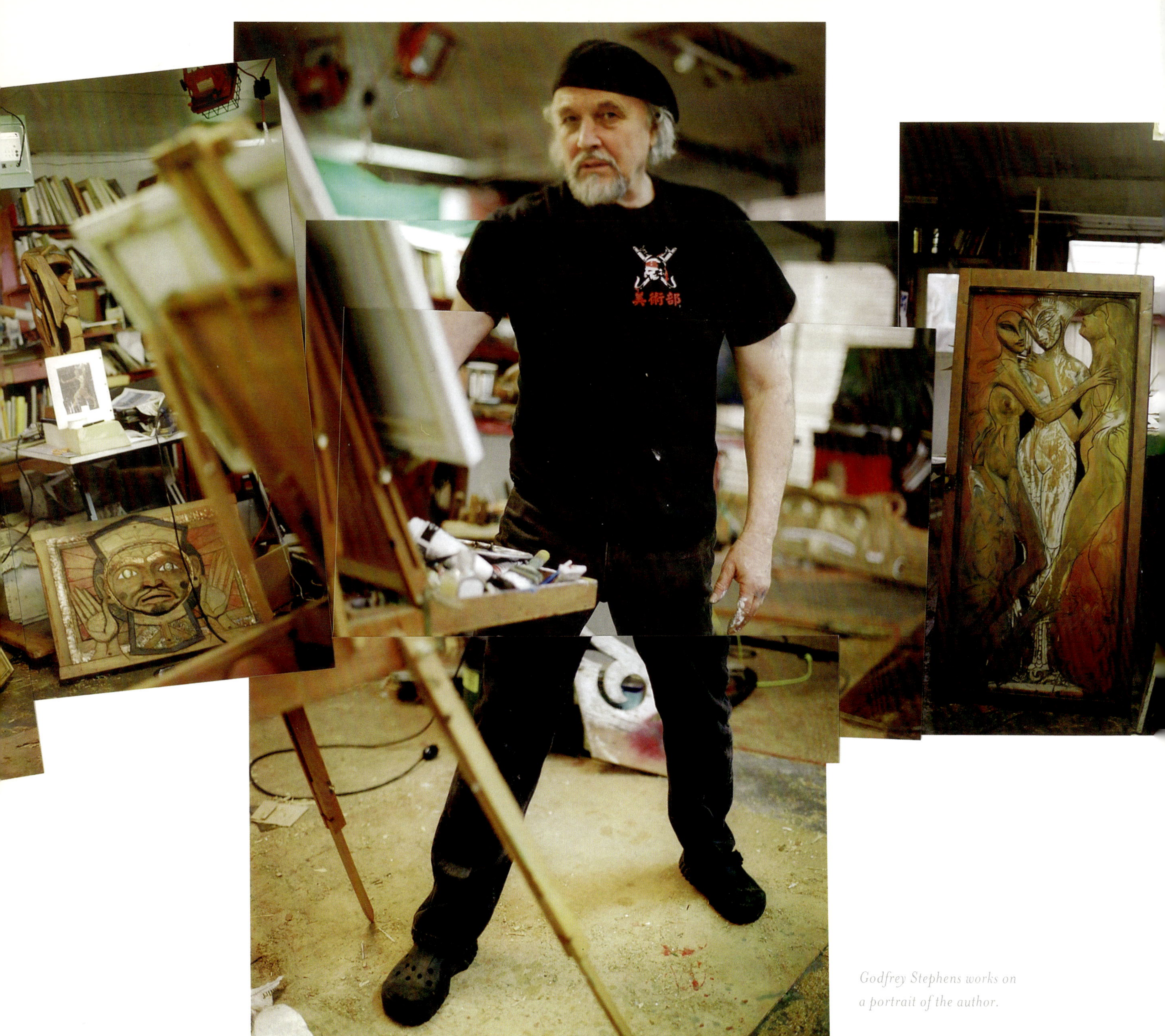

Godfrey Stephens works on a portrait of the author.

ARTISTS IN THEIR STUDIOS

WHERE ART IS BORN ✖ ROBERT AMOS

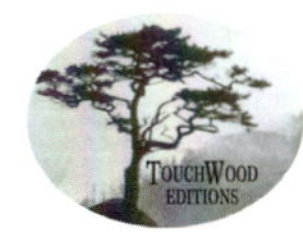

VICTORIA ✖ VANCOUVER ✖ CALGARY

TO MY WIFE, SARAH

First edition

TouchWood Editions
#108–17665 66A Avenue
Surrey, BC V3S 2A7
www.touchwoodeditions.com

LIBRARY AND ARCHIVES CANADA CATALOGUING IN PUBLICATION

Amos, Robert, 1950–
Artists in their studios: where art is born / Robert Amos.

ISBN 978-1-894898-58-4

1. Artists—British Columbia—Vancouver Island—Biography. 2. Artists—British Columbia—Gulf Islands—Biography. 3. Artists' studios—British Columbia—Vancouver Island. 4. Artists' studios—British Columbia—Gulf Islands. 5. Art, Canadian—British Columbia—Vancouver Island. 6. Art, Canadian—British Columbia—Gulf Islands. I. Title.

N6548.A56 2007 709.711'2 C2007-903953-7

Edited by Marlyn Horsdal
Proofread by Marial Shea
Book design and layout by Jacqui Thomas
Photographs of original art courtesy of the artists; other interior photos by Robert Amos unless stated otherwise.
Front- and back-cover photos by Robert Amos. Front-flap photo by Darren Stone.

Printed in Hong Kong

TouchWood Editions acknowledges the financial support for its publishing program from the Government of Canada through the Book Publishing Industry Development Program (BPIDP), Canada Council for the Arts, and the province of British Columbia through the British Columbia Arts Council and the Book Publishing Tax Credit.

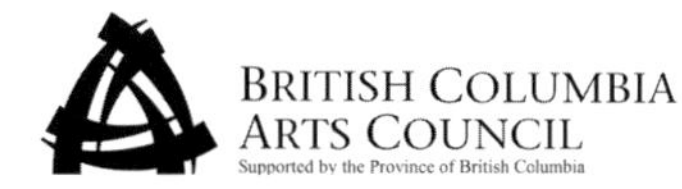

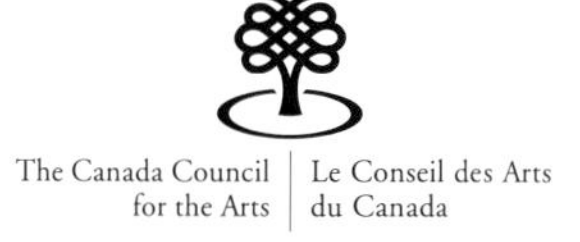

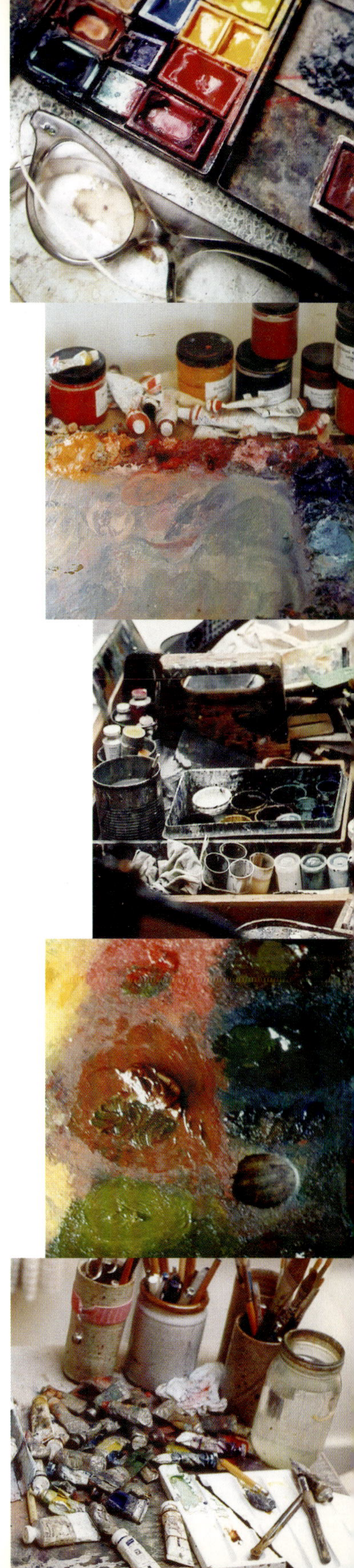

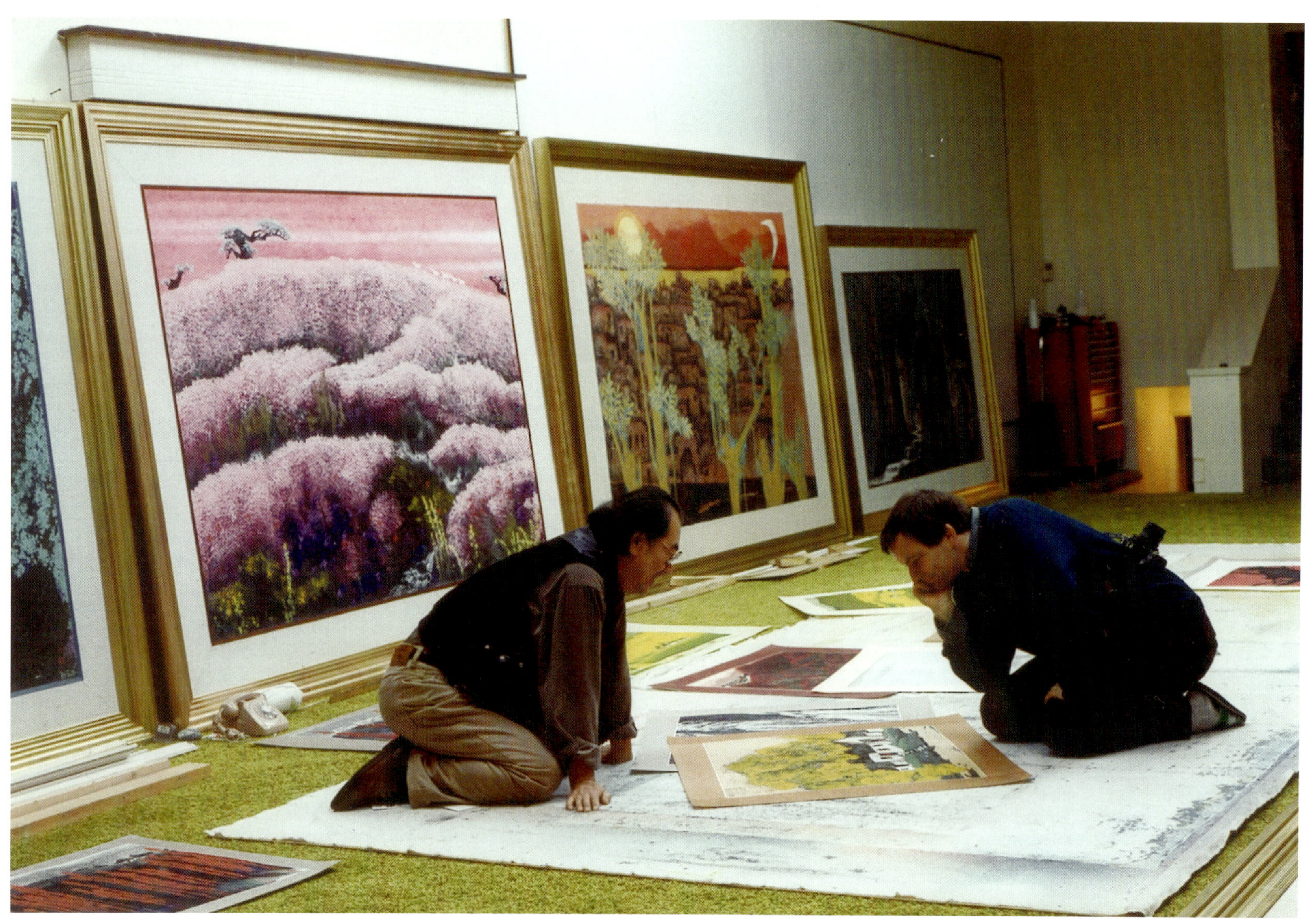

Zhang Bu and Robert Amos, 1996.

INTRODUCTION

I invite you to join me as I visit the studios of some of the most famous and interesting artists on Vancouver Island and the Gulf Islands. This book grew from the experience of writing my newspaper column, "On Art," which has appeared in the Victoria *Times Colonist* weekly since 1986.

Interviews with artists are always engaging to me, and often take place in the studio or workshop of the artist concerned. As a painter myself, I am always keen to understand something of another artist's technique and philosophy. Whether it is an architect-designed haven or a converted farm shed, every studio becomes a purpose-built "machine" for creating artworks.

During an afternoon spent with an artist I always take in a lot more information than I can write down in the 800 words my column allows. I have a sense that I am in the presence of history-in-the-making. At some point, and for my own purposes, I decided to make photographs—not of the artworks or the artist, but of the studio itself.

My style of photocollage involves a mosaic of photographed images, pasted onto cardboard and worked over with paint. This approach developed in conjunction with my work as a painter. Often, when taking photographs as a reference for a complex image, I found myself forced into close proximity to the subject. I'd pan up and down, back and forth over the field of my vision, clicking away with the camera until I'd covered everything of interest. The resulting panoramas are always irregular in shape, and it's often a mystery to me what form the image will take. When the prints come back from the photo lab I paste them together and then, using watercolours and acrylic paints, I paint in the missing parts over and around the photos.

All of the photography was done with an old-fashioned Contax SLR camera with a 35-mm lens, using 200 ASA film with available light and no tripod. I realize that with fisheye lenses, digital cameras, "stitch" programs and other technical fixes I could easily get a smoother image, but I think my way of working results in a very appealing image.

In 2005 the features editor at the *Times Colonist*, Carolyn Heiman, discovered my studio portraits and, with the encouragement of the editor-in-chief, Lucinda Chodan, two of these photocollages were published in the newspaper. I am grateful for the support of the *Times Colonist*. Shortly after the pictures began to appear, to my delight the publisher of TouchWood Editions, Pat Touchie, proposed the idea of this book to me.

It has been a daunting task to write stories about and make photos of the artists I admire. Some of my subjects were gone before I made my photographs (Emily Carr, Maxwell Bates). Others have departed since my visit (Geoffrey Rock, E. J. Hughes, Harry Heine, Myfanwy Pavelic). And many are very advanced in age. As I worked on this book, I became aware of the passage of the years and the preciousness of our short time here. Meeting these artists has been a gift, and I am grateful to those who appear in these pages.

Any errors or omissions in this project are undoubtedly my own. Throughout, I have been aware of the many worthy artists whose stories and workspaces are not in this volume and I hope to include them in future projects.

In particular I would like to thank the Seaview Foundation, whose support and encouragement allowed me to bring this project to fruition.

ROBERT AMOS — *June 2007*

ROBERT BATEMAN

SALT SPRING ISLAND

ON AN OVERCAST SALT SPRING ISLAND MORNING, THE ARTIST MET ME OUTSIDE HIS STUDIO DOOR WITH HAND EXTENDED: "BOB BATEMAN," HE SAID BY WAY OF INTRODUCTION.

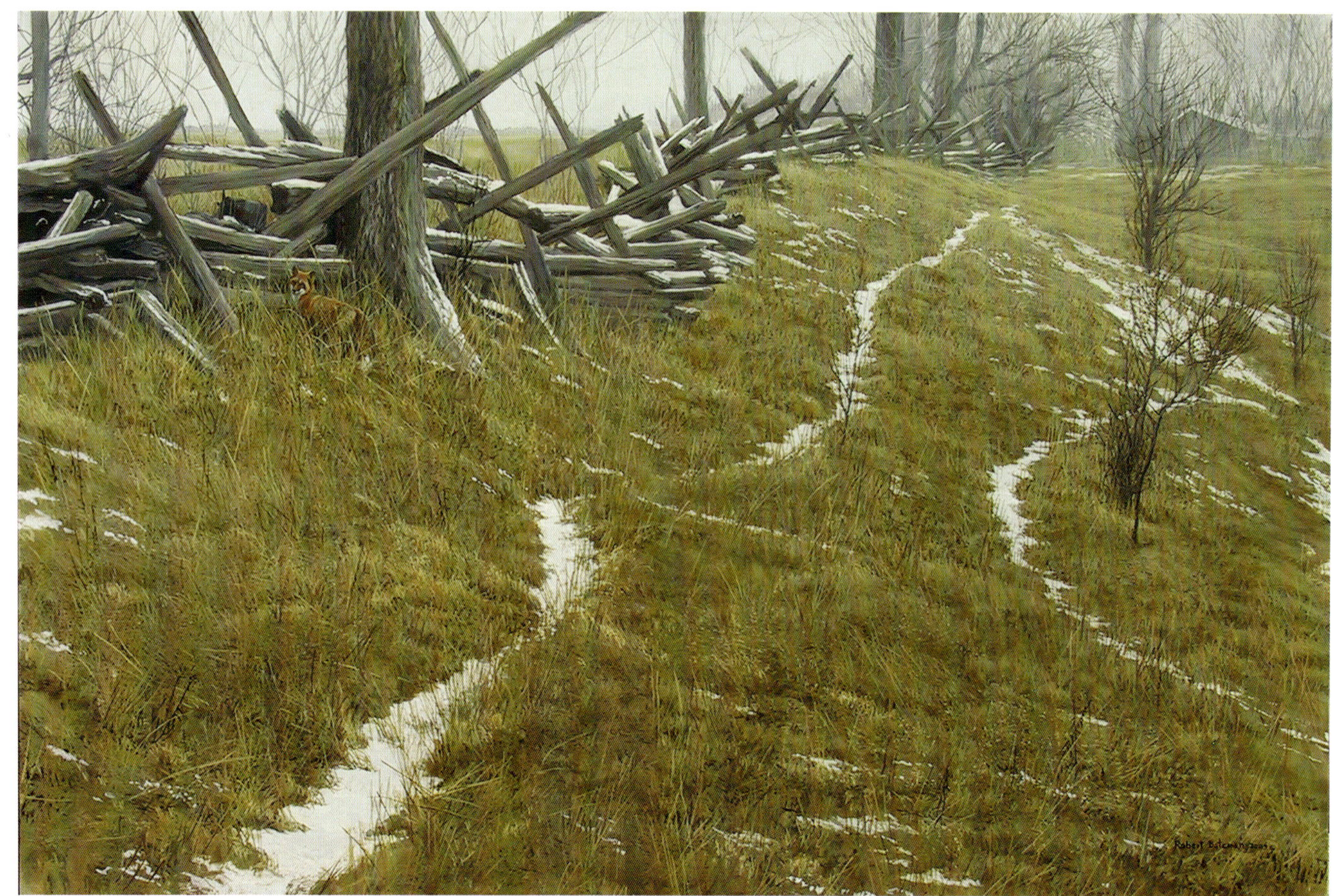

PASTURE TRAILS —RED FOX, *Robert Bateman, acrylic on canvas, 24 x 26 inches, 2003.*

We swept past the garden glade and into the hive of activity that is his studio. Bateman was not alone. Alex Fischer, the self-described "dragon at the gate," controlled the nerve centre; Kate Carson's desk in the corner was business-like; Birgit Freybe Bateman, Robert's wife, hovered over a series of her colour photographs, some of which were recently published by *National Geographic*. Clearly, the world of Robert Bateman is a group undertaking.

A high-school teacher until the age of 46, Bateman could hardly restrain his instinct to show me his world. I had come to see a collection of his paintings—virtually everything he had done in the past three years—which would shortly be sent to a gallery in Santa Fe, New Mexico.

"We'll start with the smallest," he began, and propped a masonite panel onto the easel. It was a picture of a wee mouse slipping down a branch, a design that clearly owed something to Japanese art. Bateman is a practised show-man and, after some comments, he set the first painting onto the floor beside him. It was replaced by a slightly larger one, a grey fox, silhouetted in sunlight against a greystone canyon wall.

Robert Bateman is the leading wildlife artist in the world. Because of his fame and success, there is a tendency to judge his work and his opinions with unrelenting criticism. Yet I confess that, after two hours in his studio, his skills, his philosophy and his personality disarmed me completely. He is a hard-working painter, creating pictures that mean a lot to him.

Another panel appeared on the easel—a blue thrush posed against an ancient adobe wall. Bateman took delight in revealing his methods.

"That bird wasn't there," he noted, "and the wall wasn't blue." In fact, it was a thrush of a different species that he brought out of his freezer to model for the subject. And as for the photographs, he's not coy. "I use from five to 50 photographs on the average painting," he explained.

There are many who disparage the "photo-realism" of which he is a master. But that's not what makes his art so effective. "The essence of art is a sense of mystery," he offered, quoting Hermann Hesse. By now the pile of paintings on the floor beside him must have been valued at a million dollars. But, to the man who made them, the pictures were rough and ready and sufficiently durable.

The muted hues of the next painting before us represented cow paths, zigzags in frozen grass beside a split-rail fence. As we examined it, Bateman scraped away at the surface with his fingernail, trying to dislodge a bit of paint that seemed to stand out a little. Painterly mishaps happen sometimes, to someone who invests so much time creating a believable sense of texture. He showed me a "grungy" paint roller he uses. "Don't wash it—leave the acrylic in it," Bateman advised. "Then roll it and twist it and smear it." He darted off to grab a chunk of distressed sponge and dabbed at one of the pictures, to demonstrate "the BSM"—the Bateman Sponge Method.

Like many an artist, he's rather attached to the early stages of his work. Bateman often "starts in, hoping I can leave it alone. I'd like to do a whole show of big abstract paintings that look like my paintings when they are just half-done." Yet he can't seem to hold back.

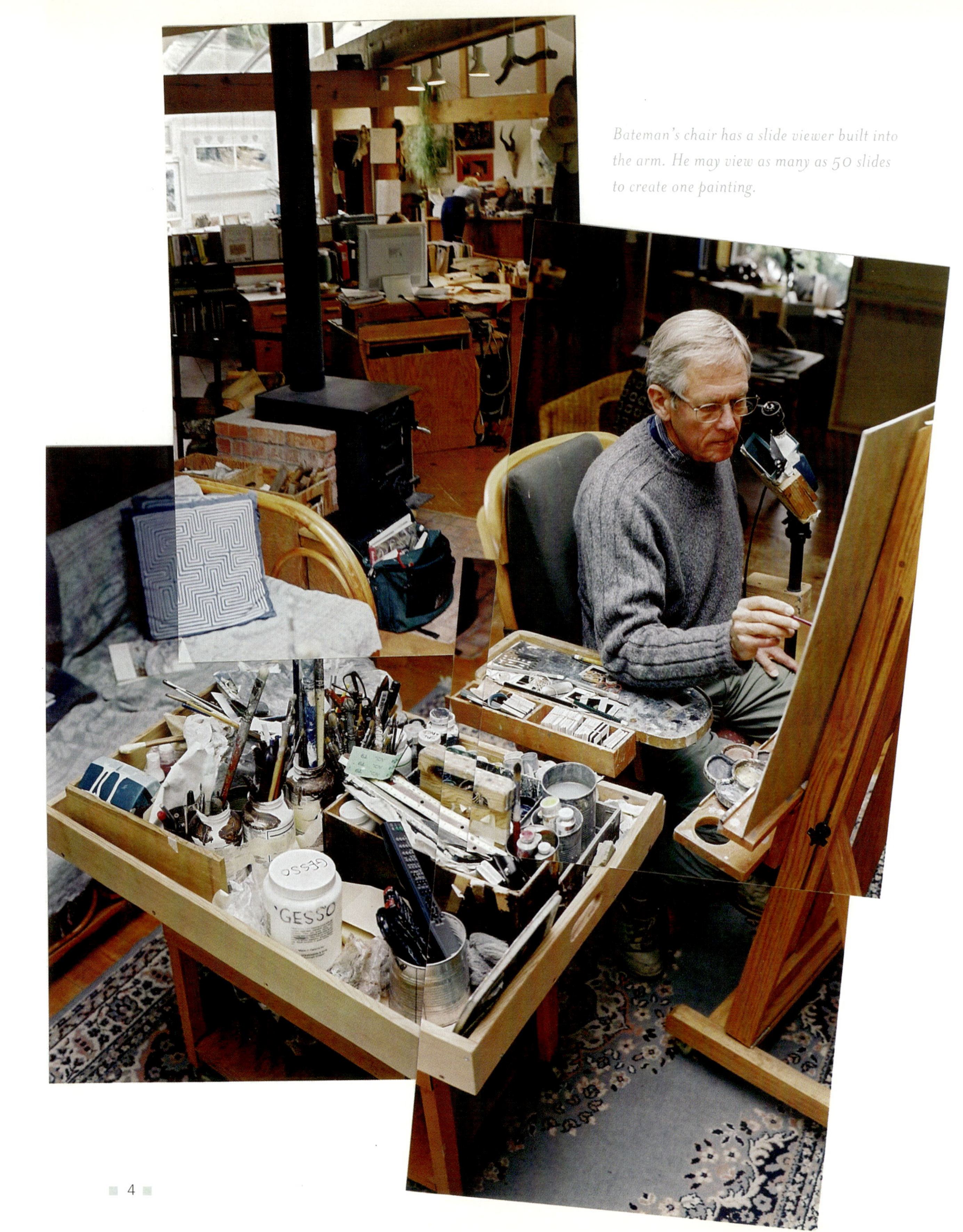

Bateman's chair has a slide viewer built into the arm. He may view as many as 50 slides to create one painting.

"I go back in," he sighed, "like trimming a hedge—or a moustache."

Next on view was a painting of a big cat on the margins of a swamp fire among Florida palm trees. Most of the picture was smoky, and the artist expatiated on his love for middle tones. Black and white almost never occur in a Bateman painting. "The secret to my work is tiny adjustments in tone," he noted.

Bateman, in his helpful and homey way, showed me how he pre-mixes many subtle tints in plastic film cans, holding three of them together with an elastic band. "That's the Martha Stewart tip," he allowed with a chuckle. His paintings tend to start out quickly, and progress more slowly as they go along. "If you weighed the amount of paint I use per day you'd find the amount steadily declining," he said.

Bateman's passions drive him to work tirelessly. These passions include a love of painting, a desire to experience the infinite complexity of the natural world and the compulsion to use his celebrity to influence us all to embrace our mother earth. "Diversity is my whole philosophy of life," he concluded. "In my writings, in my letters to politicians, that's what I worship most about this planet—the diversity of life."

Moments later I was on the ferry heading back to Victoria. All around me the coastland seemed greyed, almost monochrome. Canada geese flew by, wingtips beating not far above the waters of the gulf. Everything around me seemed touched with those "tiny adjustments in tone" to which a morning with Robert Bateman had attuned me.

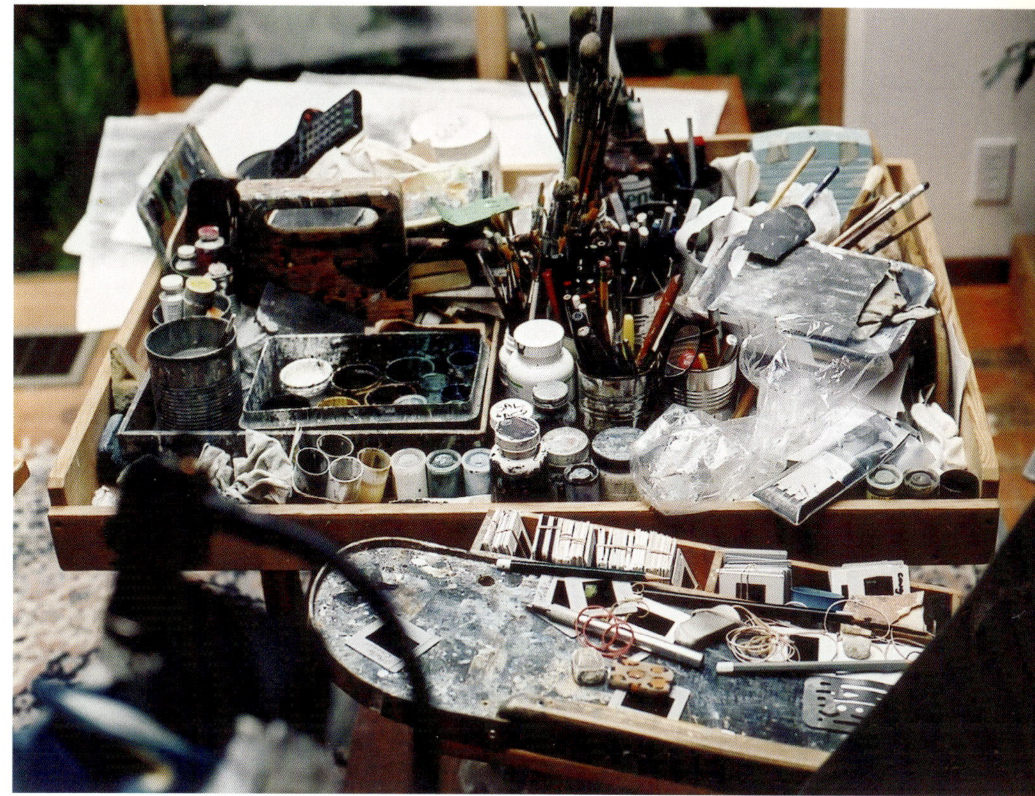

The artist's palette for mixing colours and the slides that help him create technically accurate paintings.

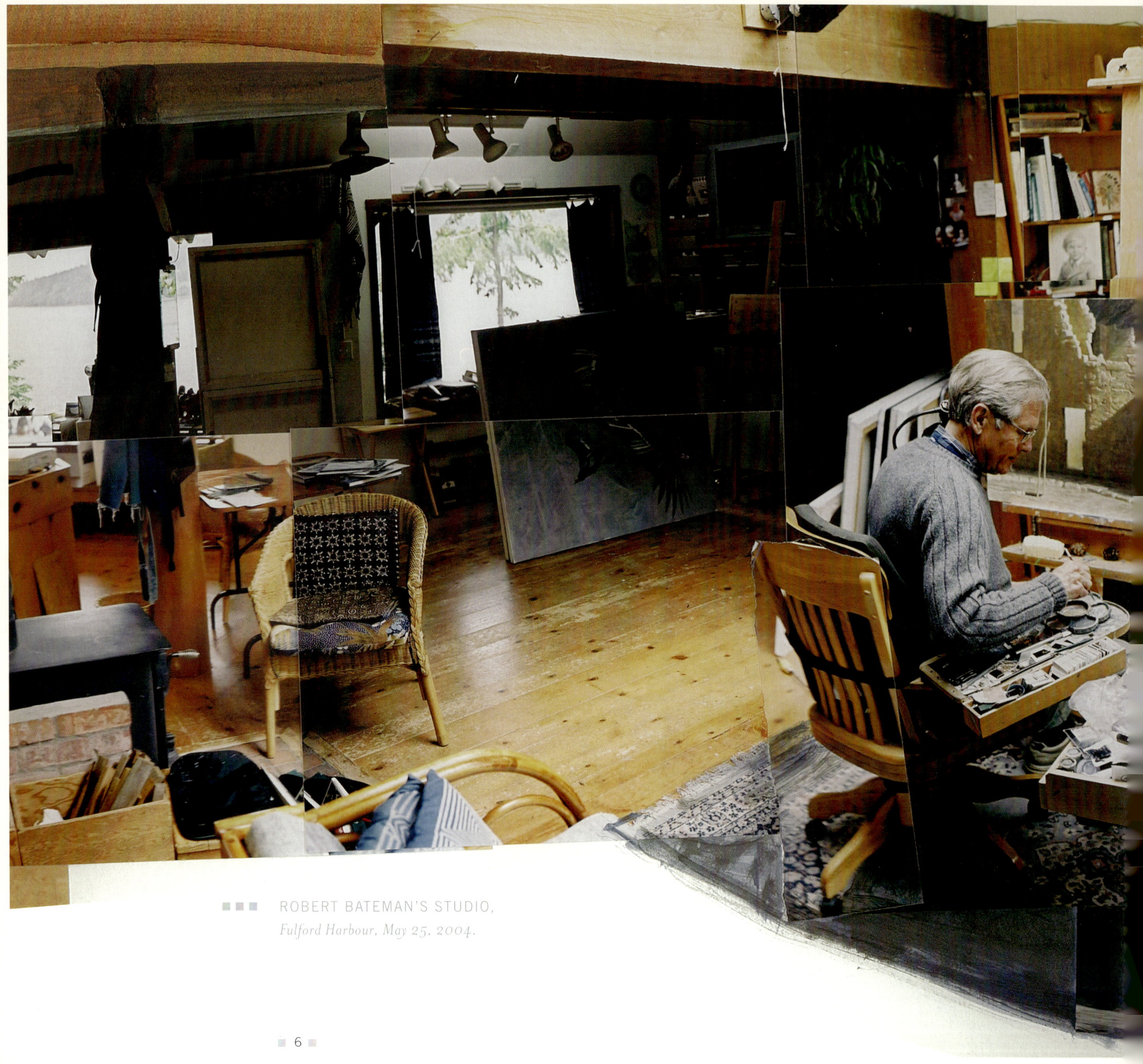

ROBERT BATEMAN'S STUDIO,
Fulford Harbour, May 25, 2004.

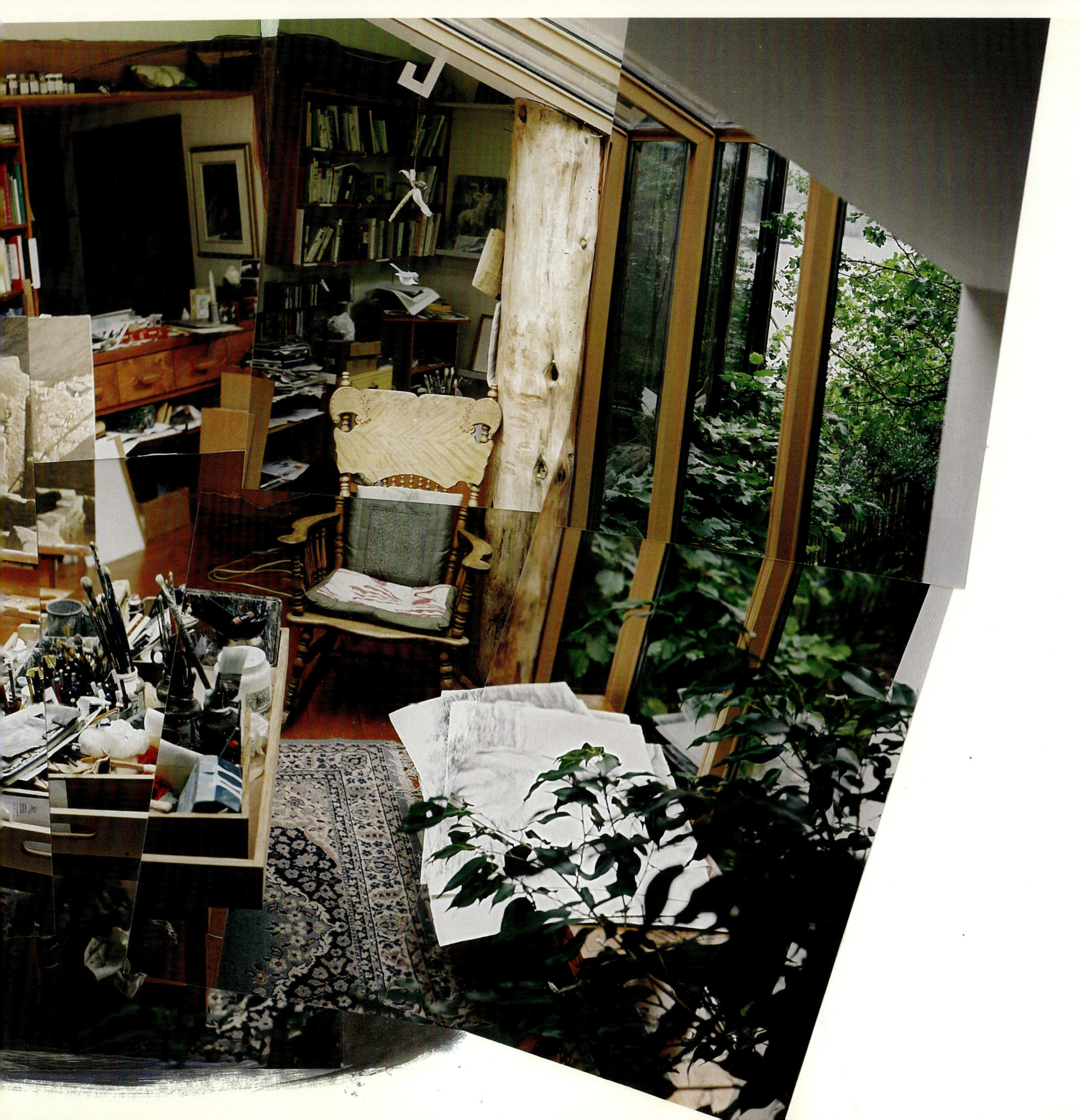

MAXWELL BATES

VICTORIA

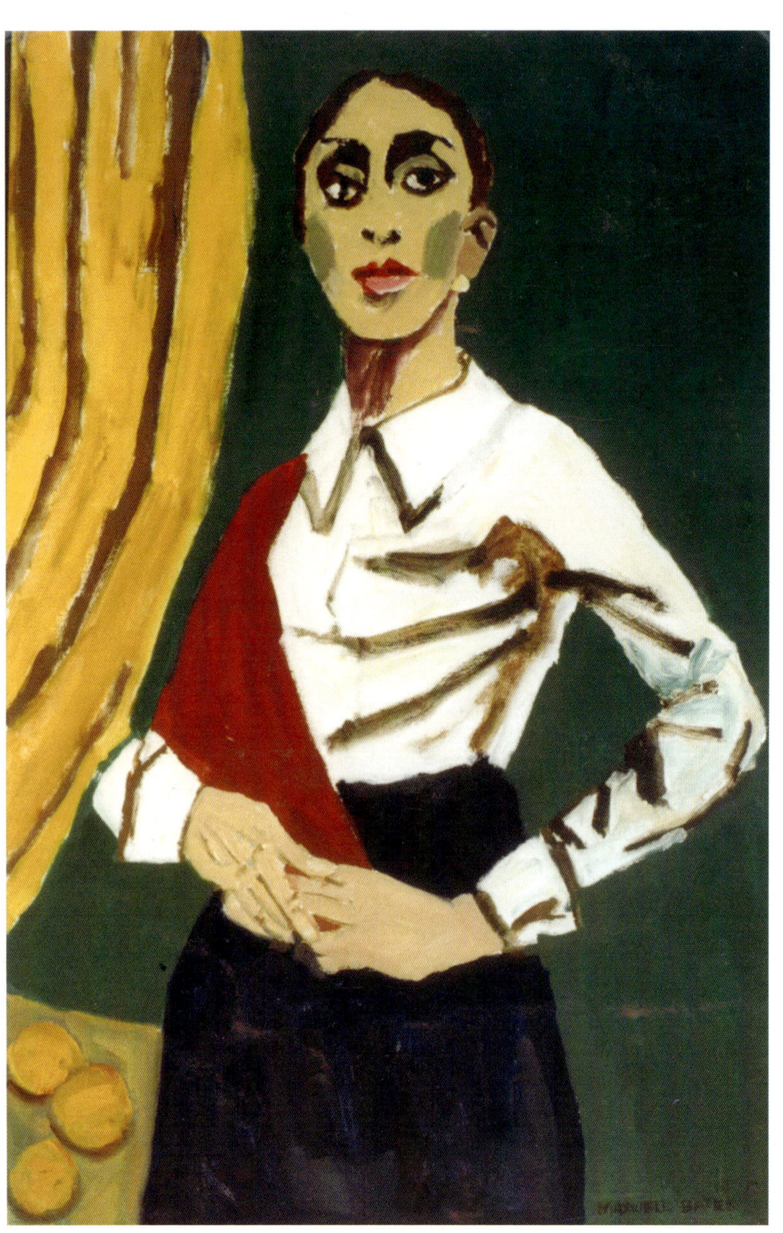

AFTER HIS DEATH IN 1980, MAX BATES' WIDOW, CHARLOTTE, KEPT HIS LAST STUDIO INTACT FOR 10 YEARS.

All the artwork had been catalogued and the material, almost 600 lots, was to be offered for sale at auction. The auctioneers invited me to help them make sense of it all. "Good painting must offer something meaningful to the spectator but it may be enigmatic. Painter and spectator collaborate unconsciously," Bates once wrote. By way of collaboration and in the interest of posterity, I made the first of my studio portraits standing on a chair in the corner of that room.

Maxwell Bates was born in Calgary in 1906, the son of an English-born architect. Young Bates was precociously talented and, after learning what he could in Alberta, he set his eyes on the prize. He was determined to get to Europe and study art and, to that end, in 1931 he worked his passage on the proverbial cattle boat. In London he sold vacuum cleaners to survive. His persistence and talent were soon rewarded when he was taken up by the rich and well-connected Lucy Wertheim; Bates showed his paintings with the prestigious Wertheim Galleries in Manchester and London.

■■■ SPANISH LADY, *Maxwell Bates, oil on canvas, 24 x 36 inches, not dated.*

Bates enlisted to fight in World War II and was almost immediately captured by the Germans. He then spent five years as a prisoner of war, working in the salt mines. It was a period that deepened his philosophical leanings. With liberation came his return to Calgary where he took up employment in his father's architectural firm. At that time, there was no market for modern art on the prairies.

Felled by a major stroke in 1961, which left him somewhat paralyzed on one side, Bates subsequently walked with a brace on his leg and smiled a crooked grin. He retired from architecture and moved to Victoria. He had been painting all along but now art took centre stage in his life.

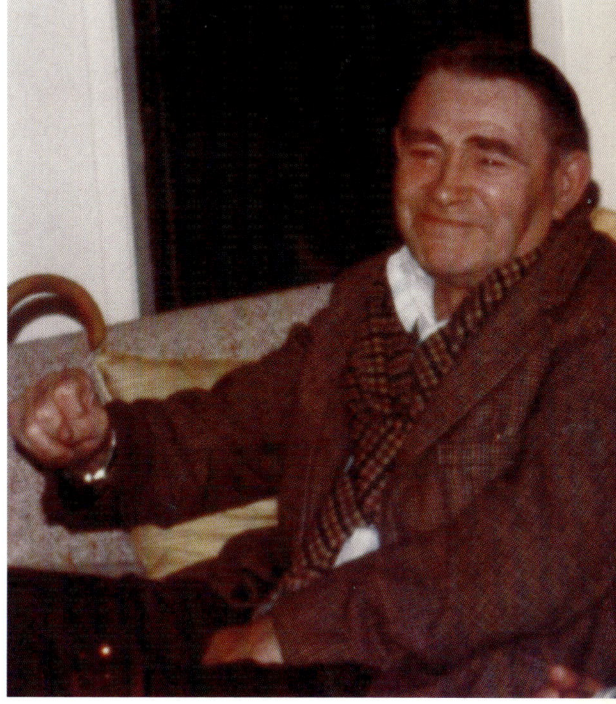

Maxwell Bates (photo by Pat Martin Bates).

Bates came from a tradition of rugged, romantic individualists who created secular works in tune with the upheaval of revolution. Eschewing patronage, in his painting Bates was answerable only to himself. "His view of humanity and of human society was sombre," the poet Robin Skelton noted. Whether it be the beggar king or the scarecrow/crucifix, everyone he painted was crippled emotionally, and some of them physically. But he was not a moralist; he was not concerned with judging or condemning.

Bates usually painted people, and he portrayed them as characters, like tarot cards come to life, like chess pieces or marionettes. Through their costumes and heraldic devices his people take on symbolic significance beyond their day-to-day personalities. His paintings of prairie pioneers standing doggedly in the wind are Canadian icons.

"Simplicity, directness, and intensity: these are the three things I am after," Bates explained.

In Victoria, painting took over his life. He joined—and named—Victoria's modernist art group, The Limners. During the 1970s his work was shown nationally with considerable acclaim, earning him an honorary doctorate from the University of Calgary. In 1980, Bates was awarded the Order of Canada. The influence of Maxwell Bates on the best minds of his community was extensive.

His paintings could quite easily "get lost" in the flux of art history. World War II cut short his career on the international scene and being a western Canadian has limited his access to celebrity. Bates, almost alone in Canada, was an Expressionist, the first truly international style. And he moved to Victoria, far beyond the mainstream of the art world. Thus, his considerable achievements as a painter have been stripped of context.

Yet Bates had a purpose for his art. It was "the artist's duty to confront our unstable world with the new values and break up those that are no longer valid and have become obstructive," he wrote. Pay attention to his paintings and you will see that purpose fulfilled. ■

Bates was a short man and didn't mind working in a basement room with a seven-foot ceiling.

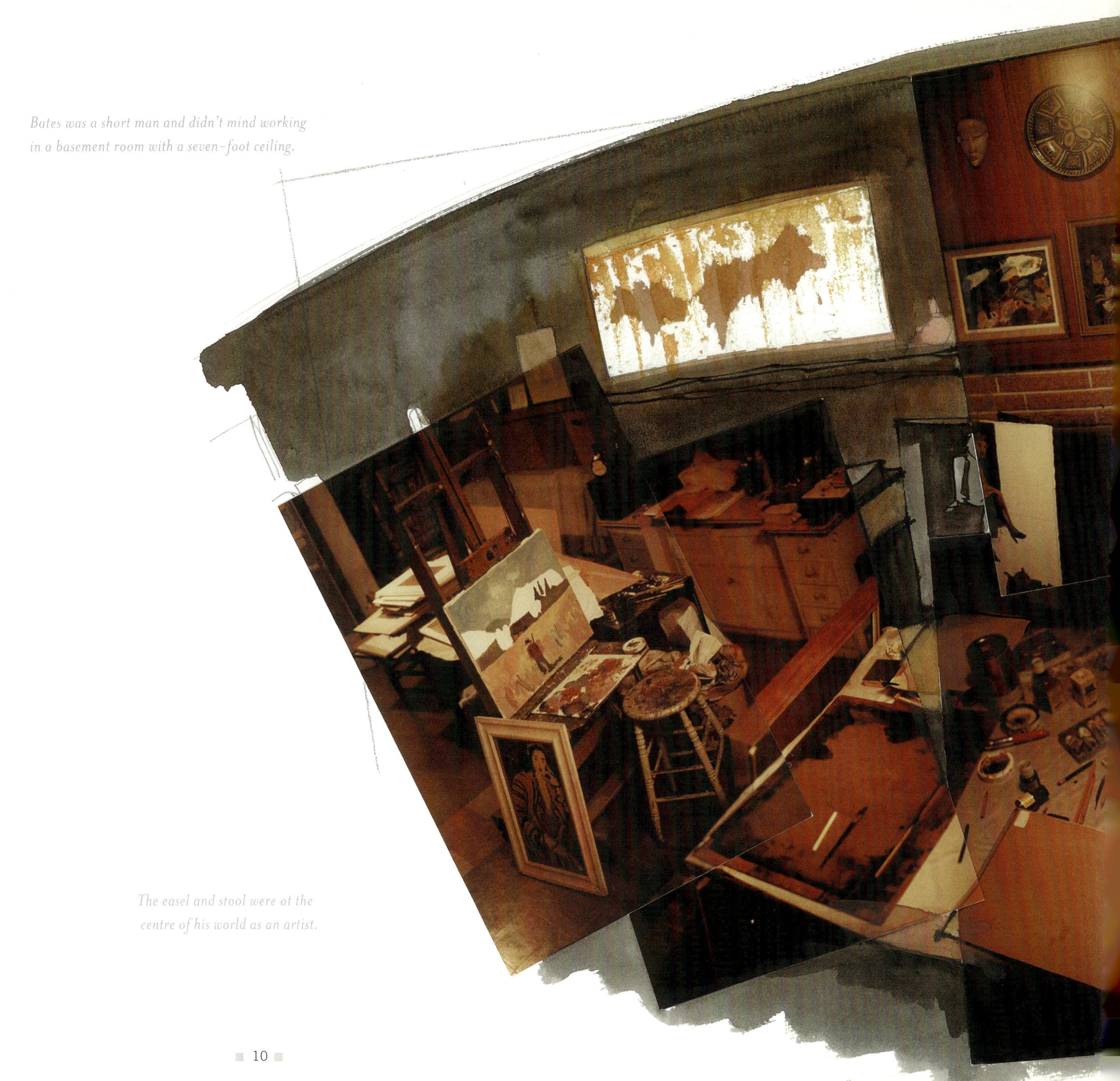

The easel and stool were at the centre of his world as an artist.

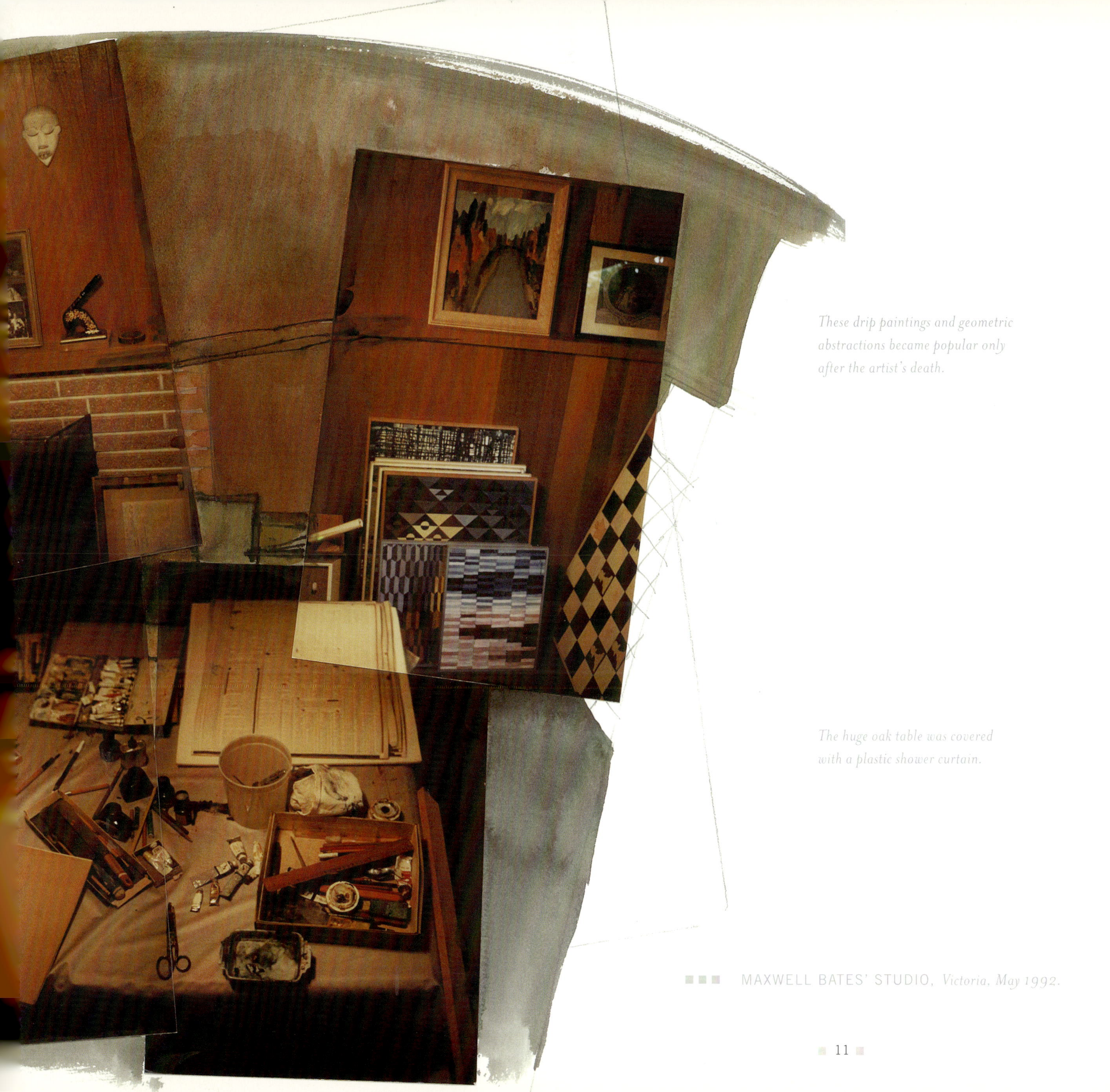

These drip paintings and geometric abstractions became popular only after the artist's death.

The huge oak table was covered with a plastic shower curtain.

MAXWELL BATES' STUDIO, *Victoria, May 1992.*

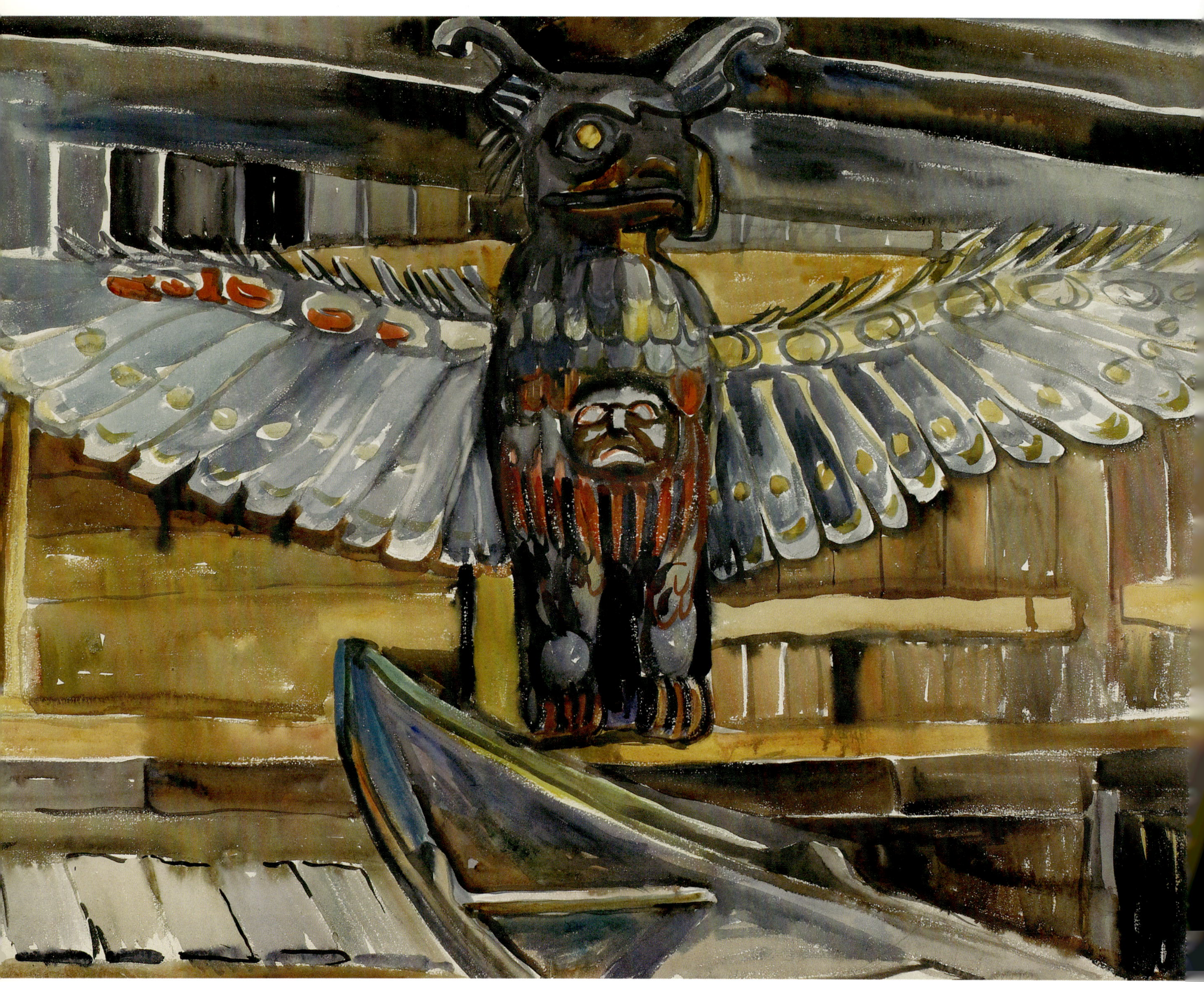

EMILY CARR

"THE HOUSE OF ALL SORTS" — VICTORIA

EMILY CARR IS NOW THE FOREMOST FIGURE IN CANADIAN ART. IT WAS NOT ALWAYS SO. DESPITE YEARS OF TRAINING IN SAN FRANCISCO, ENGLAND AND FRANCE, AND GROUNDBREAKING EXPEDITIONS TO THE NORTH COAST AND THE QUEEN CHARLOTTE ISLANDS, FOR MOST OF HER LIFE SHE COULDN'T MAKE ENDS MEET THROUGH HER ART.

Carr essentially gave up her art career in 1913 and, at the age of 41, built a small apartment building on land she had inherited at 646 Simcoe Street in Victoria. It had a studio upstairs at the back, where she expected to live quietly on the proceeds of the rents. Things didn't turn out so well, and for the next 20 years she struggled as a landlady, eventually moving out when fame caught up with her in 1936. The house remains to this day as a four-plex apartment block.

Carr's years in the building, which she called Hill House, are recorded in wry stories in her book *The House of All Sorts*. Her big, high studio on the second floor was hung edge to edge with her paintings. There was a cleared space around an open stove in one corner that served as her sitting room. A couch along one wall faced a wooden armchair which Emily and her dogs filled. A few other chairs hung on pulleys from the ceiling, ready for guests.

The space near the window was "partitioned off with furniture and boxes to make a painting nook and two canvases stood facing each other on crude, homemade easels, both draped to prevent the curious from seeing unfinished work," Edythe Hembroff wrote in her memoir of Carr, *M. E.: A Portrayal.*

"A little stairway in the corner opposite me led to a low attic room where Emily slept," Hembroff continued. "The door was open and I could see part of some dark, stark Indian eagles she had painted on the whitewashed surface of the sloping roof."

HOUSE POST, TSATSINUCHOMI, B.C.,
Emily Carr, watercolour and graphite on woven paper, 55.4 x 76.6 centimetres, ca. 1912, National Gallery of Canada, Ottawa.

Carr herself wrote, "Immediately I came into the house the attic took me, just as if it had always 'homed' me, became my special corner—the one place really my own. The whole house, my flat, even my own studio, was more or less public." When times were tight, Emily fed boarders at a table in her big room or even rented it out and lived in the basement. But the attic was her own.

"In the attic I could wallow in tears or in giggles—nobody saw," she reported in *The House of All Sorts*.

During the ensuing years Carr's studio has been reconfigured, but the attic remains much as it was. Though not open to the public, the painted roof is protected by heritage legislation.

In her artistic autobiography, *Growing Pains*, Carr wrote, "A crooked stair led to it. The stair was in the corner of my studio. I chose this [attic] room with its wide view for my bedroom. It had low-drooped walls but the centre of the room was high. Its end walls were peaked. The naked ridge pole and studding showed, because the room was unlined. Rain pattered on the cedar shingles only a few feet above my face."

One afternoon in 1999 I was standing on Simcoe Street painting a picture of *The House of All Sorts* when the owner of the house, an elderly woman dressed all in red, emerged. She came across the road and invited me to see the eagles which Carr had painted in the attic. Insisting that I fetch a ladder from the backyard, she led the way to the second-floor hallway. There, she directed me to climb up the ladder and remove the transom window over a door. I lifted out the window, which had a stained-glass image of an eagle, and climbed in.

The attic is under the roof beams in the western half of the building. Many of the floorboards were missing, and a few boxes and trunks were tucked out of the way. Light poured in from the window, which looked west over to the Sooke Hills.

"On the whitewashed underside of the roof shingles," Carr wrote in *Growing Pains*, "I painted two immense totemic Indian eagles. Their outstretched wings covered the entire ceiling." In *The House of All Sorts* she continued, "The heads of the eagles tilted upwards in bold, unafraid enquiry. I loved to lie close under these strong Indian symbols. They were only a few feet above my face as I slept in this attic bedroom. They made 'strong talk' for me, as my Indian friends would say."

Carr knew that after she left, the attic was boarded up and abandoned, much as it still is. "Old eagles," she asked in *The House of All Sorts*, "do you feel my memories come creeping back to you in your entombed, cobwebby darkness?"

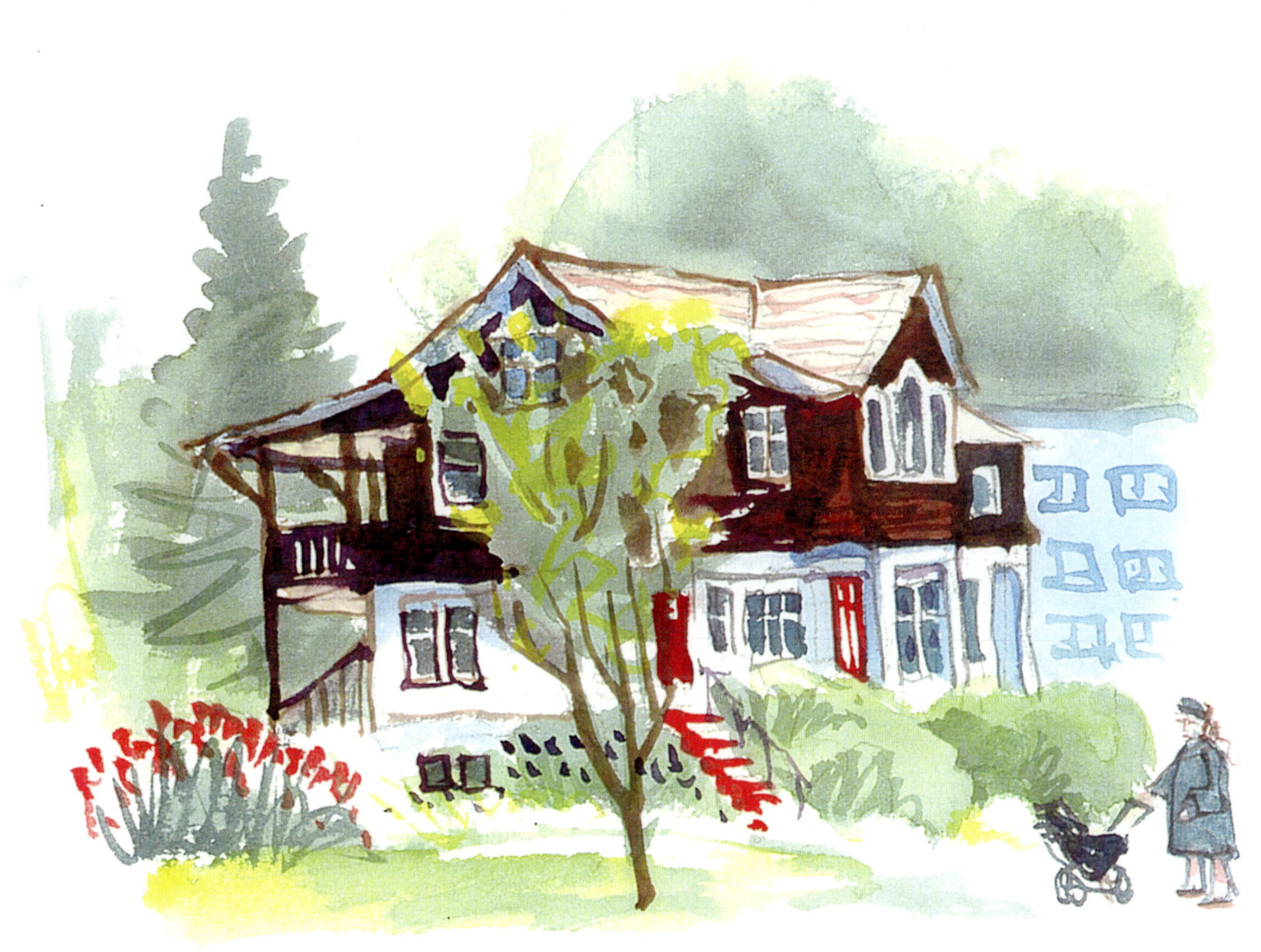

■■■ THE HOUSE OF ALL SORTS, 626 SIMCOE STREET, VICTORIA,
Robert Amos, watercolour, 4.5 x 6 inches, 2002.

The transom window, featuring a stained-glass eagle, is visible at floor level.

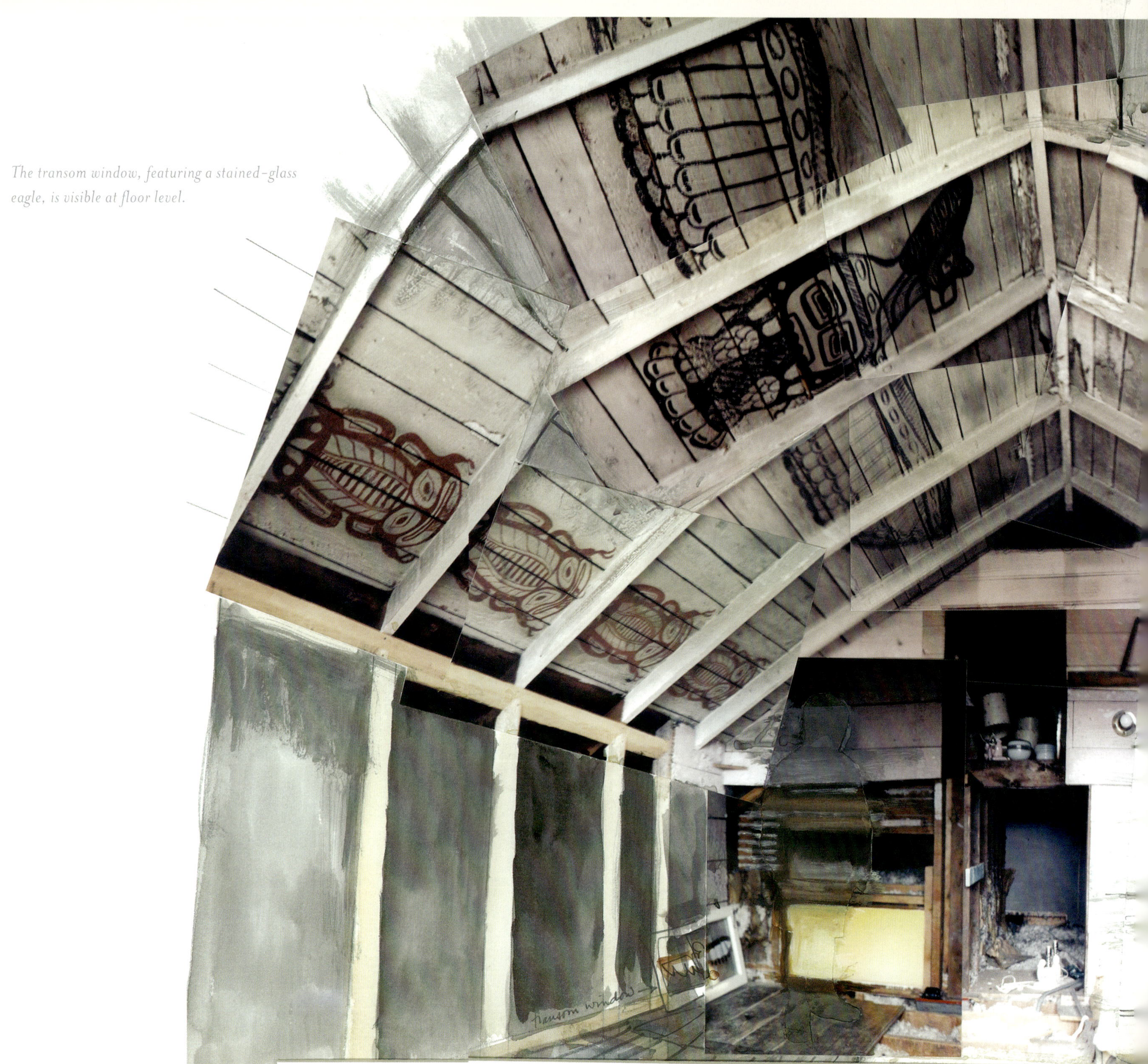

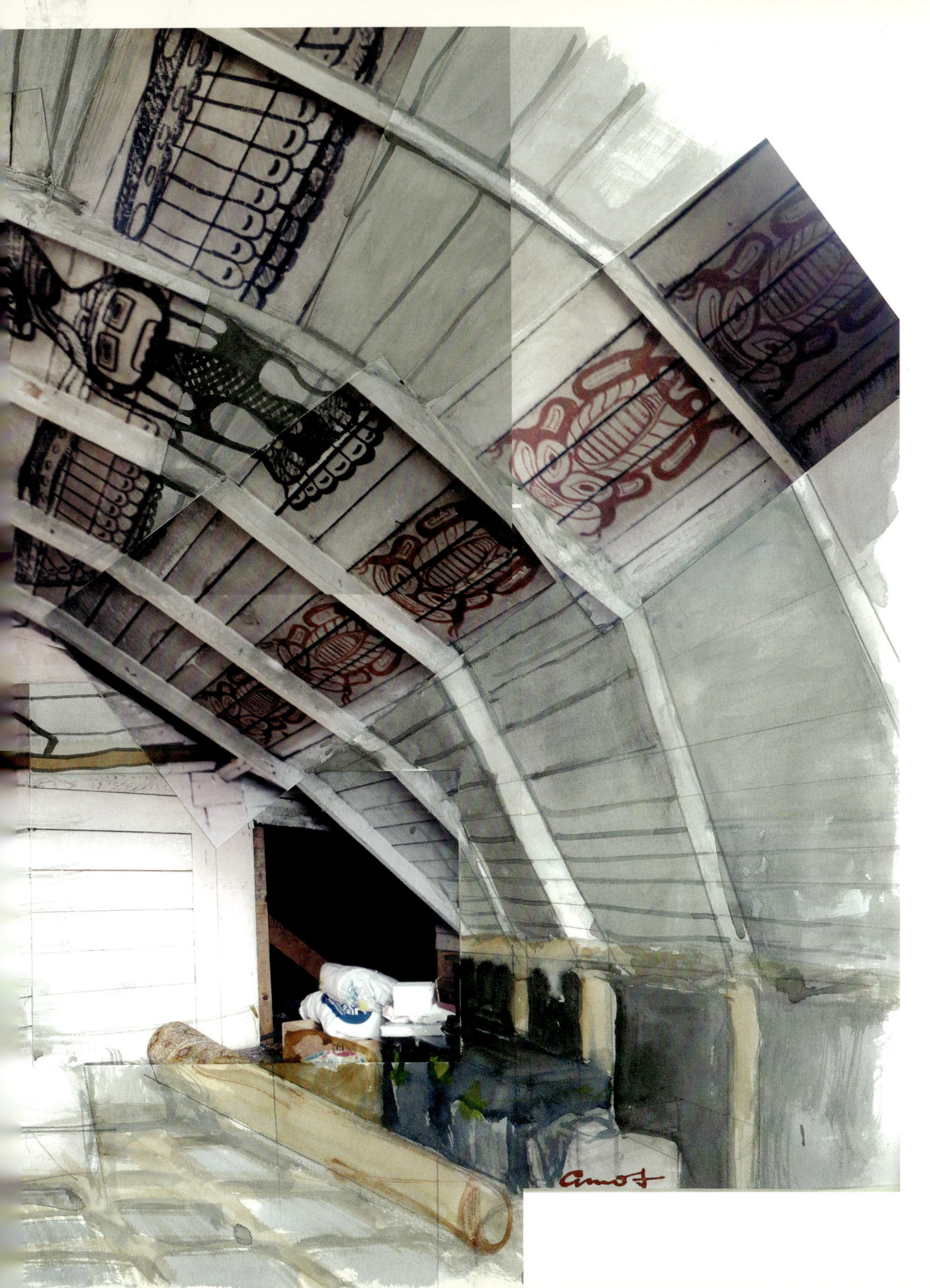

The house has a plain pitched roof, although the camera makes it appear as a barrel vault.

■ ■ ■ THE ATTIC,
THE HOUSE OF ALL SORTS,
Victoria, 1995.

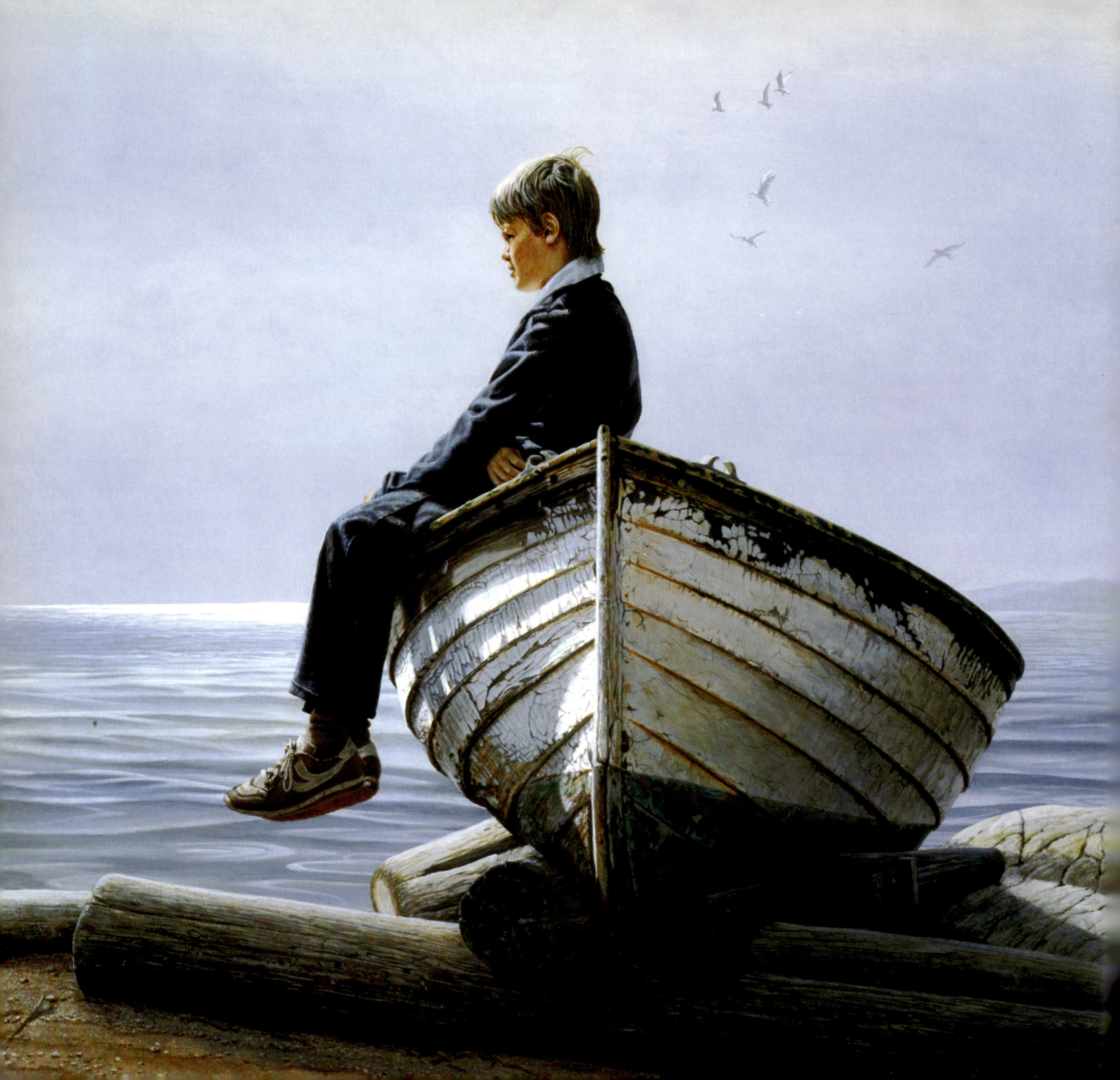

LEN GIBBS

VICTORIA

LEN GIBBS AND HIS WIFE, BETTY, LIVE IN A SUN-DRENCHED TOWNHOUSE ON THE WATERFRONT IN VICTORIA. WE SPENT AN AFTERNOON IN THEIR ATTRACTIVE LIVING ROOM, WHICH IS HUNG EDGE TO EDGE WITH A COLLECTION OF ART AND MEMORIES.

Gibbs' life story is equal parts modesty and talent. He was born in Cranbrook in 1929. When he was five his mother was widowed and he went to live in Brandon, Manitoba, with his grandparents. "Grandfather was a great influence," Gibbs recalled.

Young Gibbs played the trumpet. He admits that he has a "tin ear." When it was noticed that the congregation was "beginning to thin out," the other musicians got together and helped him find a quieter form of expression—they bought him some pencils and paper. And his art career was born.

"My grandfather had a steam tractor and went from farm to farm with the threshing crew. I'd go along and make these little sketches of field mice and the people at work. He encouraged me, and he also took me to the library." There was no art gallery in Brandon, but the lad copied everything he saw in the picture books, "Italian sculptures and all."

Drawing was relegated to the sidelines in 1945, when Gibbs joined the navy. He had mechanical ability that served him well on a Canadian aircraft carrier and he ended up in a submarine. "I thought I was smart, and talked my way in," he told me, "but really they were looking for victims."

During the Korean War Gibbs studied art by correspondence. He did his lessons while sitting on a torpedo and mailed them in from all over the globe. When he returned to Edmonton he signed on as a layout artist for the *Edmonton Bulletin*. The 80-year-old newspaper folded just two weeks later, and Gibbs then launched himself into advertising. He spent 18 years in that field, rising to vice-president of the creative department of an advertising firm, responsible for the prairie region. Through it all he continued to paint.

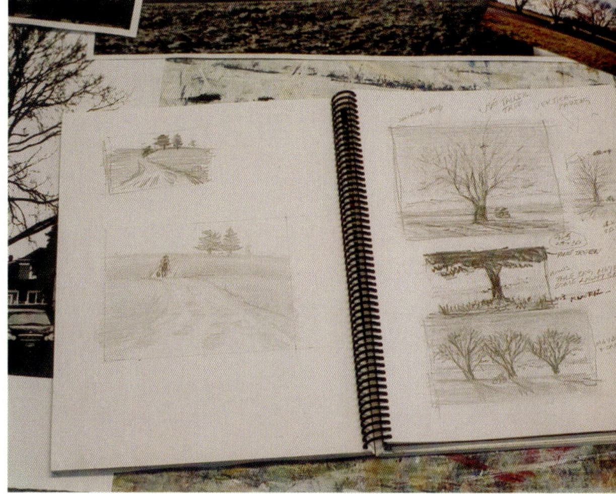

The artist's sketchbook.

CALL OF THE SEA, *Len Gibbs, acrylic, 18 x 24 inches, 1996.*

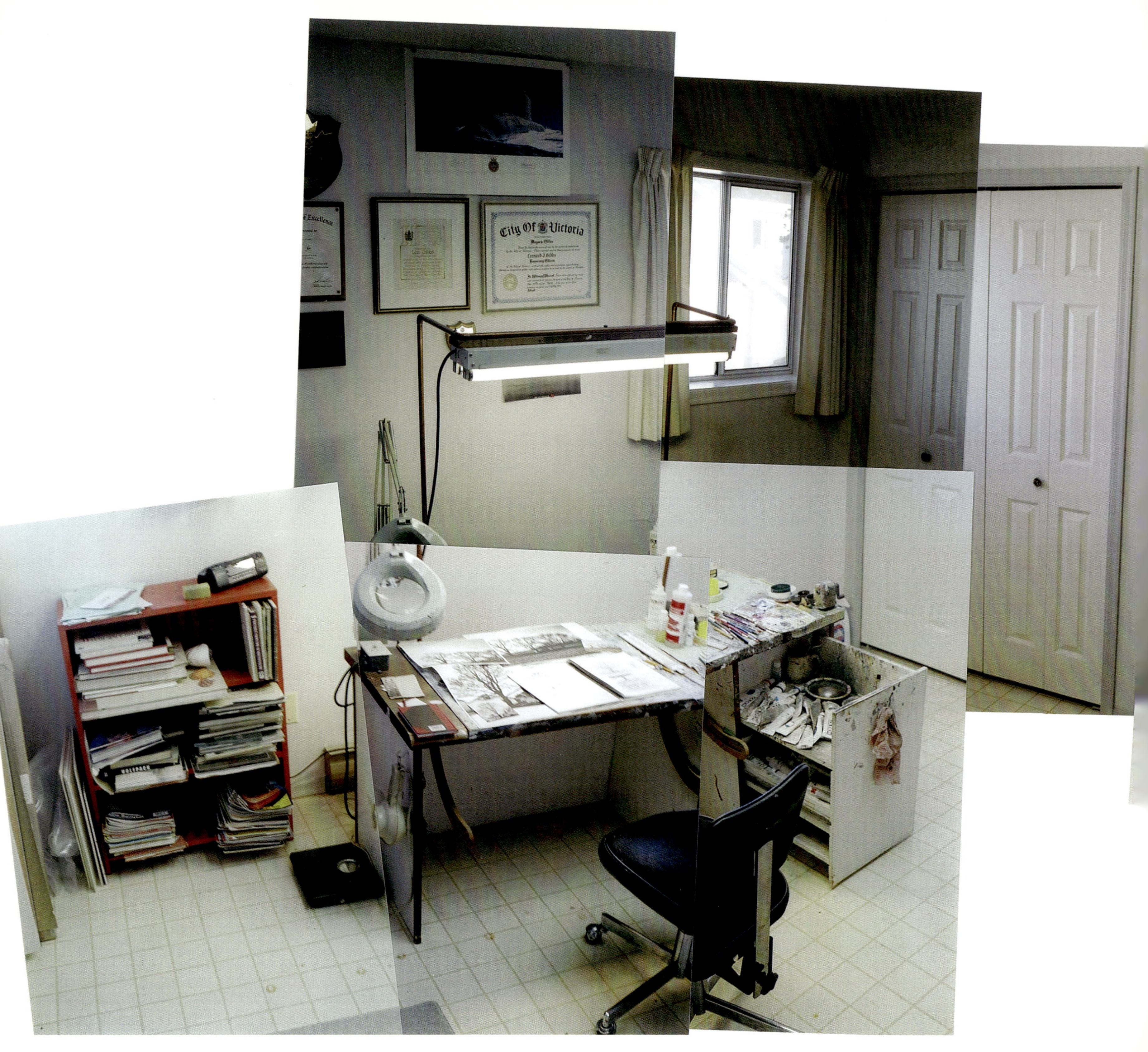
City Of Victoria

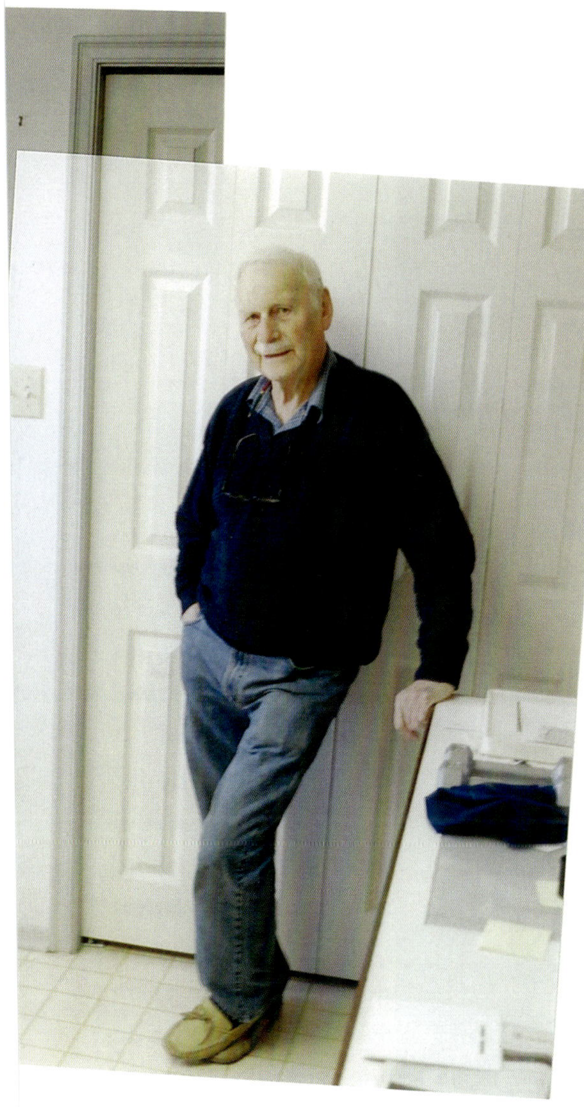

LEN GIBBS' STUDIO,
Dallas Road, Victoria, 2007.

At the time Edmonton had no art galleries, public or private, and few artists of any sort. With the awakening of national pride that came with the Canadian centennial year of 1967, Gibbs and some friends formed an artists' cooperative. Back at work, his divided loyalty was promptly noticed.

"My boss told me that I had to give up this silly art hobby and go play golf with the clients on the weekends," Gibbs chuckled. On his next trip to Vancouver, where he was directing the filming of a television commercial, Gibbs took some of his paintings into the Alex Fraser Gallery in Shaughnessy. Fraser was impressed and offered him a show. "But I don't deal with part-time artists," the dealer explained.

Gibbs made up his mind then and there. "I quit. Betty went out and got a job and we hung in there. And in November I had a sell-out show." He was now a full-time artist. Recalling balmy days he had spent on the coast during his navy career, he relocated with his wife and two children to Victoria in 1970.

Annually, Gibbs travelled to Alberta and scouted ranches, rodeos and roundups for material. "That's where the cowboy stuff came from," he pointed out. The booming market for limited-edition prints took his prairie images all over the world.

In fact, the range of subject matter Gibbs has painted is much broader. Tender scenes of children exploring the seashore; a boy spending a lazy day on the dock; a girl on a wind-swept hillside contemplating the onset of womanhood; grizzled veterans in worn clothes dreaming of past glories—these are among the sensitive scenes he confidently depicts in his homemade, untutored style of high realism.

Gibbs' meticulous paintings, carefully composed and speaking of a heartfelt sentiment, take a long time to craft. Demand from galleries in Toronto, Edmonton and the United States has always outstripped his production. His Spartan studio in a back bedroom of the townhouse contains only what is absolutely necessary, and there is no backlog of unsold pictures and failed attempts. "The fireplace is an artist's best tool," Gibbs joked.

When I asked about his influences, Gibbs thought for a while. Andrew Wyeth was one, he admitted, though he has seen his work only in reproduction. Salvador Dali perhaps had an effect as did Albrecht Durer, whose work he remembered from those books in the Brandon Public Library. "I didn't have any other influences. I wish I'd gone to art school, to broaden my experience, but if you're self-taught you automatically become a representational painter."

It's easy to forget how isolated the art world of western Canada was just a few years ago. And it's good to remember that being self-taught is sometimes the best kind of education.

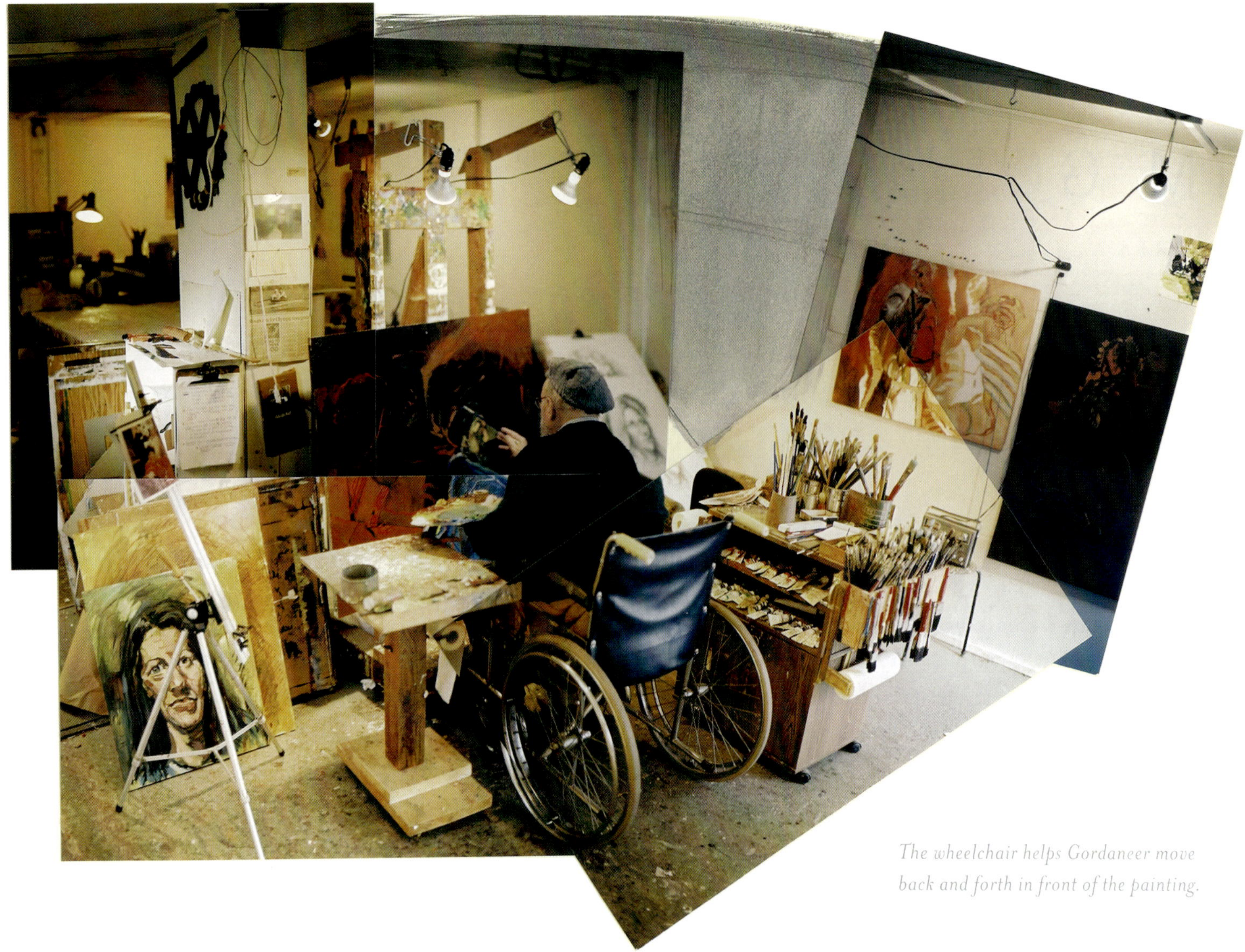

The wheelchair helps Gordaneer move back and forth in front of the painting.

still life, landscape. While the subject remained recognizable, it was plotted onto curved space—convex, concave or a combination of the two flowing into one another. This is called "topology," a study of that which remains constant within change.

Some people thought Gordaneer had gone right off the rails with these convoluted spatial forms, but in hindsight we can see that his painting practice is large enough to absorb powerful ideas and still continue to grow. In the early 1990s, a mysterious ailment caused Gordaneer to fall into a coma for six weeks, and when he emerged from the hospital he refocussed, giving up his teaching career for the pursuit of painting.

Later, with the death of Lorenz, The Chapman Group was cast upon its own resources. The experience of the philosophical exploration has had a lasting effect on the artists

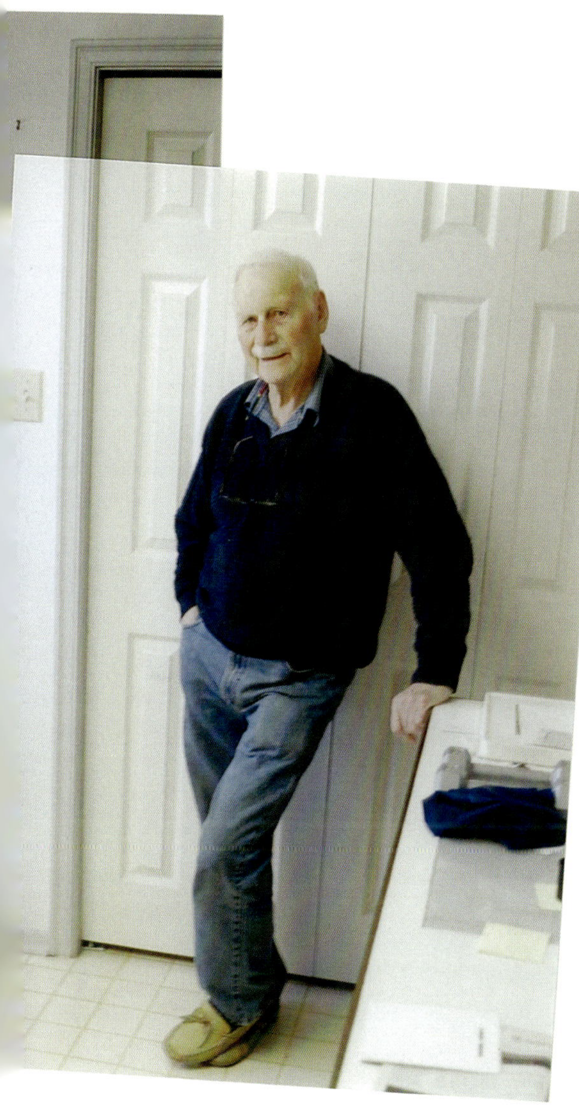

LEN GIBBS' STUDIO,
Dallas Road, Victoria, 2007.

At the time Edmonton had no art galleries, public or private, and few artists of any sort. With the awakening of national pride that came with the Canadian centennial year of 1967, Gibbs and some friends formed an artists' cooperative. Back at work, his divided loyalty was promptly noticed.

"My boss told me that I had to give up this silly art hobby and go play golf with the clients on the weekends," Gibbs chuckled. On his next trip to Vancouver, where he was directing the filming of a television commercial, Gibbs took some of his paintings into the Alex Fraser Gallery in Shaughnessy. Fraser was impressed and offered him a show. "But I don't deal with part-time artists," the dealer explained.

Gibbs made up his mind then and there. "I quit. Betty went out and got a job and we hung in there. And in November I had a sell-out show." He was now a full-time artist. Recalling balmy days he had spent on the coast during his navy career, he relocated with his wife and two children to Victoria in 1970.

Annually, Gibbs travelled to Alberta and scouted ranches, rodeos and roundups for material. "That's where the cowboy stuff came from," he pointed out. The booming market for limited-edition prints took his prairie images all over the world.

In fact, the range of subject matter Gibbs has painted is much broader. Tender scenes of children exploring the seashore; a boy spending a lazy day on the dock; a girl on a wind-swept hillside contemplating the onset of womanhood; grizzled veterans in worn clothes dreaming of past glories—these are among the sensitive scenes he confidently depicts in his homemade, untutored style of high realism.

Gibbs' meticulous paintings, carefully composed and speaking of a heartfelt sentiment, take a long time to craft. Demand from galleries in Toronto, Edmonton and the United States has always outstripped his production. His Spartan studio in a back bedroom of the townhouse contains only what is absolutely necessary, and there is no backlog of unsold pictures and failed attempts. "The fireplace is an artist's best tool," Gibbs joked.

When I asked about his influences, Gibbs thought for a while. Andrew Wyeth was one, he admitted, though he has seen his work only in reproduction. Salvador Dali perhaps had an effect as did Albrecht Durer, whose work he remembered from those books in the Brandon Public Library. "I didn't have any other influences. I wish I'd gone to art school, to broaden my experience, but if you're self-taught you automatically become a representational painter."

It's easy to forget how isolated the art world of western Canada was just a few years ago. And it's good to remember that being self-taught is sometimes the best kind of education.

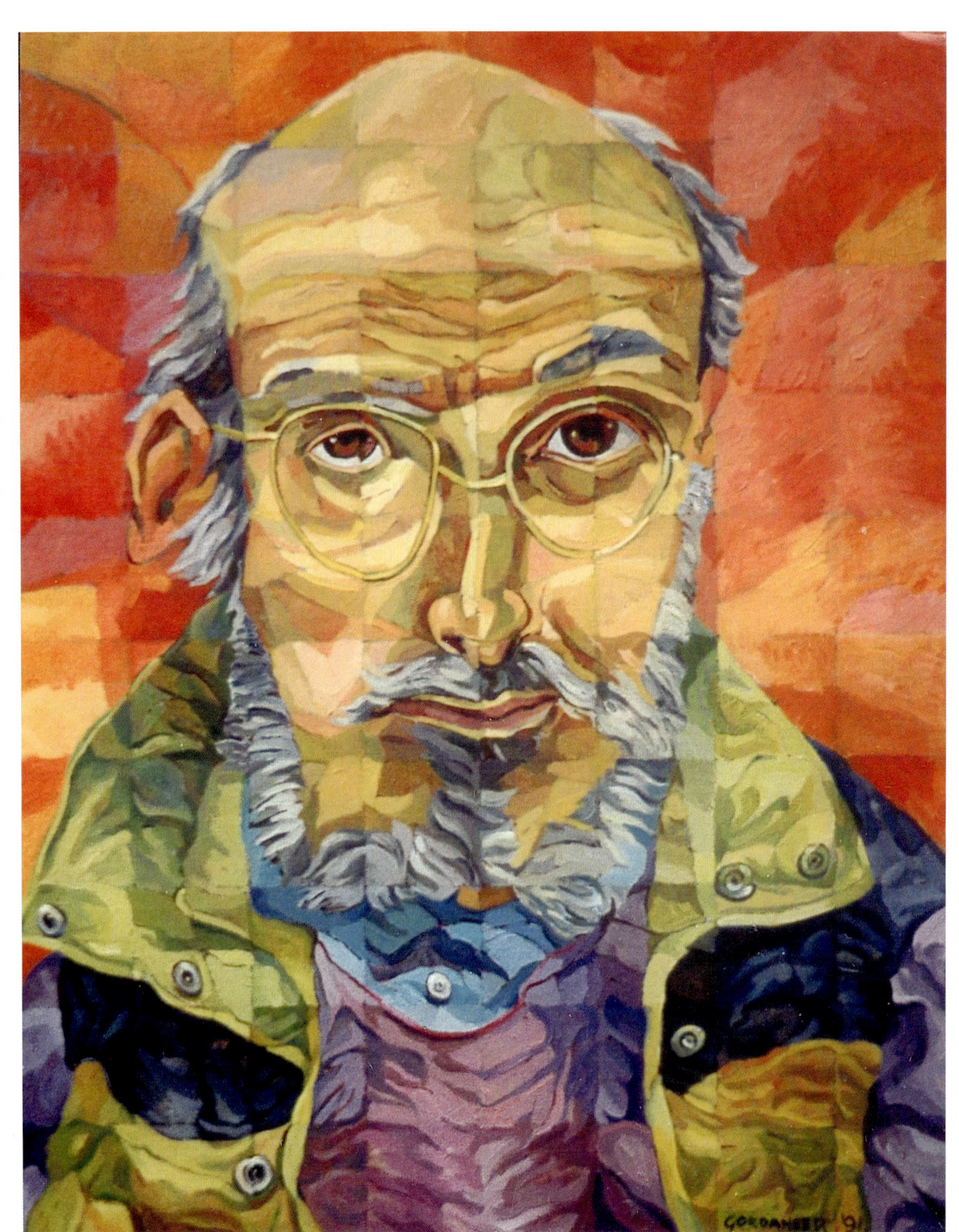

SELF PORTRAIT,
Jim Gordaneer,
oil on canvas,
24 x 30 inches, 1991.

JIM GORDANEER

VICTORIA

JIM GORDANEER LIVES AROUND THE CORNER FROM ME. I WALKED OVER TO HIS FAIRFIELD HOME ONE MORNING, WENT AROUND THE BACK AND KNOCKED ON THE DOOR OF THE GARAGE IN THE OVER-GROWN YARD. THE ARTIST, BUNDLED UP IN A KNITTED HAT AND WARM CLOTHES, LET ME INTO A WORLD OF COLOUR.

Gordaneer works in a comfortable, paint-encrusted space that has seen huge production over the years. There are scarcely any windows in his studio. A few naked spotlights illuminate various corners. Gordaneer's world is all about painting, and has been for more than half a century. His engagement is with line and colour, and as far as he is concerned, the public can take it or leave it.

Born in Toronto in 1933, Gordaneer started as a maintenance man, pupil, then teacher at Kitchener's Doon School of Fine Arts. An active member of the Ontario Society of Artists, he developed in the jazz-tinged 1960s, in the milieu of Harold Town, Gordon Rayner and Michael Snow. In 1975 Gordaneer and his wife, Miria, moved to Victoria. He has continued his career with sales and shows in galleries, commercial and private, across the country. In Victoria he has made his most valuable contribution as the foremost teacher of oil painting, enlightening students at the university, the community college and the Victoria College of Art.

In the 1980s, Gordaneer and a number of his young associates engaged in a lengthy exploration of visual representation with philosopher Raymond Lorenz. They were dedicated to escaping the strictures of our usual system of perspective, in which straight lines appear to converge at the vanishing point. The Chapman Group, as they named themselves, set out to create highly resolved pictures of all types of imagery—figurative,

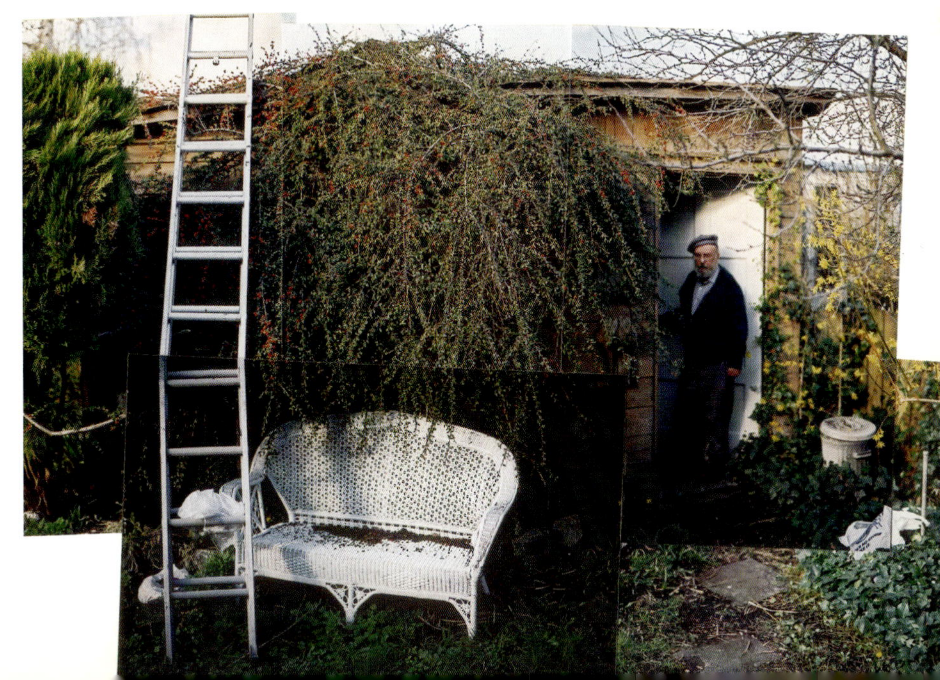

Jim Gordaneer outside his studio, Fairfield, Victoria.

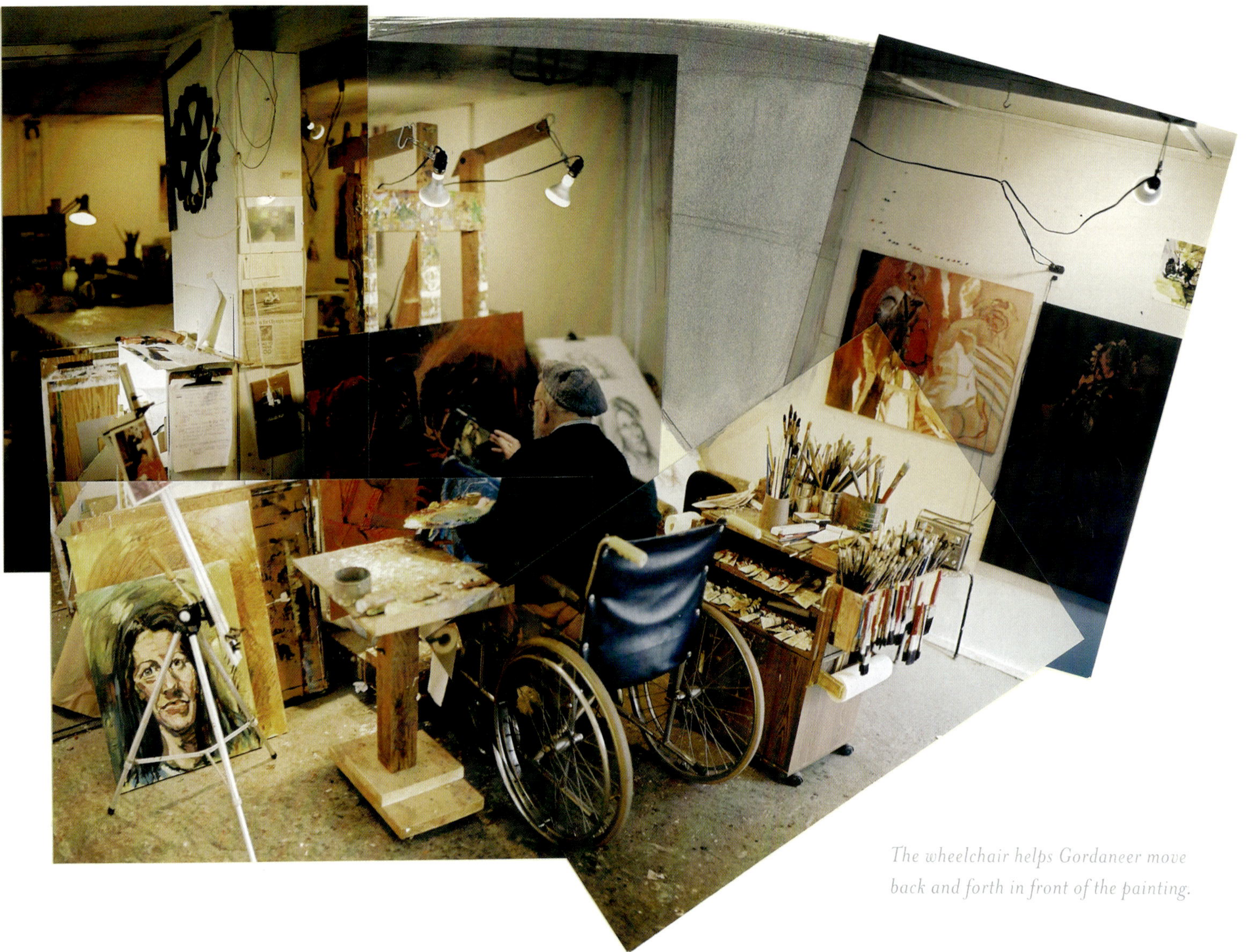

The wheelchair helps Gordaneer move back and forth in front of the painting.

still life, landscape. While the subject remained recognizable, it was plotted onto curved space—convex, concave or a combination of the two flowing into one another. This is called "topology," a study of that which remains constant within change.

Some people thought Gordaneer had gone right off the rails with these convoluted spatial forms, but in hindsight we can see that his painting practice is large enough to absorb powerful ideas and still continue to grow. In the early 1990s, a mysterious ailment caused Gordaneer to fall into a coma for six weeks, and when he emerged from the hospital he refocussed, giving up his teaching career for the pursuit of painting.

Later, with the death of Lorenz, The Chapman Group was cast upon its own resources. The experience of the philosophical exploration has had a lasting effect on the artists concerned, but as Gordaneer says, "We all had to kick the ladder out from beneath us."

Since then Gordaneer has made a habit of painting outdoors in his Fairfield neighbourhood. Setting up his easel in front of the most ordinary scenes, he paints the back alleys and boulevard trees in a provocative and loopy sort of way. Larger and more considered work is created in his studio. He spends the finest hours of his day, every day, painting.

Gordaneer's long career has left the painter's ego untouched. He enjoys talking about his work, but the real dialogue goes on between brush and canvas. He keeps his eye open for the telling juxtaposition of a burnt orange and a screaming Irish green, a tender baby blue and freely brushed stripes of warm, pink flesh.

When I last visited him, the artist was hobbling about on worn-out knee replacements, but he eagerly hoisted 30 large painted panels into place to show me the fruits of his current labours. This time they were huge faces, each a metre tall. Mind you, the subject is not at first apparent. These heads have an explosive, centrifugal force that blows apart the fragments of which they are made. Bits of landscape, costume and pure painterly gusto cavort in a rhythmic dance, anchored by only the slightest physiognomic reference.

Lest his paintings become too factual, he works by turning the canvas around and around. This habit results in the surging dynamic of the painting. "When I work on it rightways up, I am conscious of the figuration. When I work on it upside down, then I'm thinking of the space," was his explanation. "I see the painting and the subject matter as a sort of dance. I work back and forth."

And we are left to consider the sheer exuberant game of painting, played here by a wily master. Like a pool shark, Gordaneer has in his time chased the ball all over the table. He knows all the angles and still remains fascinated by the challenges of the game. Not for him the easy answer of a "likeness" or a "formula."

There has been a lot of talk about the end of painting, but Gordaneer continues to paint, even if his life's work creates storage problems. "I think I will always be here—pushing pigment around," he concluded with a smile. It's hard to think of an artist who has pushed it further. ■

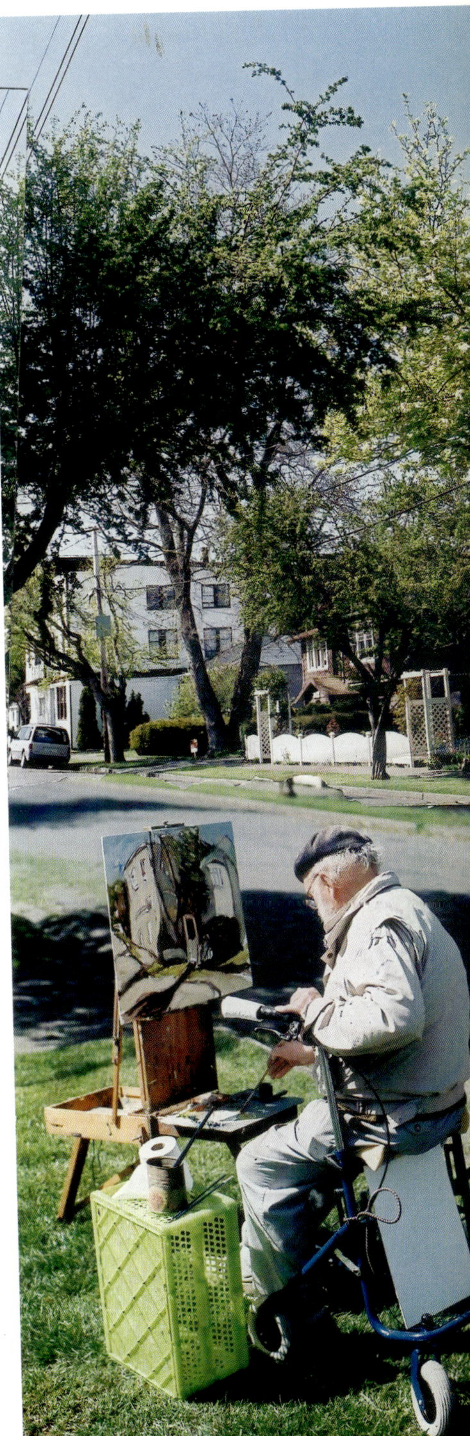

Gordaneer painting on Linden Avenue near Chapman Street, Victoria.

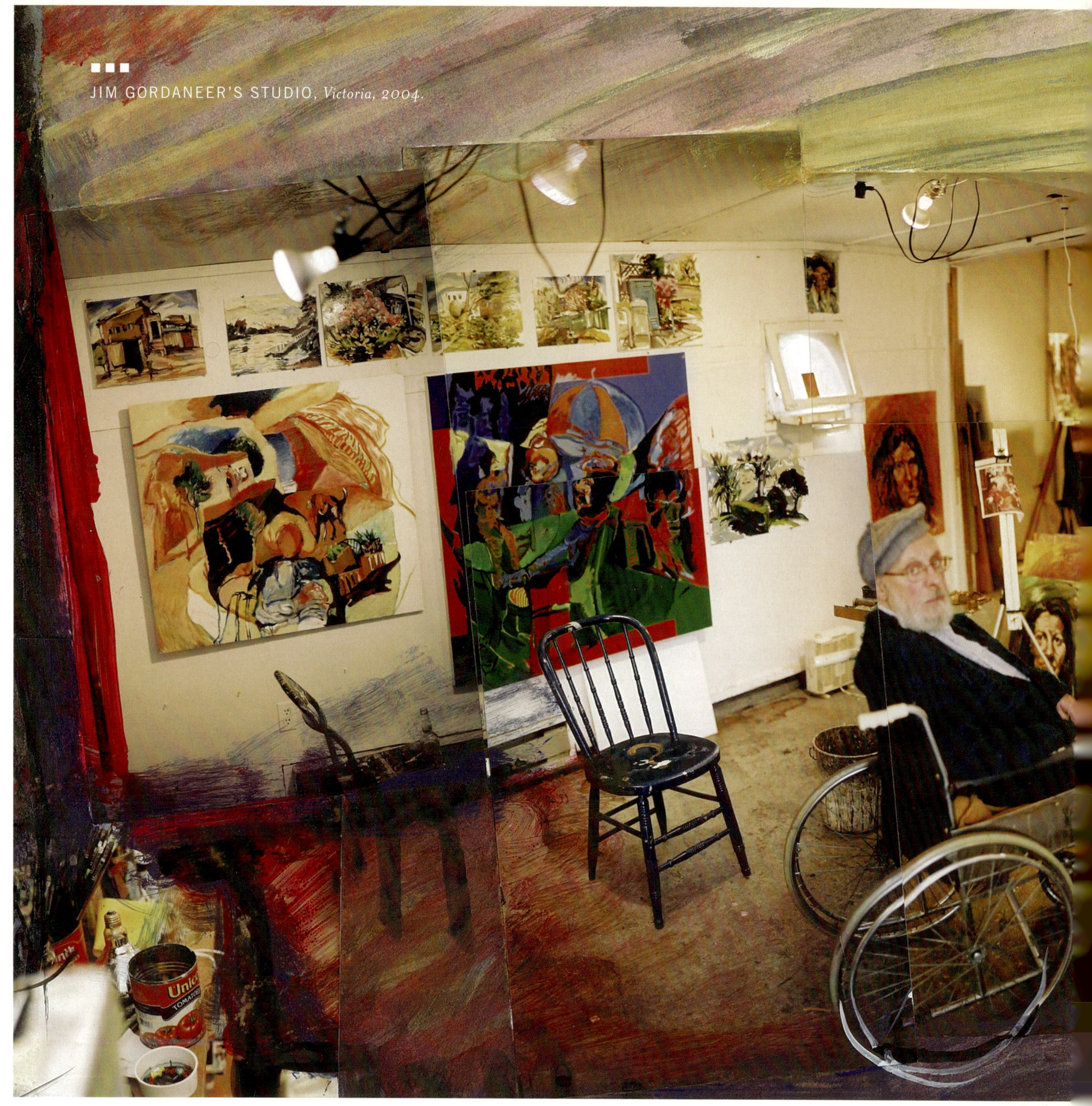

JIM GORDANEER'S STUDIO, *Victoria, 2004.*

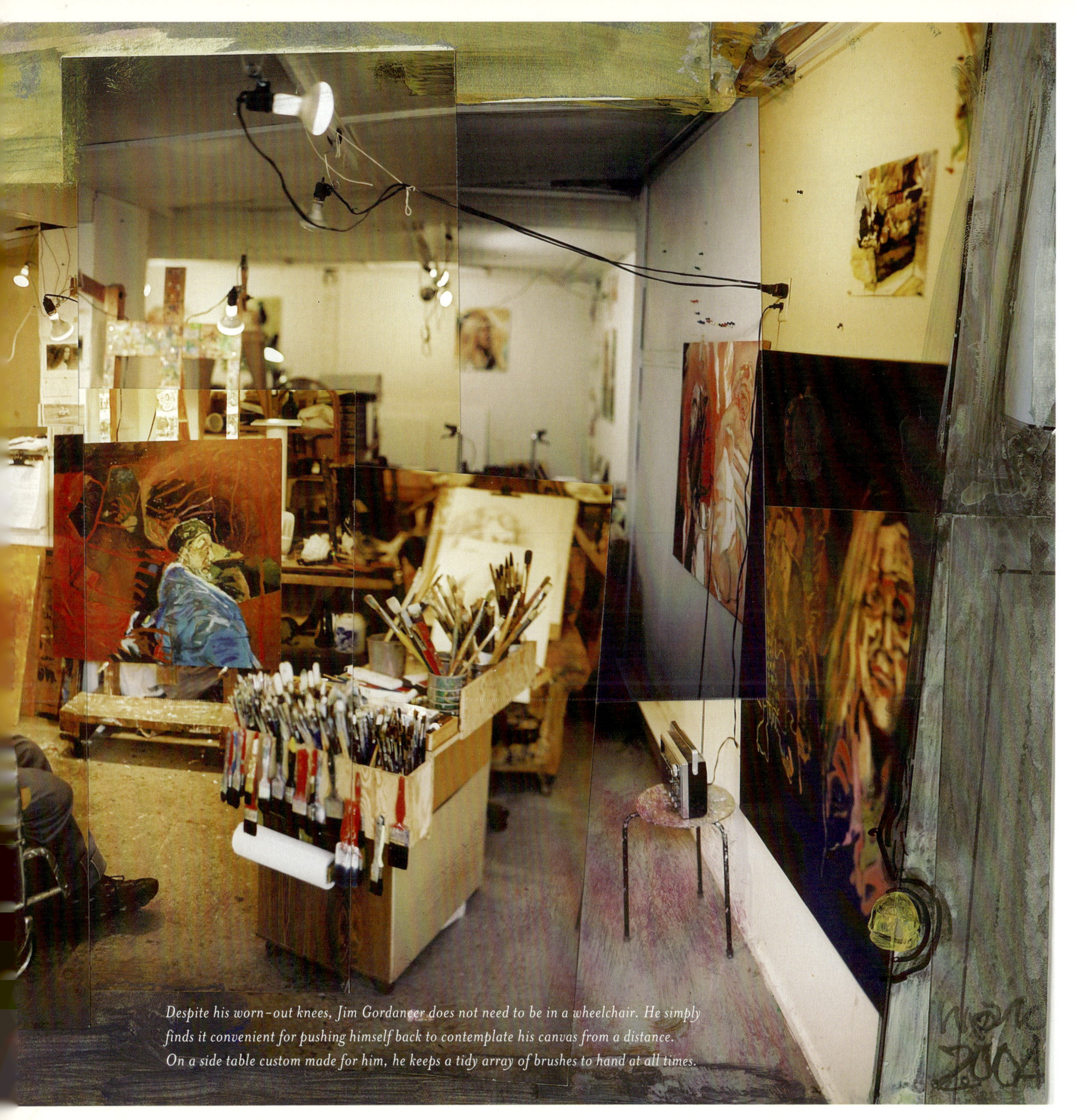

Despite his worn-out knees, Jim Gordaneer does not need to be in a wheelchair. He simply finds it convenient for pushing himself back to contemplate his canvas from a distance. On a side table custom made for him, he keeps a tidy array of brushes to hand at all times.

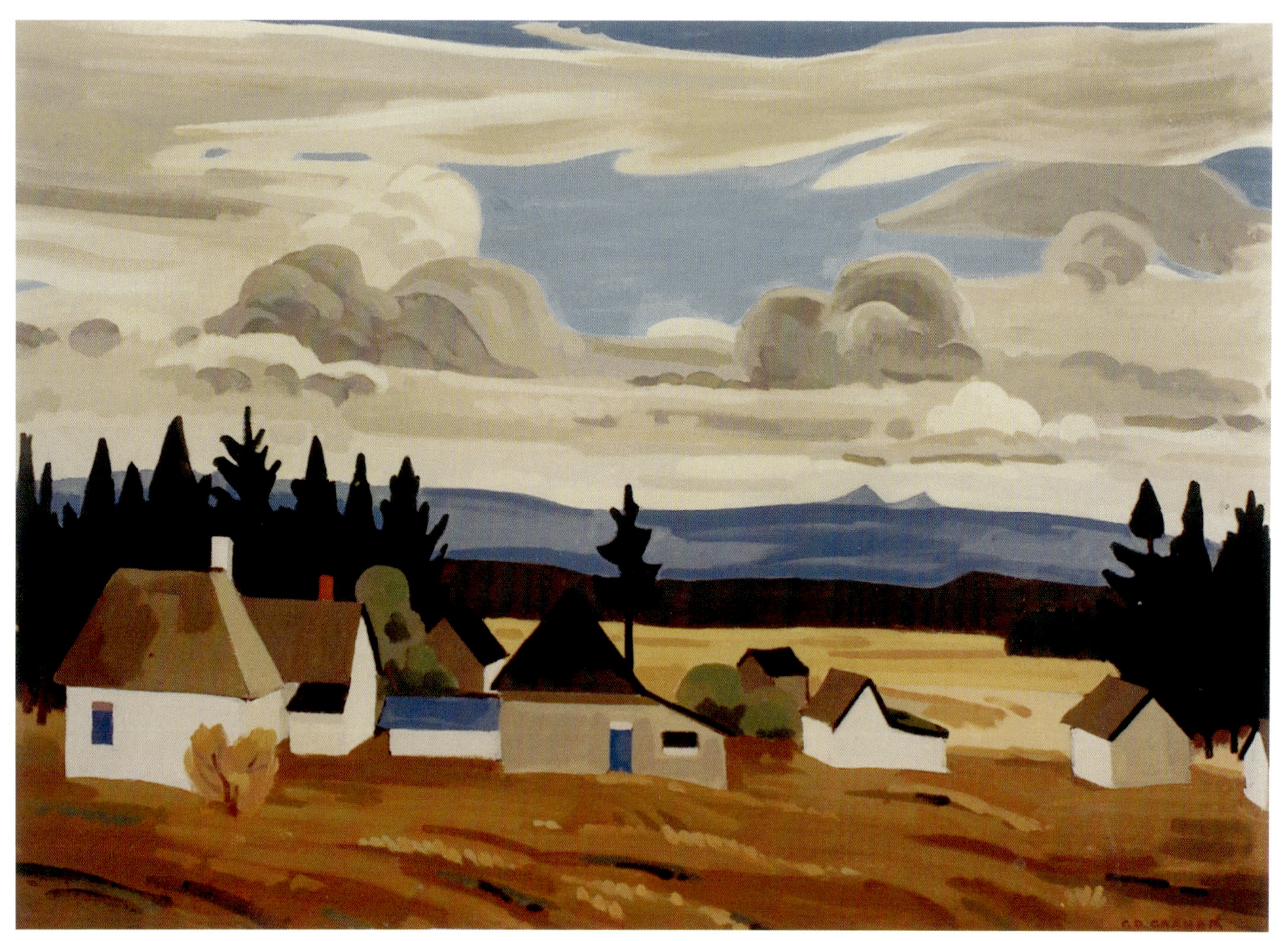

■■■ NORTH SAANICH, *Colin Graham, ink, 4 x 9 inches, not dated.*

COLIN GRAHAM

NORTH SAANICH

COLIN GRAHAM AND HIS WIFE, SYLVIA, WELCOMED ME TO THEIR SUPERB WEST COAST MODERN HOME PERCHED 20 METRES ABOVE THE WATERS OF DEEP COVE AND 20 KILOMETRES NORTH OF VICTORIA.

Our conversation took place by the picture window, though when it was time to paint, Graham retreated to a cluttered spare bedroom where he sat beneath a skylight and communed with his muse.

To photograph his studio I cleared away an accumulation of books and pictures from the side window and then went outside. I crawled through the rhododendrons and photographed the artist through that window, as he contemplated his next picture.

Graham was born in Vancouver in 1915 and attended Shawnigan Lake School. His own interest in art was piqued in his childhood by the sight of a Lawren Harris painting in a tent at the Pacific National Exhibition. Some years later, he was invited to Harris's Belmont Avenue home in Vancouver, for one of the Thursday evening soirées Lawren and his wife, Bess, held for young people. "He had one of the best gramophones," Graham recalled fondly.

After graduating in history at Cambridge University Graham pursued a Master of Art degree at Berkeley. As an art educator he stayed on in California until he was invited to become the first director of the Victoria Art Gallery, now the Art Gallery of Greater Victoria, a position he held from 1951 until 1974.

Graham's stewardship of visual art was deft. His own enthusiasm for artists such as Lawren Harris, A. Y. Jackson, Margaret Peterson, Herbert Siebner and Maxwell Bates was balanced by a recognition of the prevailing tastes of Victoria. A master of the anecdote, Graham still tells tales of leftover Edwardians "passing over in pained silence all this dreadful modern stuff."

He remained at the helm of the Victoria gallery until ill health forced his early retirement but he continued to share his expertise there as curator emeritus until 1978, at which time he received an honorary doctorate from the University of Victoria. He

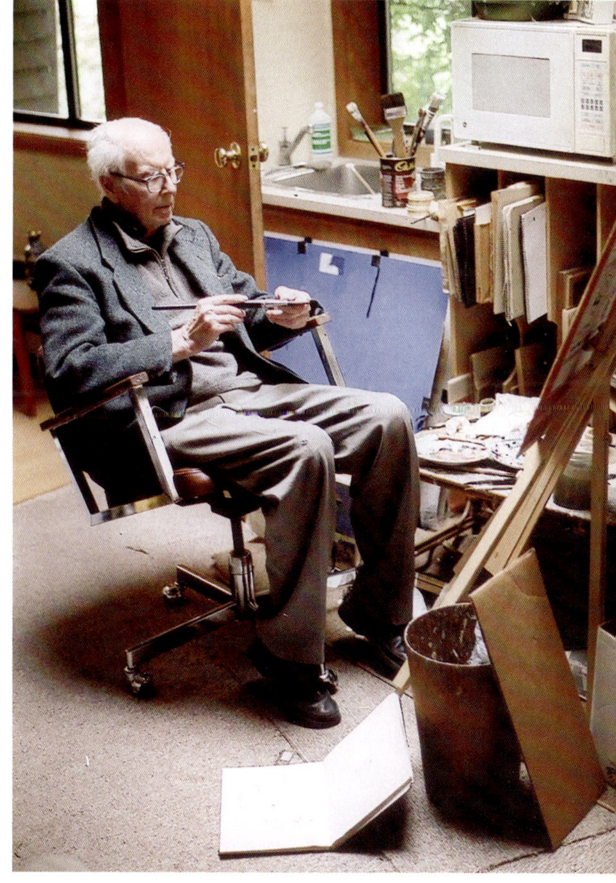

Colin Graham in his studio, 2006.

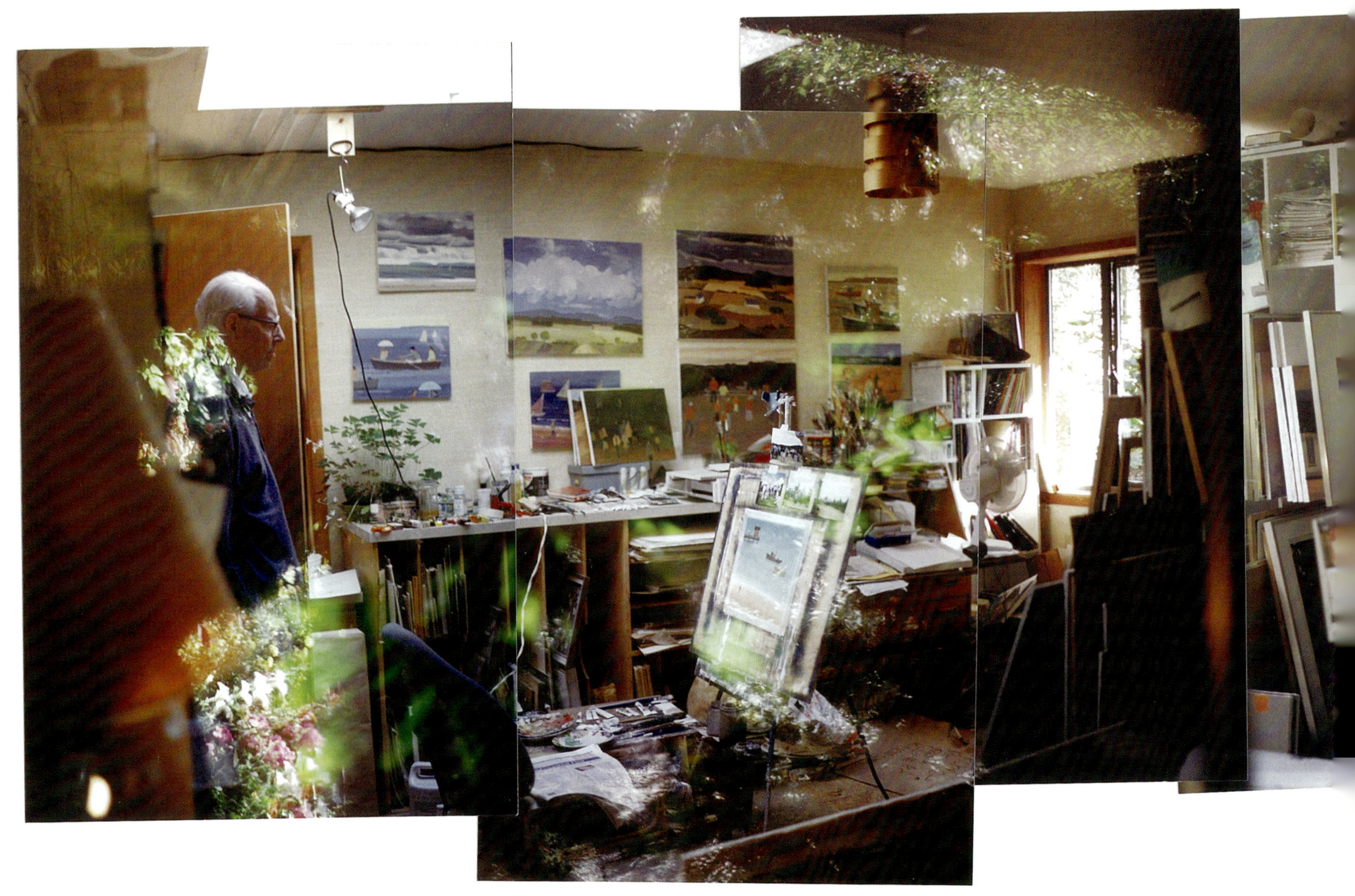

COLIN GRAHAM'S STUDIO, *Deep Cove, October 15, 2006.*
Reflections of the garden lend context to the photo.

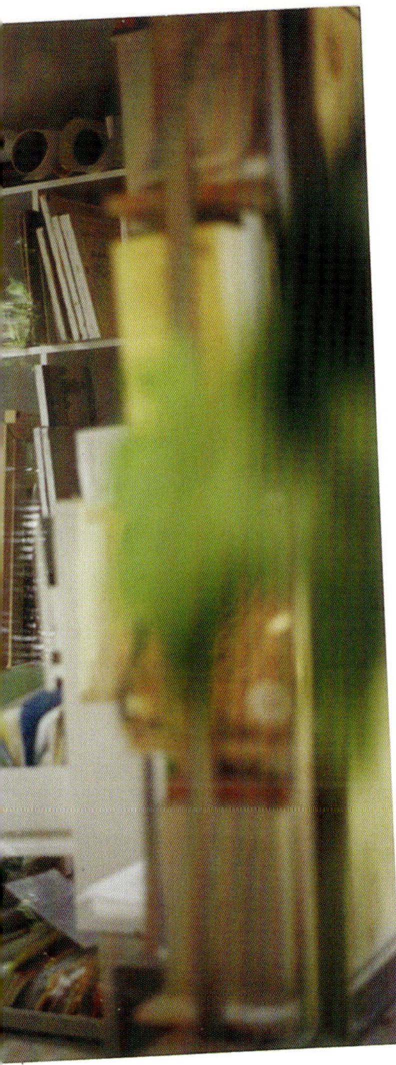

then retired to write and to paint, or, as he put it, "To add to the world's store of bad paintings."

In his studio, Graham was self-effacing. "I call these my 'Thurber wine' paintings," he quipped. "As James Thurber has one of his characters say, 'It's just a naïve little wine but I think you'll be amused by its presumption.'" In fact, Graham's paintings are mellow and matured, with a splendid bouquet. Using gouache (an opaque watercolour), casein (a tempera with milk solids as its binder) or oil paint, he creates images of gentle, blended colours, rich in harmonious middle tones.

His years at the gallery were crucial to this talent. "Being so close to all the exhibits," he noted, "I began to get close to what a reasonable painting consisted of, the fundamental structure of the painting which related the colours and forms in a coherent whole." He achieved this essentially abstract goal with landscape, becoming a "landscape painter with abstract influences."

Since retirement Graham has had to fight fatigue. Unable to stand for long periods of time, he hit on the idea of driving to scenes he wished to record. He'd sketch from the roadside and later, at home, transpose these drawings to canvas from a comfortable chair by his easel. He perceptively mines the casual sketches, which gives him the freedom not to be dominated by the subject.

"A colour sensation will start me going," he noted. Like the tonality of a musical composition, certain colour relationships are the foundation of a Graham painting. A master of subtle tones, he can mix a perfect mauve or taupe.

Being at heart a modern artist, Graham is conscious of the integrity of the picture plane, for, to him, all paintings are basically arrangements of colour and tone on a flat surface. Of course he is rendering "space" in his landscapes, but he keeps up a constant dialogue with "flatness" and avoids modelling and shading his forms. "That's apt to destroy colour," he explained.

We may sometimes glimpse the looseness of Dufy or the incipient cubism of Cezanne in Graham's paintings. Perhaps due to his contact with Chinese art, clouds and trees are rendered in a shorthand that speaks of experience distilled, rather than nature delineated. Written symbols—a house, a cart—are arranged on the paper in a way that implies space with deceptive simplicity. He recalls the words of a teacher: "avoid visual journalism."

With accustomed modesty, Graham calls himself "a very minor painter," yet this attitude has freed him from nagging ambition. Blessed with a certain colour sense, and not having a family dependent on his artistic income, Graham summed it all up: "I just set out to enjoy myself."

"I start out the day with an absolutely blank mind," he told me, sitting in his bedroom-sized studio. Books and storage racks crowded the walls. In the centre a low chair and easel presented a palpable sense of the creativity that has gone on here. In the past 15 years, close to a thousand paintings have left this studio to add their measure of beauty and serenity to the world.

TED HARRISON

VICTORIA

TED HARRISON WAS BORN ON AUGUST 28, 1926, IN THE VILLAGE OF WINGATE IN COUNTY DURHAM, ENGLAND, AND TRAINED IN ART AT THE WEST HARTLEPOOL COLLEGE OF ART.

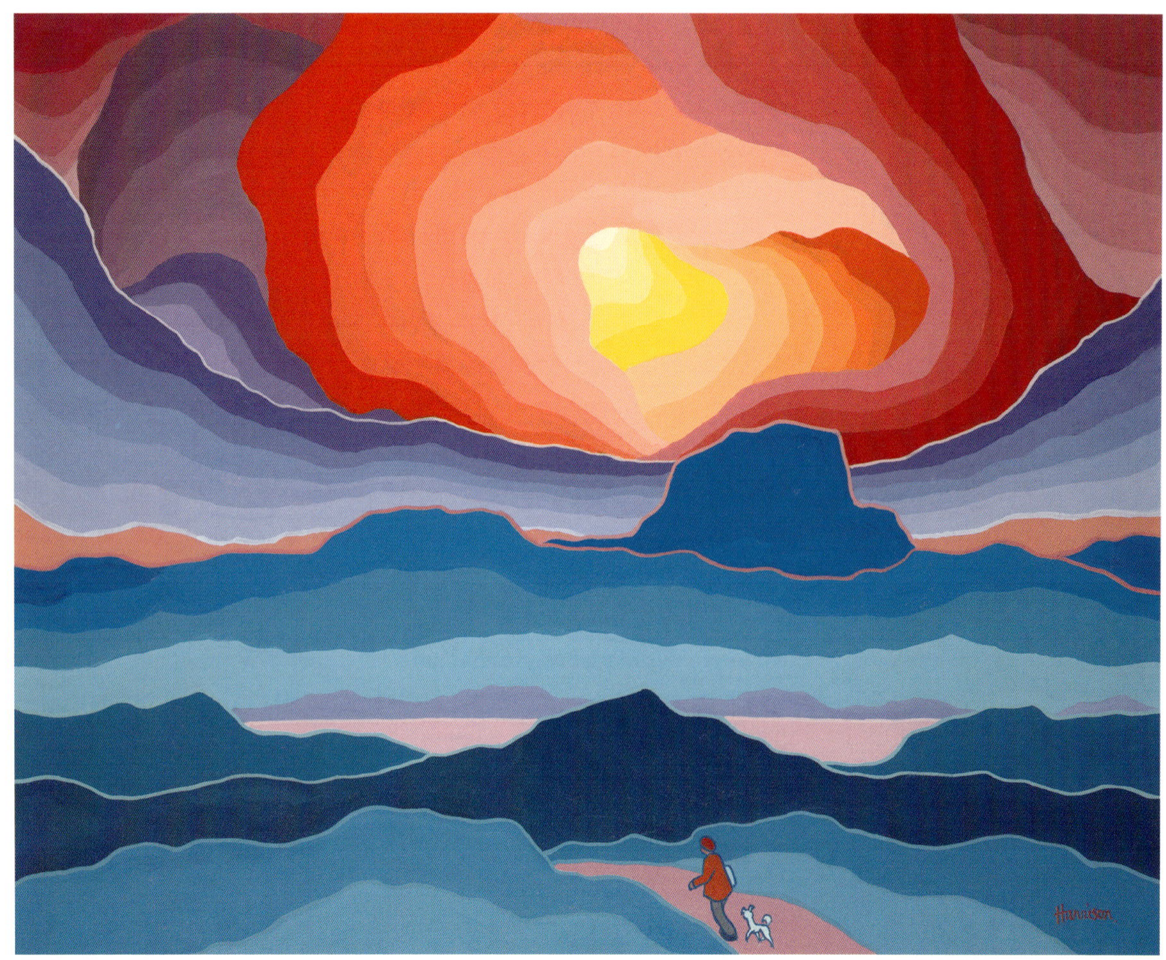

WALKING ALONE, *Ted Harrison, acrylic, 24 x 30 inches, 2000. Harrison painted this for the Alzheimer Society, in memory of his wife, Nicky.*

He saw wartime service in India but after the war there was no work for an artist so, with his wife, Nicky, he went to teach in the South Pacific. In 1967, the Harrisons decided to finish their careers in Canada and landed up in the Yukon. Living in Carcross and Whitehorse, Ted created his unique and colourful style, influenced by the vast space and colours of northern life.

Harrison was discovered there in the 1970s and brought to the attention of the nation and the world. His paintings have since become a defining image of Canada's north. His illustrations for books of Robert Service's poems, *The Cremation of Sam McGee* and *The Shooting of Dan McGrew*, brought him international fame and opened the way to a life of considerable creative freedom.

Recently I asked Harrison's business manager, Irene Davies, about marketing his work. She replied, "We don't have to do marketing. Every elementary-school teacher in the country makes sure every child is aware of Ted." The children are delighted to discover this accessible artistic style and the joy that is included in all of Harrison's work.

Seeking a more moderate climate, the Harrisons moved to Victoria in 1993. It was there, in their comfortable ranch-style home on a leafy cul-de-sac, that I photographed them in 1997. The two oldsters and their terrier, Maggie, greeted me. The dog was named after Margaret Thatcher—"She never stops yapping," Ted explained. The household was suffused with an uproarious sense of fun.

Harrison's studio was the sunroom over the garage, flooded with light and facing the backyard beneath a canopy of Garry oak trees. A creative clutter surrounded the artist. Visible in the foreground of my photograph is a big bag of birdseed, an exercise machine and some of the paper plates that served as palettes for Harrison's acrylics. Artworks from students and children jostled with beautifully crafted artifacts from the couple's travels.

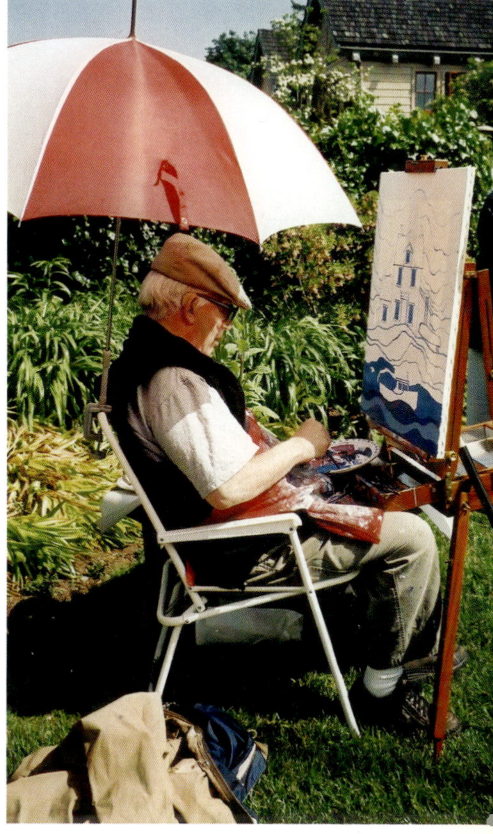

Ted Harrison at Painter's Lodge, Campbell River, 2002 (photo by Sarah Amos).

A computer and a radio keep Harrison company during the long hours he puts in, working to meet the demand for his work. He admitted that when he's not looking at the canvas, he's probably watching the Turner Movie Channel.

Harrison was proudly offering me a bottle of beer, with one of his own paintings on the label, when the phone rang. He took the call and his face fell. "It was my dealer," he explained after he hung up. "The show isn't next month. It's next week."

Back to the drawing board. While Ted returned to work I set about making my photographs. "You're not going to take my picture," Nicky challenged me from the doorway. She was holding Maggie and looking my way when I clicked the shutter. Harrison recently told me he wished I had taken a picture of his sweetheart looking "a little less ferocious," but by now both Nicky and Maggie have passed on.

Harrison is in demand as a public speaker and at an annual event in Campbell River called Painters at Painter's Lodge, he is a star attraction. He's honed his comic timing in front of audiences of reluctant students in classrooms all over the globe. I noted some of the questions and answers:

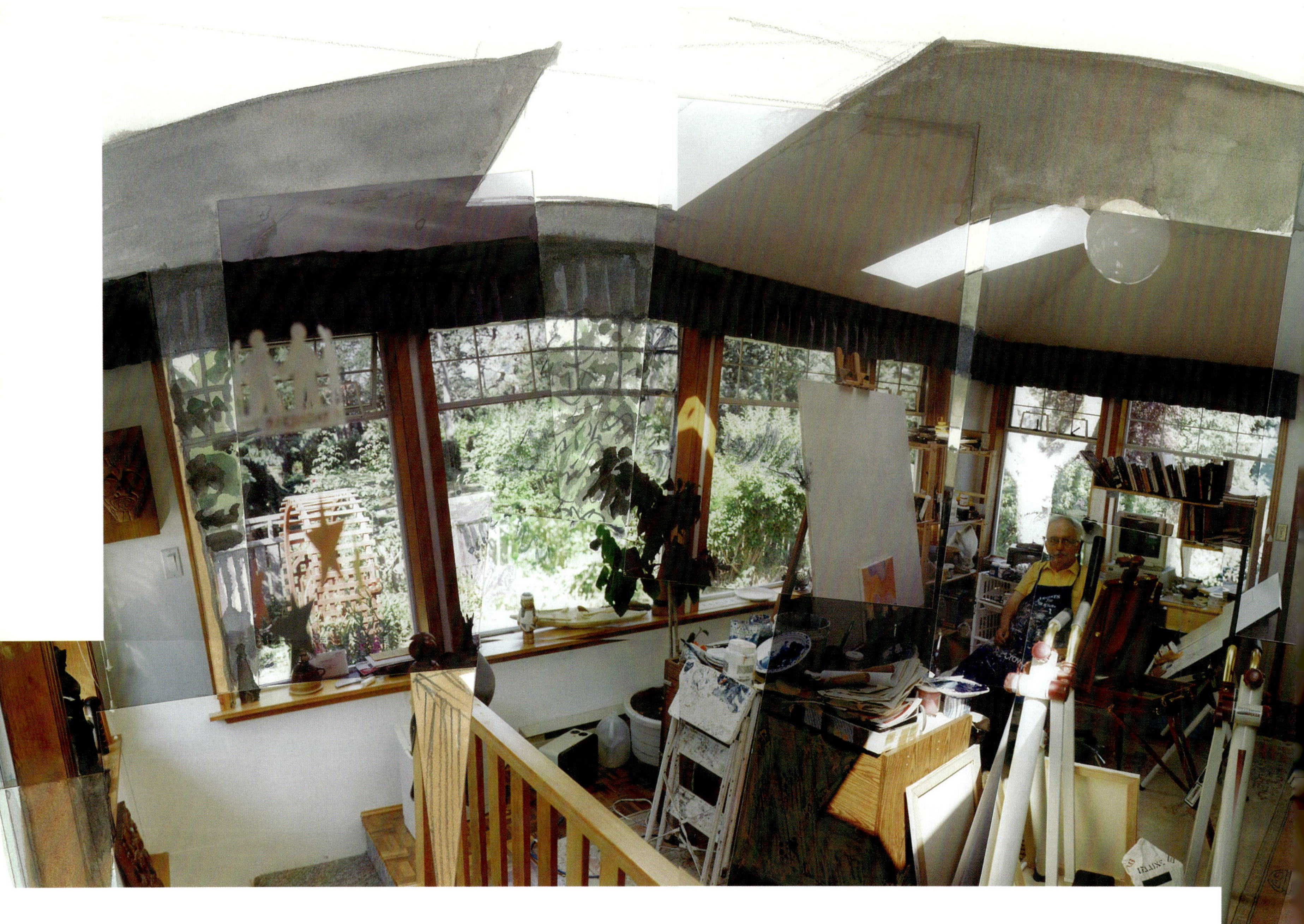

What was your best moment as an artist?

I guess it was the moment when I realized that your art could be anything you wanted it to be. It could be a blue moose, or a pink dog. One day someone pointed out to me that there was a mistake in one of my paintings.

"What's the mistake," I asked.

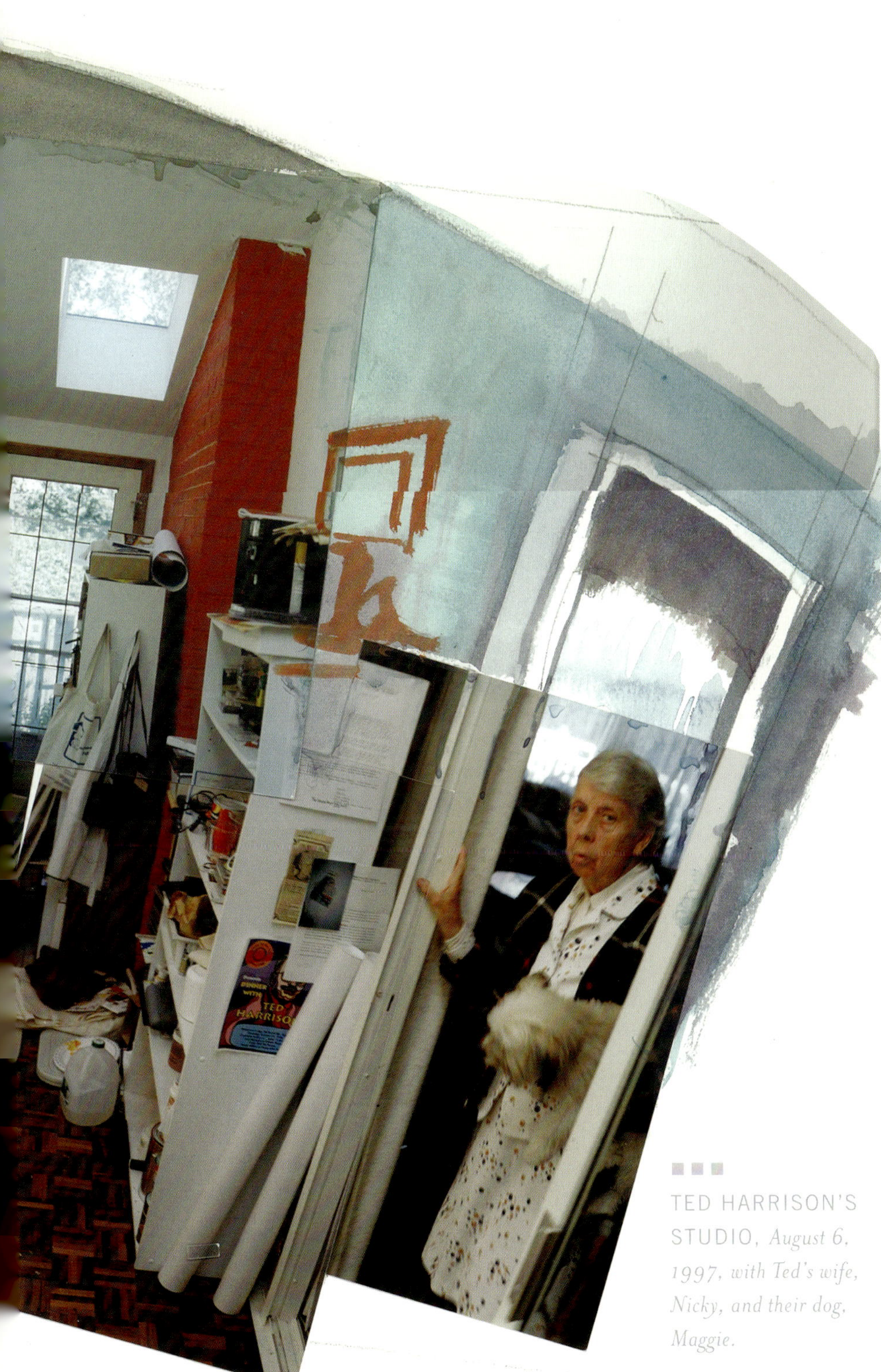

TED HARRISON'S STUDIO, *August 6, 1997, with Ted's wife, Nicky, and their dog, Maggie.*

"Well," he said, "you painted two men carrying a dead moose. Any idiot knows that two men can't carry a dead moose."

"Yes," I told him, "but this is a *blue* moose. And two men can carry a *blue* moose." If it's a blue moose, you can wrap it up and put it in your pocket. And when you get it home you can dip it in the bath and it will come back as a full-sized moose.

Do you dream in colours?

When I sleep I use a CPAP machine because I have sleep apnea. And now I have better dreams than I ever had, because it keeps the oxygen going to my brain. I hadn't known that it wasn't reaching my brain before. Now, my dreams are so colourful and entertaining that I'd be willing to pay an entertainment tax. I won't divulge the content.

What do you do with your time when you aren't painting?

Since I lost my wife to Alzheimer's I've gone on the board of the Alzheimer Society, so that takes a lot of time. And I listen to CBC Radio's *Ideas* program every night at 9:00. I like to watch the History Channel on Thursday evenings. I enjoy listening to the music of Beethoven and baking bread.

What type of bread do you bake?

The best!

Do you ever paint abstract paintings?

Me? I like to paint houses, people, dogs, birds ... If I left those things out, my paintings would be abstract paintings. I like looking at abstract paintings; I don't like doing them. I grew up in Britain during the Depression. It was a very humanistic place, where people really mattered. If I lived in New York, I'd be trying to keep away from people and I'd probably paint abstracts. But I think the world needs more humanism.

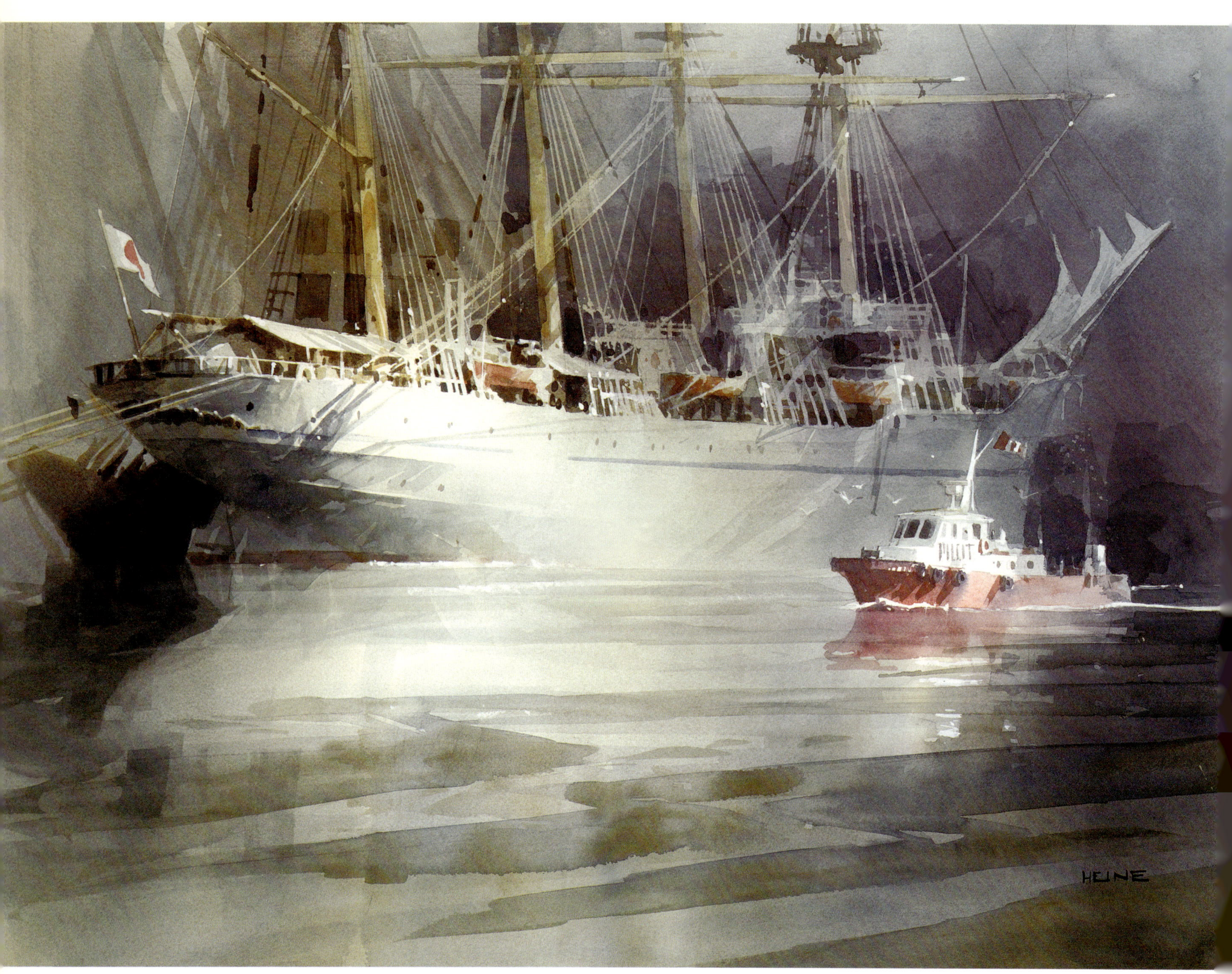
HEINE

HARRY HEINE

SAANICH

ON THE WAY TO HARRY HEINE'S STUDIO I CONTEMPLATED THE VIEW ACROSS SAANICH INLET, A PLAY OF LIGHT AND MIST I RECOGNIZED FROM MANY OF HEINE'S PAINTINGS.

His studio was in Brentwood Bay, in a converted garage at the back of the family home. This simple building housed both a workshop for building and carving things and also his shipshape painting studio.

Once I was inside, Heine proudly showed me the latest model of his super-efficient travelling paintbox. He then took me into his fluorescent-lit painting room. The misty day outside and the greenish cast of the lighting within lent a suitably marine atmosphere to the proceedings. The studio's ambience reminded me of a ship's cabin, with all the gear stowed in cleverly designed cupboards and drawers, ready for action.

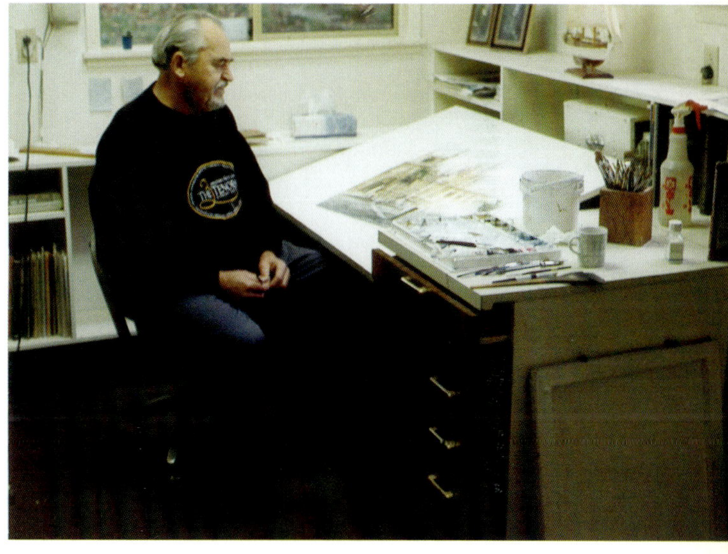

Harry Heine in his studio, Brentwood Bay.

The tables were littered with sketches he had made when he led a recent art trip to Spain. "People spend too much time copying photographs," he fumed. His pleasure was to make lightning-quick studies in watercolour or pencil on the spot and then work from them in the studio to make the finished painting.

Surprisingly, there is often less detail in his large works than in the sketches. This was evident in a view of the Alhambra Palace near Granada, a subject of ferocious complexity. When drawing on the spot, Heine wasn't daunted. "The confidence comes from my old trade, architectural rendering," he noted. The finished work was dramatically simplified.

Large studio watercolours require a lot of patience, waiting for washes to dry. Heine told me he loved to listen to Beethoven and Mozart while contemplating his next move. Our day together was time off for him, and he let himself enjoy an abundance of cigarettes and conversation.

■■■ NIPPON MARU, OGDEN POINT, VICTORIA, *Harry Heine, watercolour, 20 x 28 inches, not dated.*

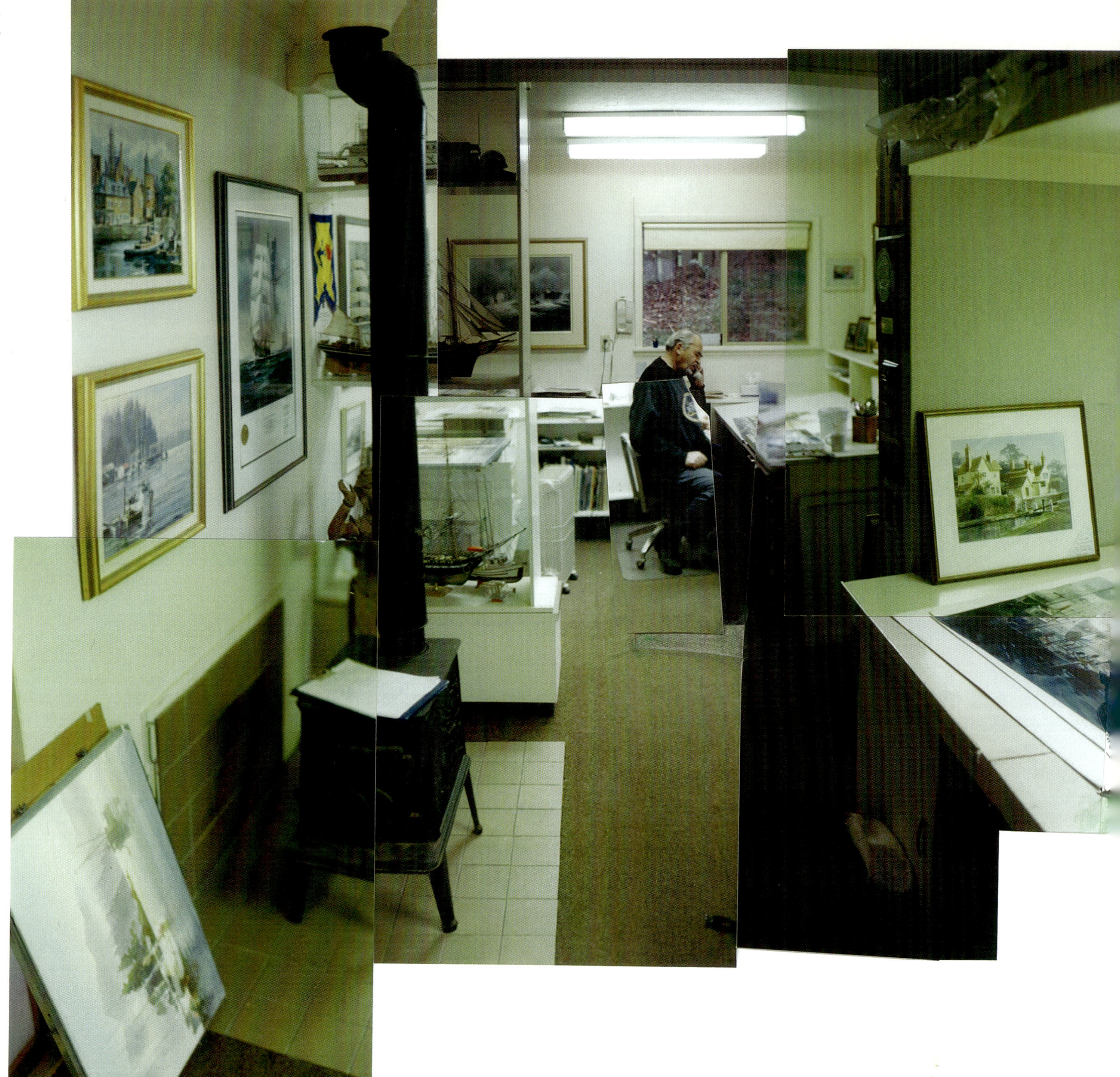

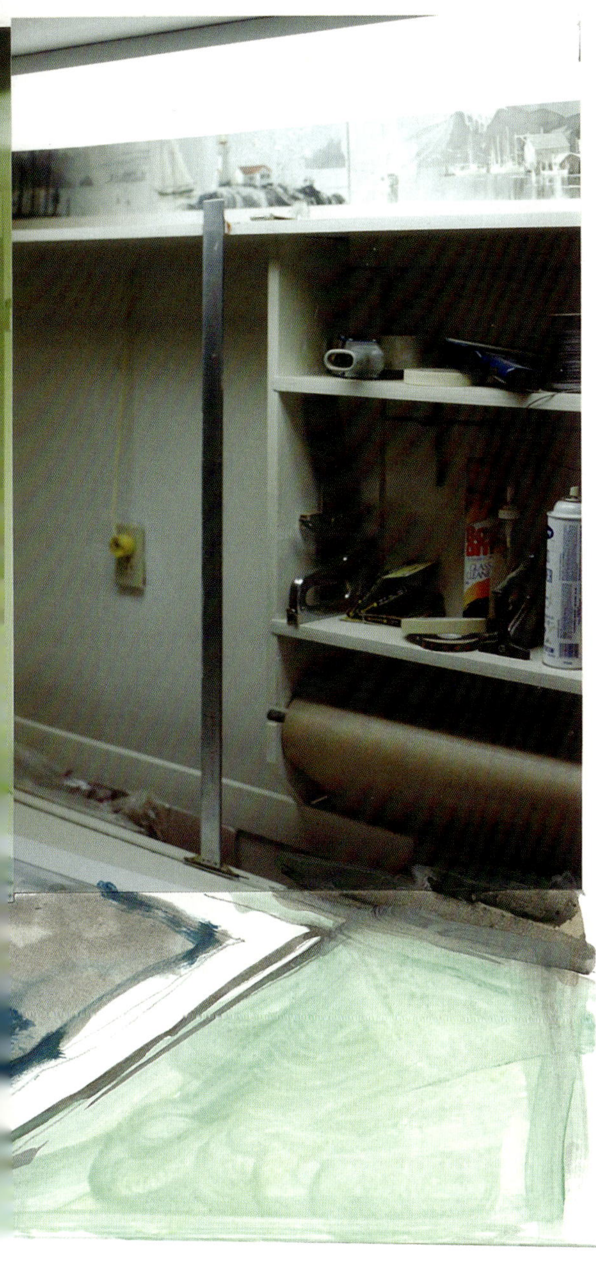

HARRY HEINE'S STUDIO,
Brentwood Bay, November 18, 1997.

Heine was born in 1928 and spent his early working years in the disciplined atmosphere of commercial art, starting as a staff artist with the Alberta government. Later he did a number of murals for an Edmonton design company and became the director of Designs of Canada, Ltd. Though he always painted in his free time, his move to Vancouver Island in 1970 signalled his emergence as a full-time exhibiting artist. On the coast, he gravitated toward painting ships.

The Alberta murals didn't contain many ships. "I didn't set out to become a marine artist," the prairie boy laughed. His first commissioned painting of a ship was Captain Cook's vessel of exploration. By 1980 he was elected to the Royal Society of Marine Artists, the first and only Canadian member. He exhibited regularly with the RSMA in England and at the Mystic Seaport Museum in Connecticut.

Heine painted the Victoria-based sail-training schooner *Robertson II* and a thousand other vessels, mostly local working ships. Through his sincere interest, he became a life member of the Sail and Life Training Society in 1991 and honorary life member of the Vintage Vessel Registry of the Maritime Museum of British Columbia in 1996.

In later years Heine led painting tours to Italy, China, Germany, France, Java, Bali, Russia, Mexico, Austria, Thailand and England. Working out of doors kept his style loose—when he got comfortable he felt a tendency to "noodle," he told me. "The danger is in being overwhelmed by details and overworking the bold statement of light and form. There's a temptation to put it all in."

I commented on his dextrous handling of mist and vapours. Gesturing toward the forested slopes of Brentwood Bay, Heine informed me that he started "doing mist and fog to get rid of all those damned trees!"

Harry Heine died in 2004. Though not an intellectual, he opened people's eyes to the world around them—non-artists, amateurs and talented painters alike. His was a great life, and he shared it generously.

MARTIN HONISCH

CHEMAINUS

CURIOSITY BROUGHT ME TO THE CHEMAINUS STUDIO OF MARTIN HONISCH. MY ADMIRATION FOR HIS GLAZED OIL PAINTINGS IS GREAT, BUT THEY HAVE A DARKNESS OF TONE THAT, IN THE BRIGHTLY LIT GALLERY, PUZZLED ME. HOW DID THEY LOOK IN THE STUDIO WHERE HONISCH CREATED THEM?

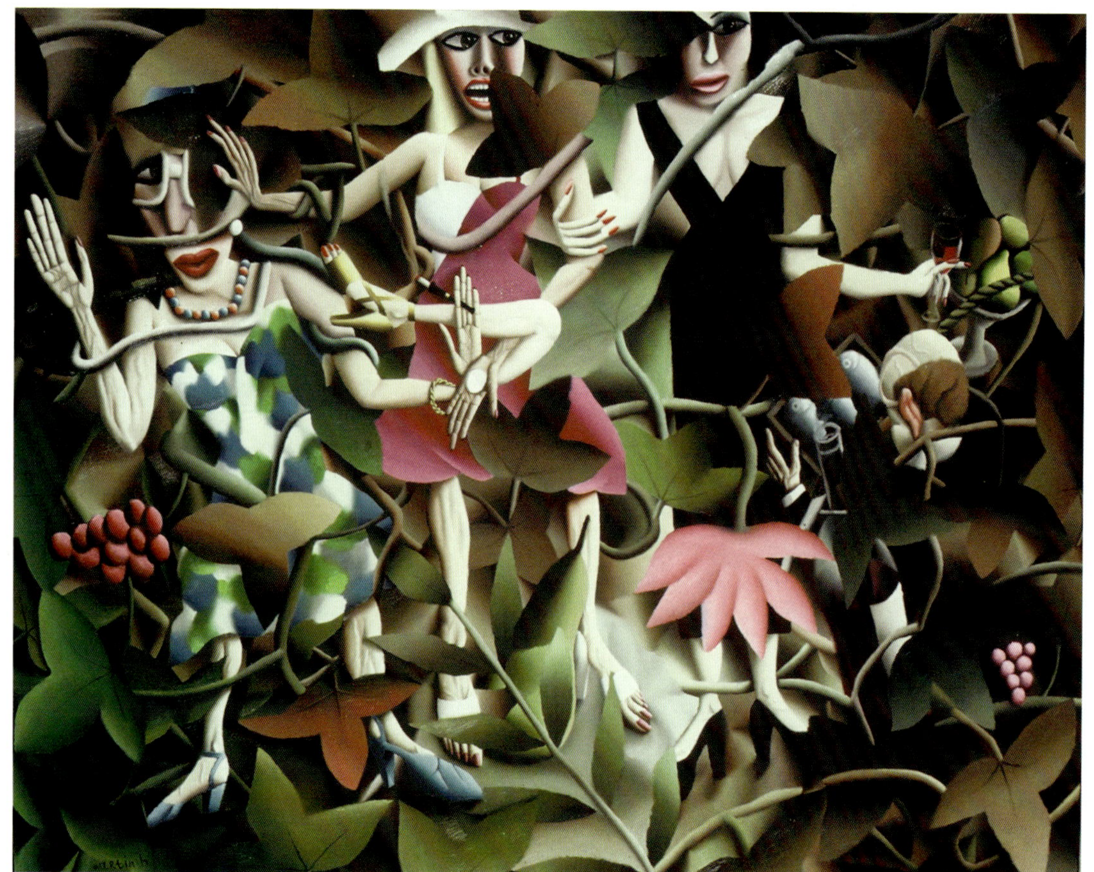

SHUT-DOWN AT LINDERHOF,
Martin Honisch,
oil on canvas, 45 x 57 inches, 1986.

Honisch paints by a north window in the sitting room of his family's modest home on a quiet street. He does not share the avid commercialism of the well-known Chemainus muralists. At home, he appeared as a bearded *paterfamilias*, right down to the pipe and slippers, as he sat amid a stack of art books in his well-worn easy chair. The essentials of the oil painter's craft were spread before him.

Martin Honisch was born in 1942 in the region known as Moravia. While Moravia has been part of many political constructs—Austria, Czechoslovakia, Germany—Honisch saw it not as the scene of the current events of the day, but as a place that had been part of an ancient and traditional world, a continuation of European civilization as it had endured for more than a millenium. His home was, unfortunately, at the crossroads of the old world and the new. The old fell to pieces in 1945.

"Wartime leaves marks on a child who grows up in it," he told me. In the face of the Russian invasion of Hungary, he fled with his family to Vancouver, arriving in 1957. During the 1960s Honisch studied art at the University of British Columbia and on scholarship at the University of Hamburg. And then a different sort of revolution rearranged his world. Honisch sees flower power and the anti-Vietnam era as a continuation of the effects of World War II, for, as he said, "Those were the babies who were bombed on."

Travel through the Middle East to India and Nepal followed, and years of bold experiments in art and living. Then, in 1973, he moved to Kitimat in northern B.C. and began eight years of secondary-school teaching. Through the summers he took a Master of Education degree in Bellingham, with a thesis on oil painting technology. Already a very good painter, Honisch was slowly learning the sublime discipline of oil painting. He and his wife, Usha, were married in the Punjab in India in 1979 and have two children.

Honisch's painting is based on a firm outline. At heart he loves form best, naming Cezanne and Poussin as inspirations. He works within a spatial format he calls "a sculptural bas-relief approach." Each element is brought up close to the picture plane and modelled there, as if in clay. These forms are not illuminated by a single external "light source"; instead, the artist gives us selective lighting that seems to emanate from certain significant points of the composition.

Honisch paints with an Old Master technique as fine as any you'll see. His dark glazes create a rich profundity of tone. He has striven for—and largely achieved—the limpid clarity of Van Eyck. His image bank is stocked with Gothic churches, cobbled squares, ruins, saints and soldiers. World travel and his untrammelled imagination are ever-present sources. "Most of my paintings are based on imagery seen while dreaming or having my eyes closed. When I was younger I wasn't aware of my inner life," he noted. But now he cultivates his subconscious, clearly previsualizing each of his paintings.

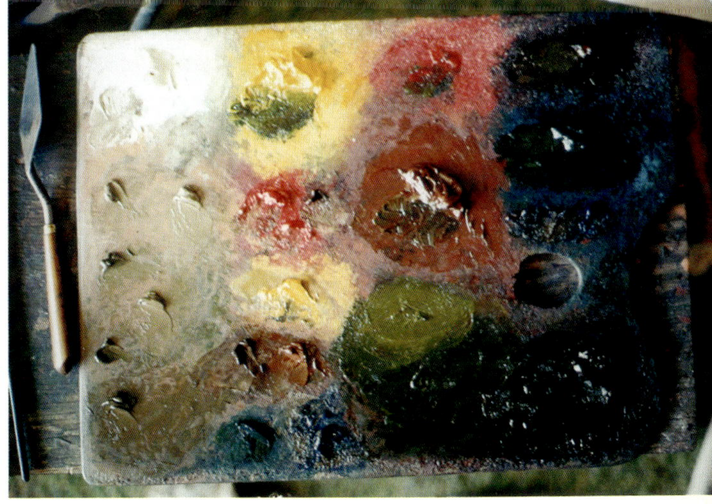

Rich dark hues of oil paint are carefully set out on Honisch's palette. He uses these islands of colour to create glazes with his paints, the basis of his sonorous and sombre style.

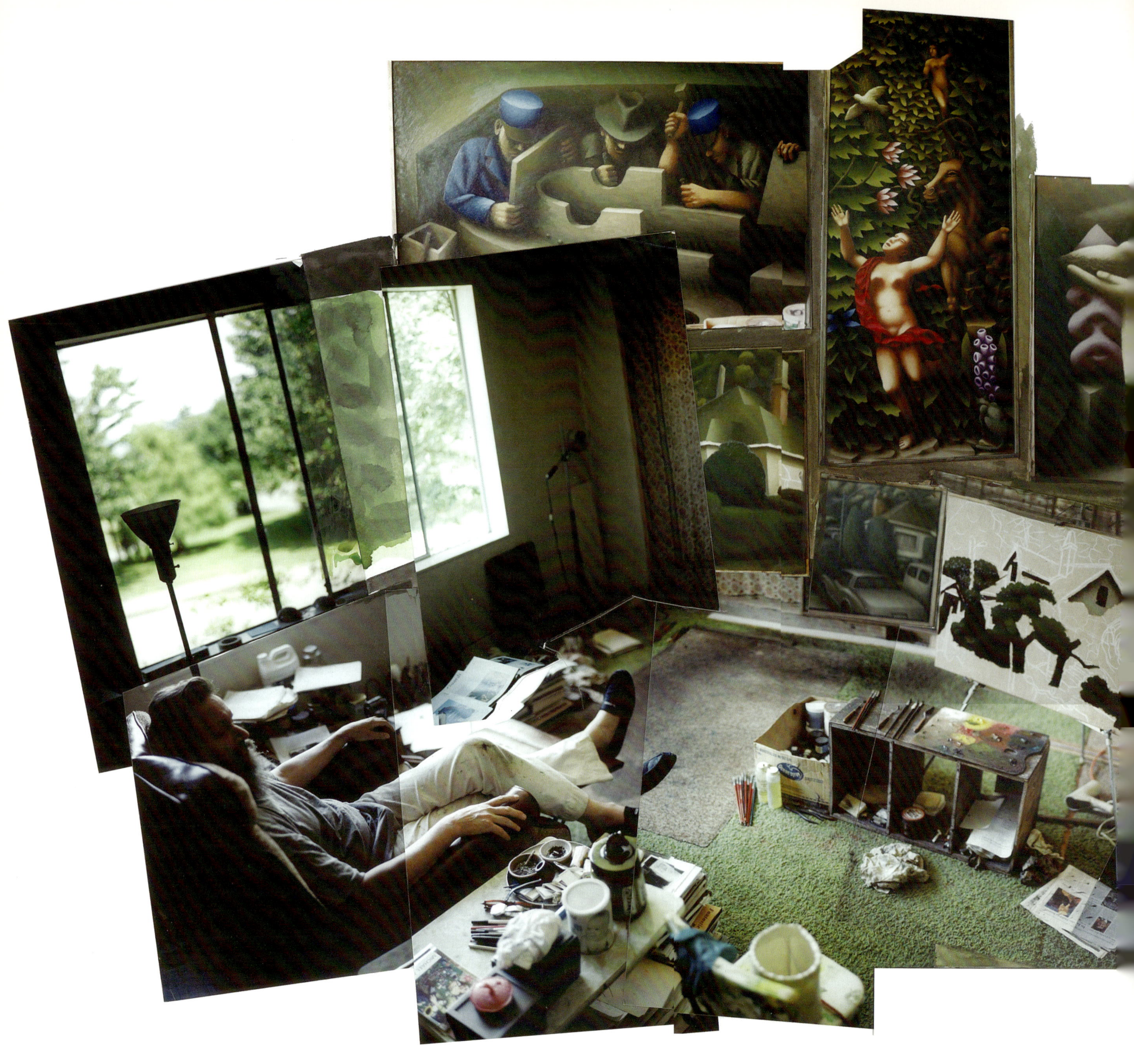

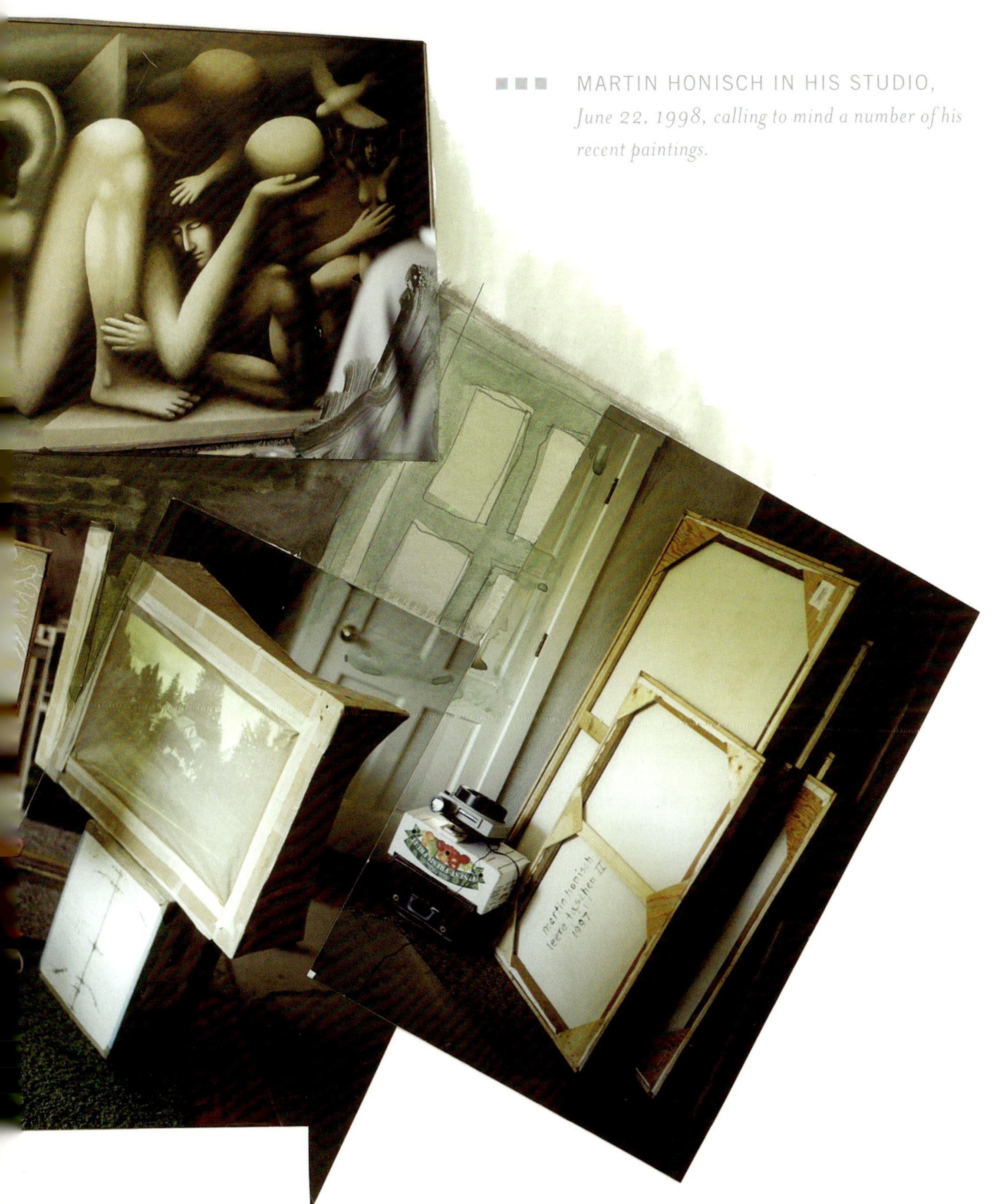

MARTIN HONISCH IN HIS STUDIO, *June 22, 1998, calling to mind a number of his recent paintings.*

"I would venture to state that the fantastic is at the root of all art and ought to occupy a central position, reflecting the basic fact that life and the world are inherently fantastic, weird and wonderful," Honisch explained.

When I was there he was working on a painting of an unusually ordinary suburban scene. A slide projector threw his source image onto a rear-projection screen made of a cardboard box and tracing paper. The painting was developing on a piece of masonite perched on a spindly easel, the first elements blocked in with chalk. Slowly, the haunting scene was taking form in sombre oil glazes.

The wall opposite the artist was hung with an Indian-print bedspread and I had neglected to photograph it. Later, for my photomontage, I collaged in that space a number of the paintings which I had photographed that day in the studio, as if they were appearing before the artist's mind's eye.

Honisch's well-wrought dreams are perhaps too intense for the local market, but that doesn't sway him from his task. Numerous exhibitions of his work have taken place at the Bau Xi Gallery in both Toronto and Vancouver, at the Surrey Art Gallery and the headquarters of the World Bank in Washington, D.C. Those who appreciate fine painting would do well to pay attention to his art.

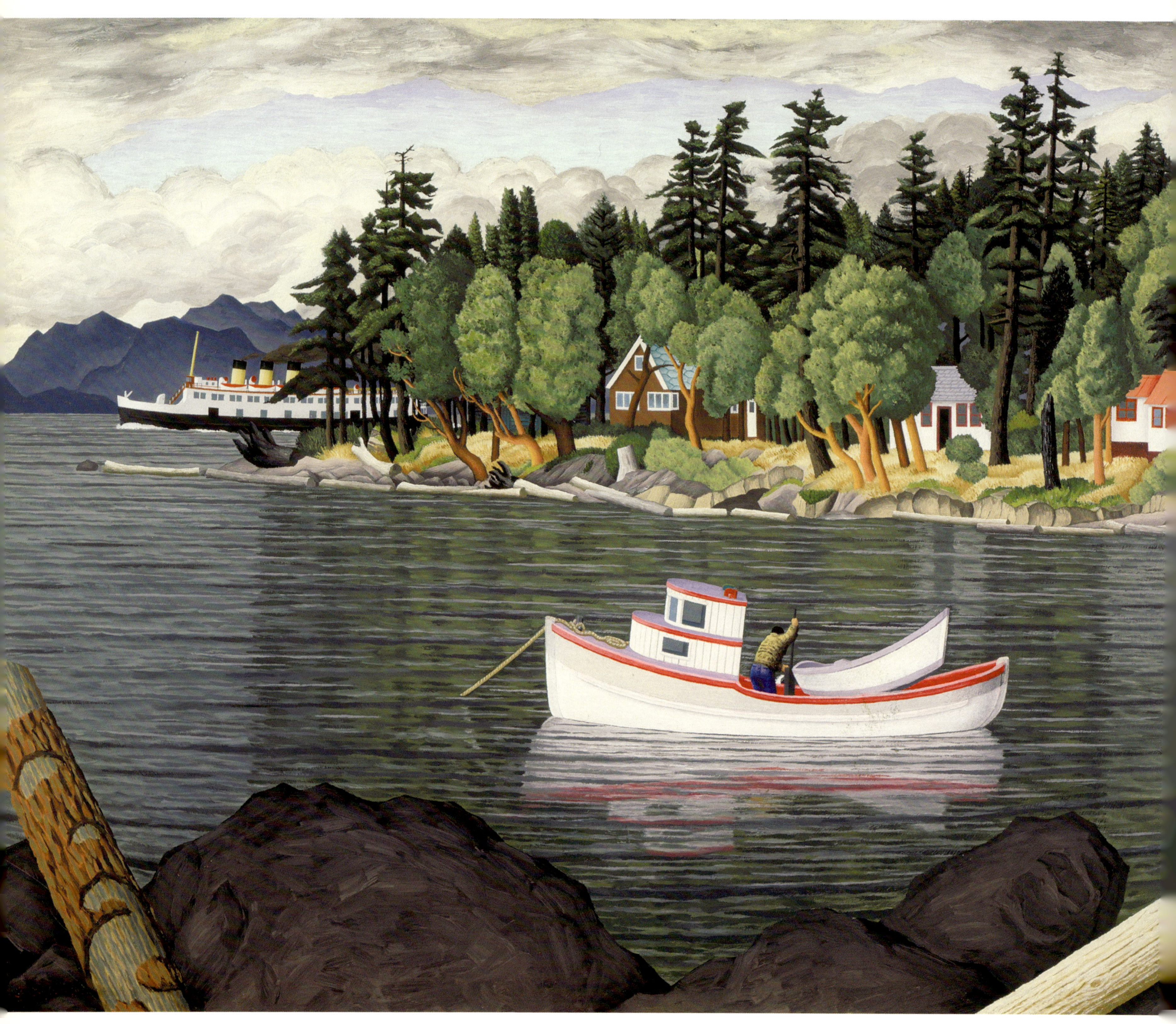

E.J. HUGHES

DUNCAN

E.J. HUGHES IS GONE. WE'LL NEVER SEE HIS LIKE AGAIN. NEXT ONLY TO EMILY CARR, HUGHES WAS THE ARTIST WHO SHOWED US THIS PLACE.

Hughes was born in North Vancouver in 1913 and lived almost all his life on southern Vancouver Island—in Victoria, Nanaimo, Ladysmith and Duncan. A landscape painter, Hughes gave us images of island waterways that ring true. Coastal steamships, government wharfs, booming grounds and fishboats—we see them as if through his eyes.

There was a gentlemanly air about Hughes, a respect for his craft and the people he met, which seemed to be of another time. He learned to draw and paint in the proper, old-fashioned way—a sort of observational realism—under Charles H. Scott at the Vancouver School of Decorative and Applied Arts. By the time he graduated in 1933, his aims and attitudes were set.

A series of unusual circumstances sheltered Hughes and allowed him to nurture his profound powers of concentration. Despairing of earning a living as an artist, he enlisted in the army in 1939. War intervened and he spent more than six years in diligent effort as a war artist. Never sent to the front, he had much detailed material to paint and no worries about food or shelter.

In 1946 he and his wife, Fern, settled in Victoria, but after a few years of struggle they fled to the quiet of a cabin near the West Arm of Shawnigan Lake. There, in storybook style, Hughes was discovered by Emily Carr's dealer, Max Stern, the owner of Montreal's Dominion Gallery. Stern made Hughes a verbal offer to buy everything the artist produced. This arrangement continued to their mutual satisfaction until Stern's death in 1987 and beyond. (The gallery finally ceased operation in 2000.) By his own choice, Hughes was left alone, avoiding openings and customers.

Sometime after Fern's death in 1974, Hughes gratefully accepted Pat Salmon as his loyal intermediary, and he was able to get on with his work undisturbed, quietly and patiently.

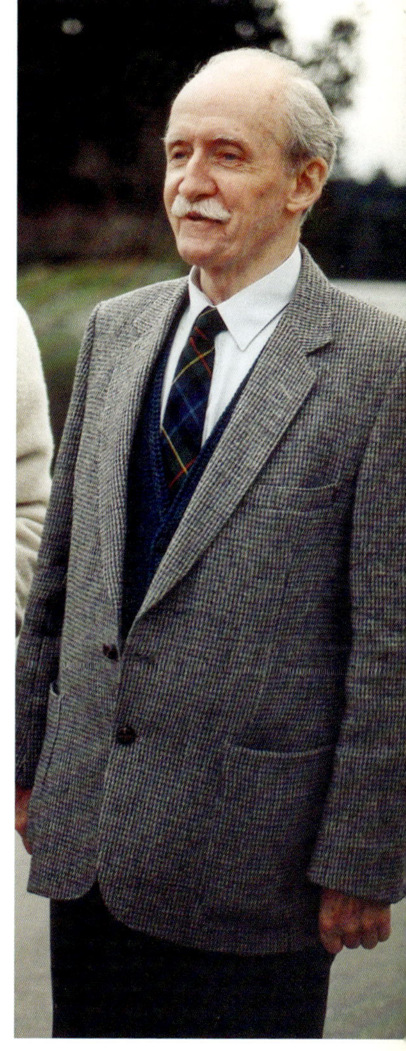

E. J. Hughes, 1994.

■ ■ ■ TAYLOR BAY, GABRIOLA ISLAND, *E.J. Hughes, oil, 24 x 30 inches, 1952.*

Hughes poses with his recently completed watercolour Trees on Savary Island *(2004). In the foreground, note his carpenter's pencil wrapped with string, at hand for drawing a compositional grid, and razor blades ready for sharpening the pencil. His cherished sable brushes all lie neatly with their tips exposed to the air for drying. Before him on the easel is a print of his early oil of* Trees on Savary Island *(1953), available to copy.*

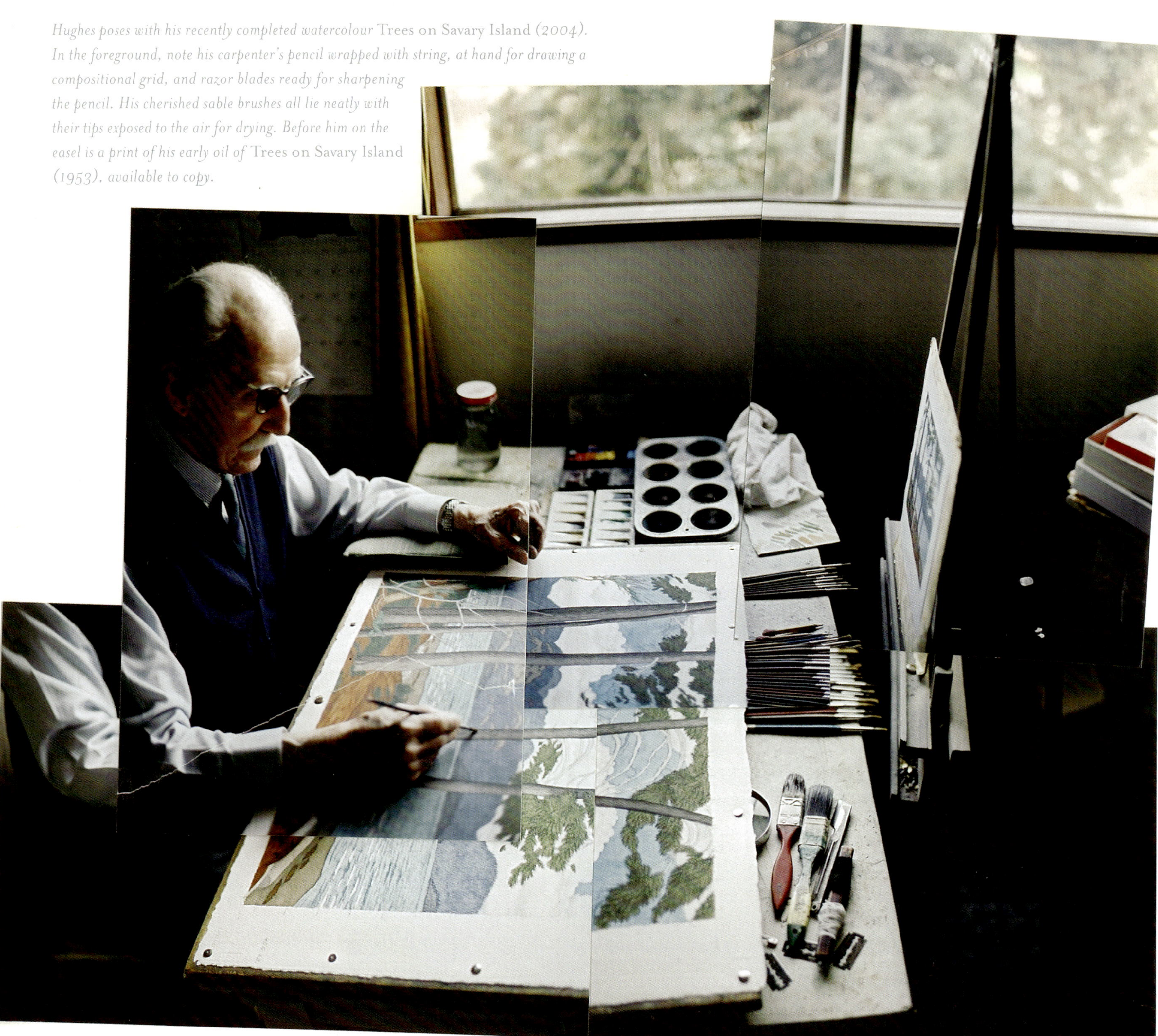

The Dominion Gallery positioned Hughes brilliantly, selling his work to the National Gallery as early as 1951 and placing it in most of Canada's great national collections, both public and private. Without Hughes' active involvement, his career climbed steadily, eventually resulting in two honorary doctorates, the Order of Canada and the sale of one of his early canvases at auction in 2004 for $920,000.

On Vancouver Island, Hughes cherished a sort of anonymity. Regulars at the Dog House Restaurant in Duncan recognized him as a local, with his blue eyes, neat moustache and tweed jacket. When I was first invited to visit his singularly modest suburban home I found nothing of the grand man. There he lived alone in an ordered bachelor existence, with shag carpet and wood-grain wall panels still in place from the 1960s. His collection of his own art included just two early drawings of his wife and a framed poster. He treasured two woodcut prints by Walter J. Phillips. The only visible mark of his success was a large new Jaguar parked in the carport.

Hughes' studio was the spare bedroom, with a table and easel drawn close to a single north window. He retired here to paint every afternoon, six days a week. The furnishings of his studio never changed. His sable watercolour brushes were poised over the edge of his desk to dry. Razor blades for pencil sharpening and string for gridding off his drawings were at hand. For close work he put on a pair of glasses that had belonged to Fern many years before; one of the arms was mended with string.

He took Sundays off and, in his active years, took some time every fourth summer to drive to picturesque locations nearby and accumulate new material for his paintings. On site, Hughes would sit in the front seat of the car and draw, giving two days to a careful pencil study. On the third day, he made a written "colour map." What he absorbed there he brought home to his studio, translating these notes into oils, acrylics or watercolours as much as 65 years after the fact. Miraculously, his concentration never wavered.

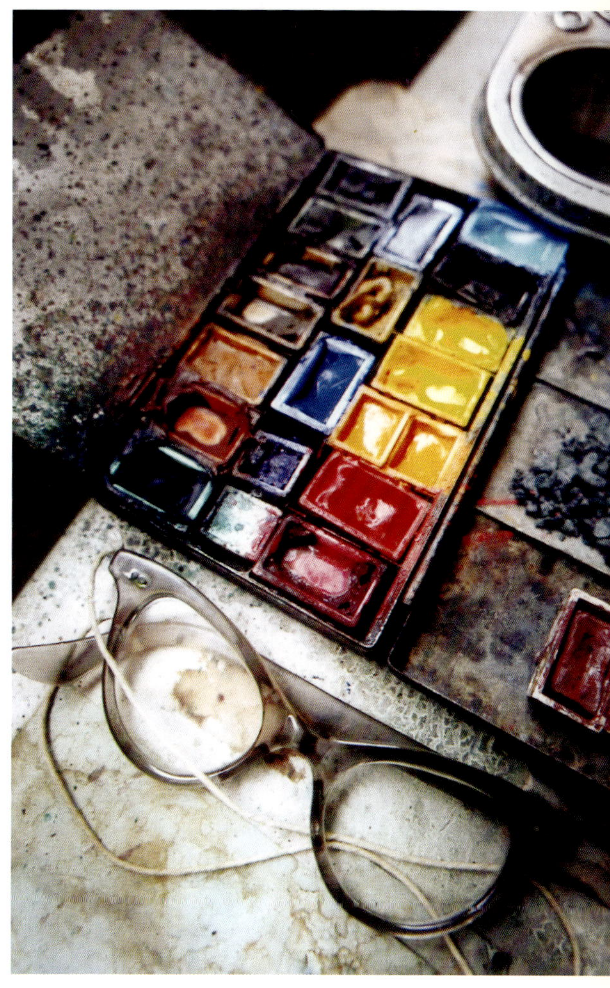

Watercolour palette and glasses, E. J. Hughes' studio (photograph by Darren Stone, reproduced by permission of the Victoria Times Colonist*).*

The paintings are utterly representational and speak of something beyond photography. There is memory and experience encoded in every brush stroke, heart and soul in every carefully considered wave crest and tree limb. There is no haste or shortcut. Without irony or anxiety, he fully conveyed the innocent joy he felt in a perching seagull or a flag blowing in the breeze.

It's unashamedly picturesque, and yet his work commands the respect of our highest authorities. In the definitive book, *E. J. Hughes*, which accompanied a national touring exhibition in 2004, Ian Thom wrote, "Links can be made between his work and a variety of traditions, but this does not explain the singular power of his art to affect the psyche. Hughes' oeuvre is a great deal more sophisticated than it might

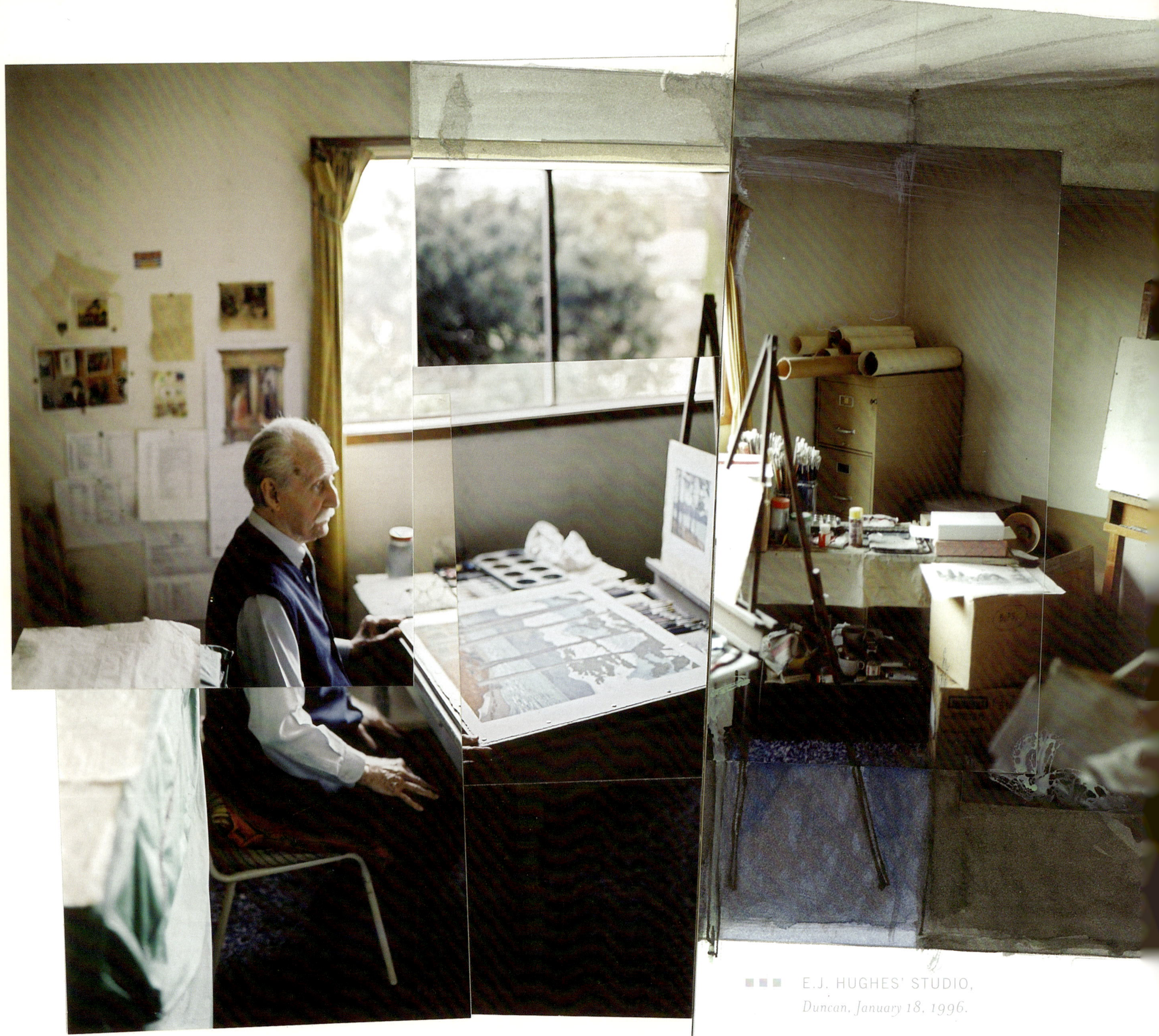

E.J. HUGHES' STUDIO,
Duncan, January 18, 1996.

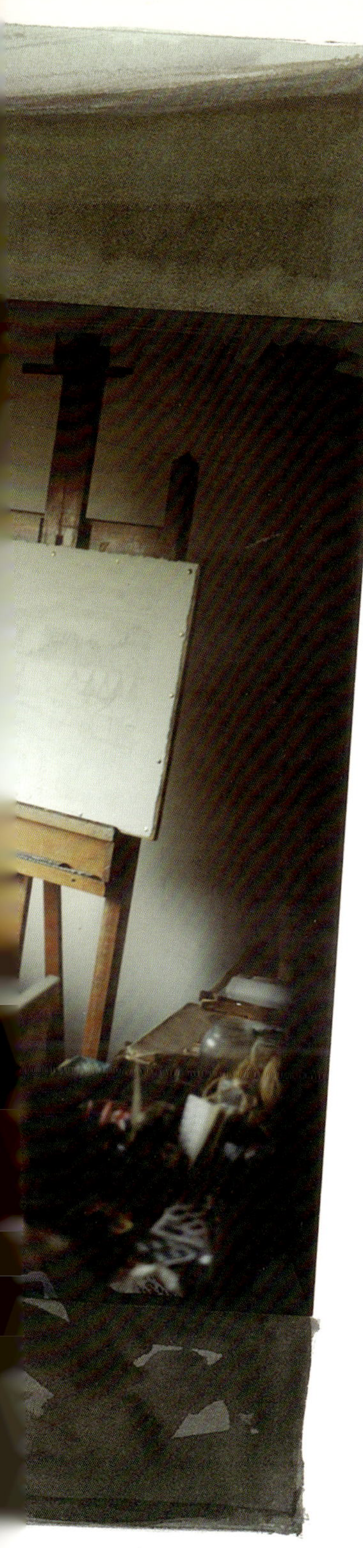

initially appear ... the work is too subtle and too complex to reduce to a simple description."

The work of an artist is a gift to us all. We see the world through his eyes, and our view is changed. To our lasting benefit, E. J. Hughes showed us the corner of the world in which he lived. ■

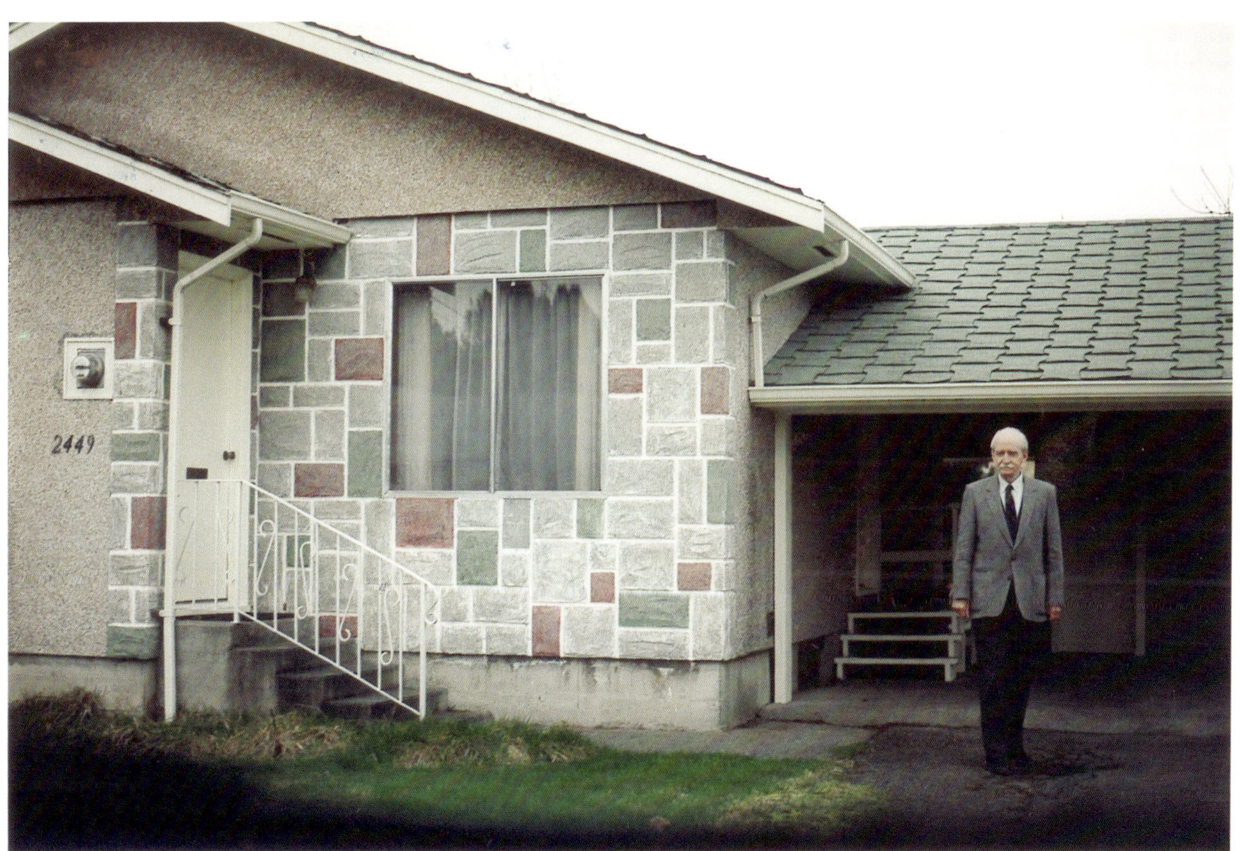

Hughes lived for the last 25 years of his life in a little house that mirrored his modesty. Located on a quiet street on the east side of Duncan, it suited his needs and tastes perfectly. In this photo, he had come out to wave goodbye in his courtly way as I drove away.

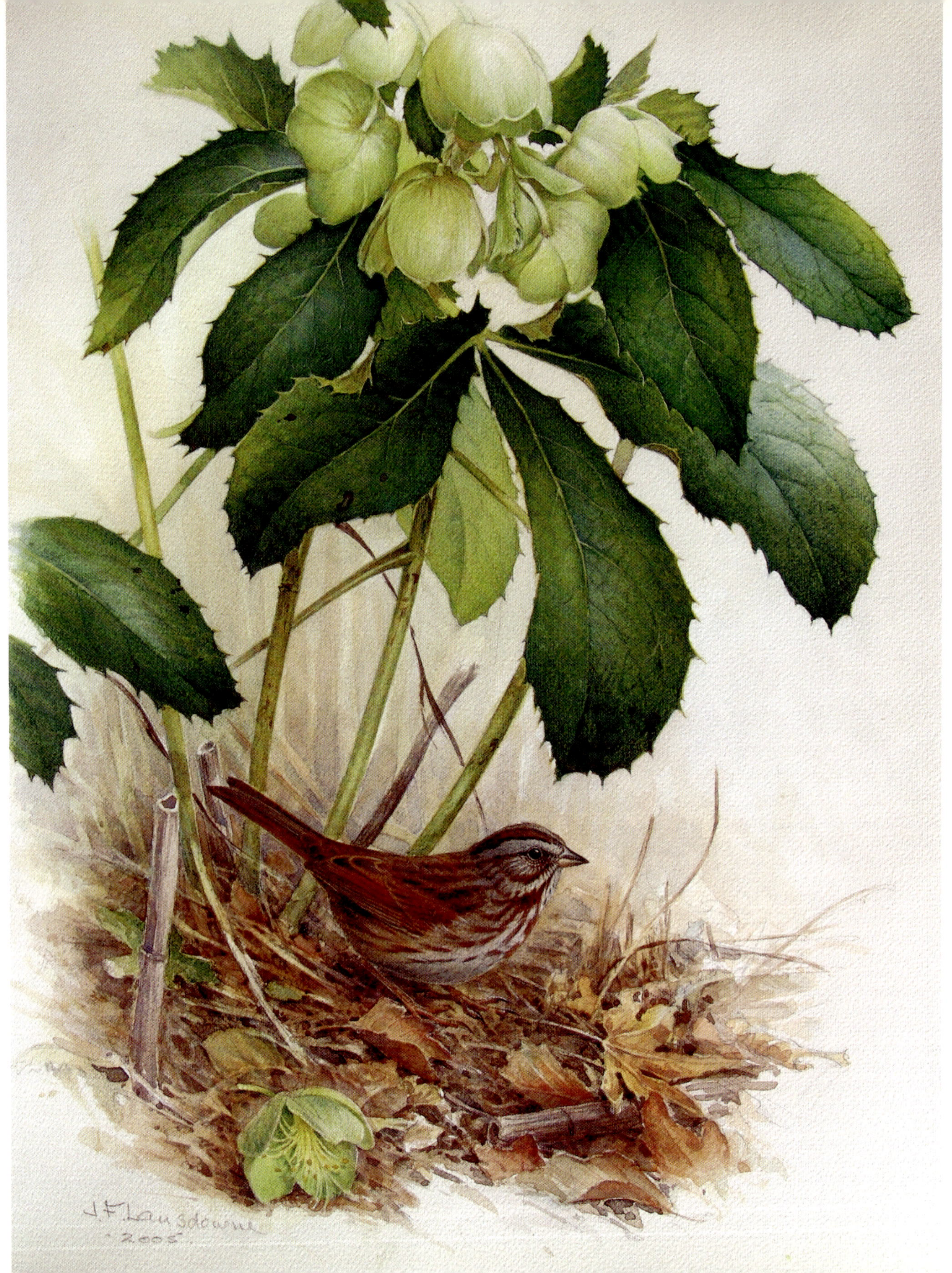
J.F. Lansdowne
"2005"

FENWICK LANSDOWNE

VICTORIA

FENWICK LANSDOWNE IS PERHAPS BEST KNOWN TO THE GENERAL PUBLIC FOR THE SERIES OF BOOKS CONTAINING HIS PAINTINGS OF MANY OF THE BIRDS OF CANADA.

His large-format series, "Rare Birds of China," was a decade-long project in which he recorded the bird species most threatened by environmental hazards and habitat loss in that country.

I met him in the quiet cottage he used at the time for his studio in Victoria's Oak Bay neighbourhood. Clearly this artist is not voluble. "I don't have a lot of penetrating insights," he began in a quiet, almost diffident tone of voice. His intentions were obvious—to represent birds as accurately and sympathetically as possible.

The details of Lansdowne's life have been told often. He was born in Hong Kong in 1937; an attack of polio at the age of 10 months left him partially paralyzed. He lived in the Far East until 1940, when he and his mother moved to Victoria. His relative immobility, combined with the encouragement of his mother, who was herself an artist, set him on his life's course.

Lansdowne's mother left a legacy of hundreds of her painted ceramic birds in Victoria homes. Certainly she encouraged her son to draw and paint but, he says, "I would have done it anyway." As for his art education, "I had no training whatever at any time." When he was a young man, he was advised not to go to art school and "spoil his natural talent."

Among the heroes of his early painting days were Allan Brooks, Luis Agassiz Fuertes and Archibald Thorburn; much later came his admiration of John James Audubon. While Audubon was good at painting "dead" birds, some people feel that Lansdowne's subjects come to life in his paintings.

During his youth Lansdowne attended St. Michael's University School and Victoria High School. He also pursued his interest in birds at the British Columbia Provincial Museum (now

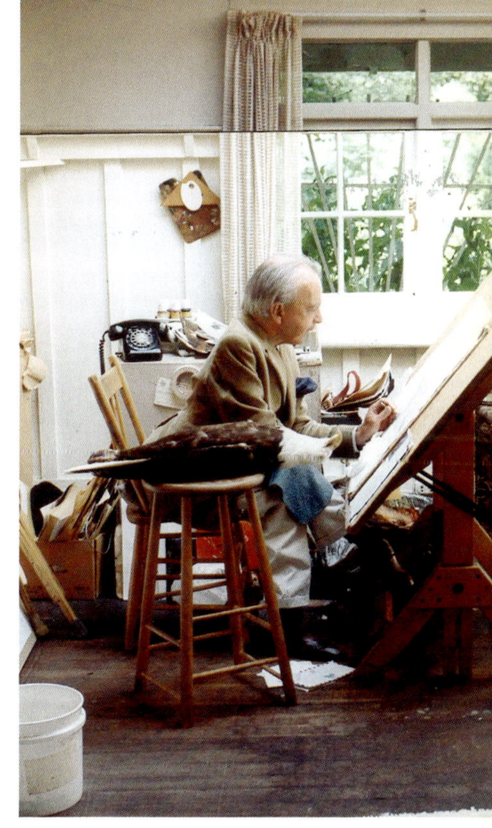

Fenwick Lansdowne in his studio cottage, Oak Bay, Victoria.

SONG SPARROW, *Fenwick Lansdowne, watercolour, 15¾ x 11½ inches, 2005.*

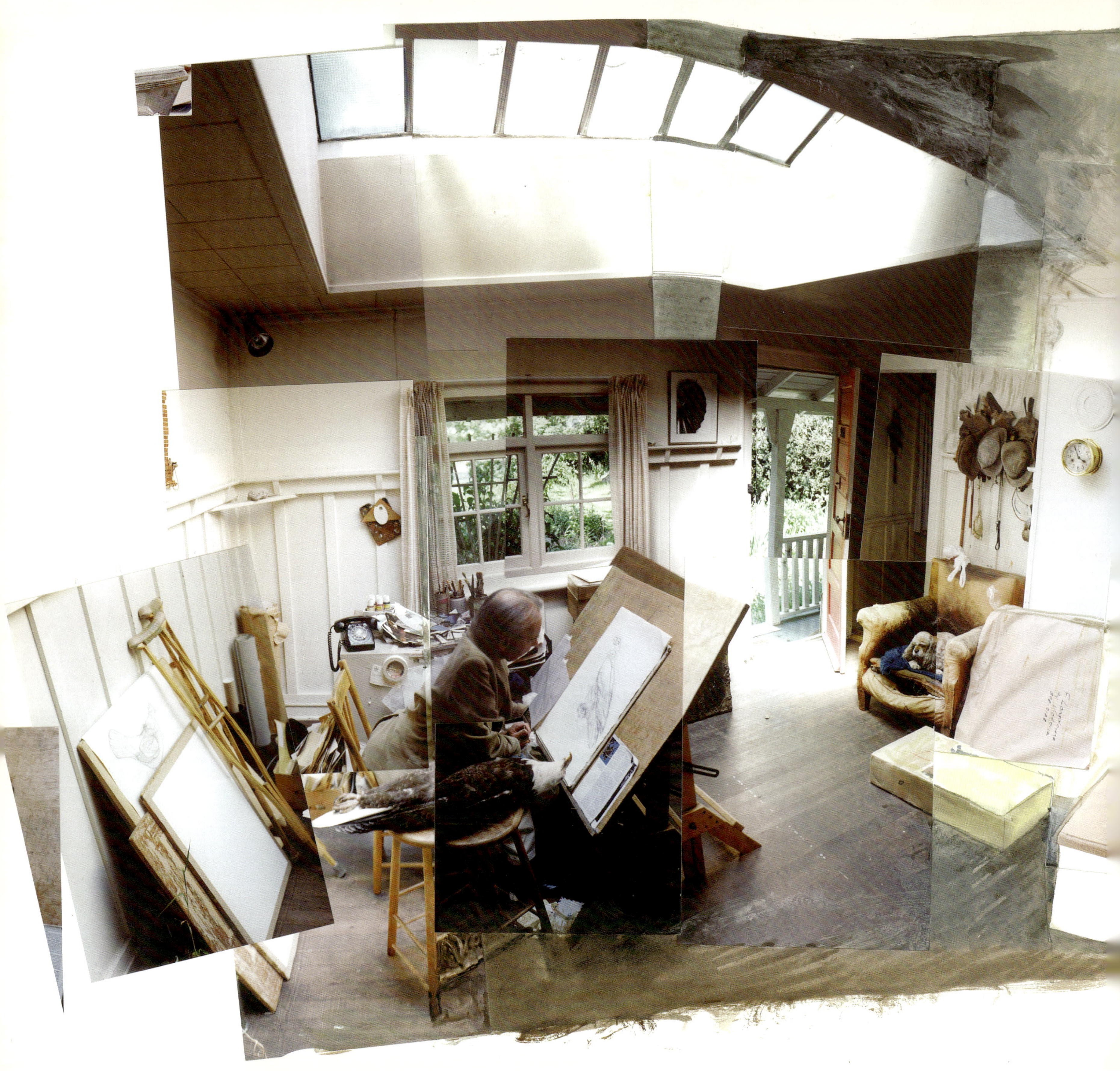

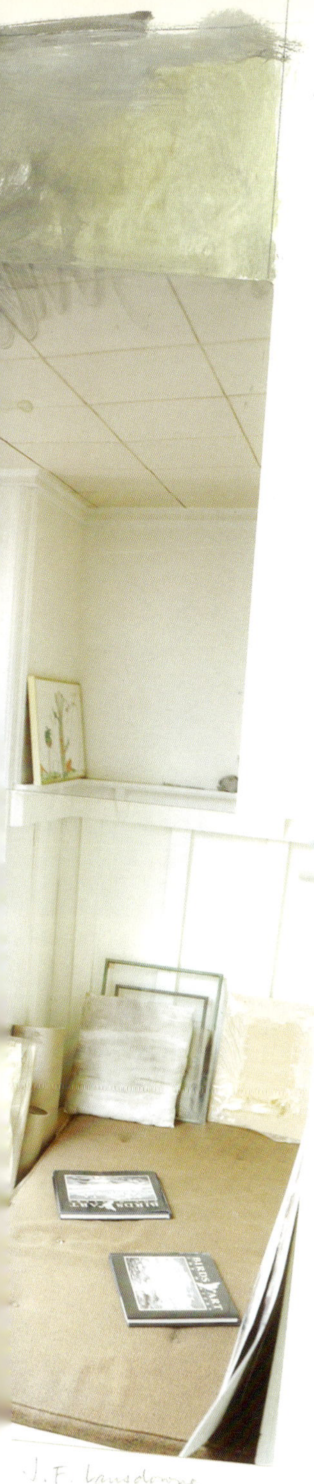

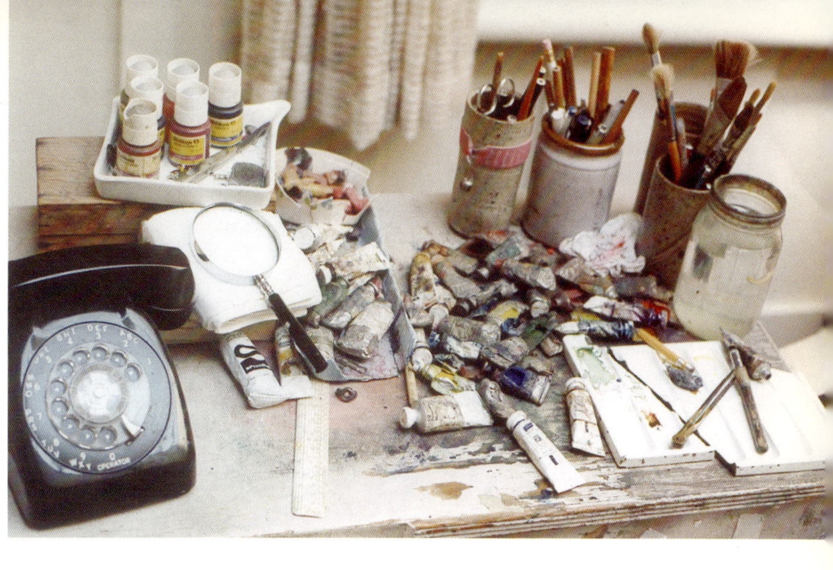

FENWICK LANSDOWNE IN HIS STUDIO,
Victoria, May 1996.

the Royal British Columbia Museum) and in the field. With his friend Robert Genn, the landscape painter, he drove across the Okanagan looking for road kills, stopping to scoop up the wings and tail feathers of hawks and bluebirds and orioles.

His precocious early talent landed the 20-year-old Lansdowne a show at the Royal Ontario Museum in Toronto in 1957, where his potential was noticed almost immediately. His career took off, with exhibits following at Audubon House in New York and the Tryon Gallery in London. Since then, he has been shown almost everywhere in the world where ornithological art is honoured. The Leigh Yawkey Woodson Art Museum in Wausau, Wisconsin, is such a place and Lansdowne exhibited there annually from 1975 to 1987.

He has received almost every honour that can come to a painter in this country, including the Order of Canada, and has produced major books on birds. In the introduction to *Birds of the West Coast, Volume 2*, His Royal Highness Prince Philip wrote, "Fenwick Lansdowne has the exceptional ability to capture such moments with a seemingly effortless assurance but which can only come from intimate knowledge, immense care and remarkable talent."

The day I visited Lansdowne, he was painting an eagle. A skin was lying to hand, along with a clipping from a magazine. After miscellaneous jottings to get an idea, he made a complete line drawing. He then transferred it with tracing paper to a sheet of watercolour paper taped to his drawing board. Though the results are radiant, his materials are humble—at his left hand were a few dried-out tubes of watercolour paint and a broken china palette. "The bird is completed first, and I drop the wash in around it," the artist explained.

The eagle is not simply an accurate painting in colour and detail. The feathers seem soft and radiant, pulsing with the sheen of life. This artist alternates between layers of detail and wash, trying "to retain some clarity and depth of colour."

Regarding his work habits, he mused, "Some people can apparently paint for 17 hours at a time. If I'm doing something really complicated, a duck with fine venation for example, I'm exhausted after six hours. That night I go to sleep and the pattern comes again and again and again, and I keep repeating widgeon feathers, widgeon feathers, all night long." It took him more than four weeks to paint this widgeon, an image about as big as my two hands.

When I commented on his patience, he told me, "I'm not what you call a spontaneous person. I work better on a regular routine." His days are long, but not busy. "Most of it, of course, is sitting around waiting for a wash to dry," he smiled.

Lansdowne had answered all my questions and seemed bemused by my intrusion. As he had predicted, I uncovered no secrets or revelations. But the message is profound: Stay home, work hard, do what you love and it is possible to achieve great things.

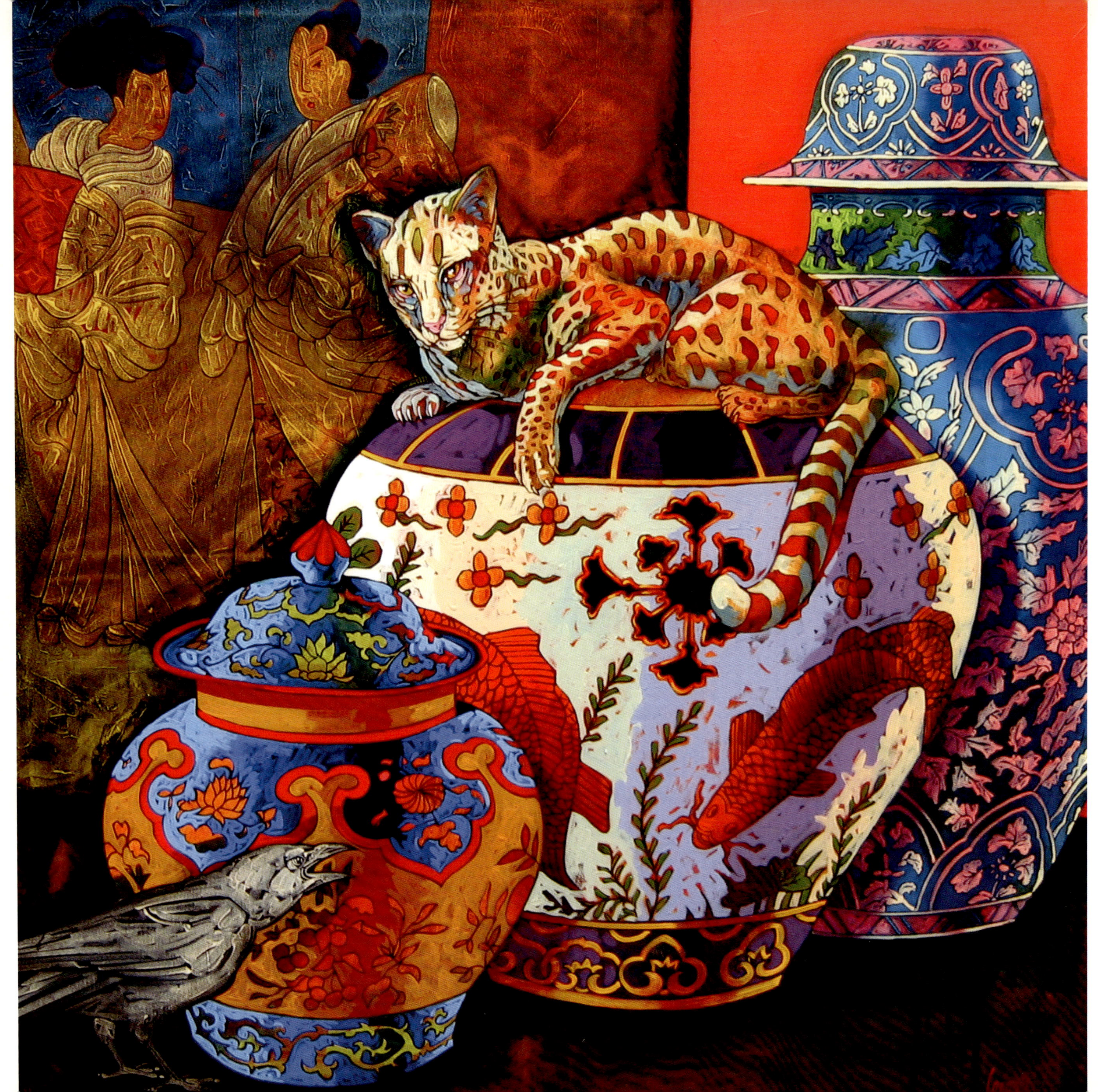

GRANT LEIER & NIXIE BARTON

YELLOW POINT

THEY PAINT, THEY GARDEN, THEY SHOP LIKE MAD. THEY'VE ALREADY BEEN ON TV—TWICE! GRANT LEIER AND NIXIE BARTON ARE A POST-WARHOLIAN BRADY BUNCH WHO HAVE SET THEMSELVES UP AS A SUBURBAN ROADSIDE ATTRACTION AT YELLOW POINT.

It's a gallery, a store, a garden and a home, and if you haven't been there, you owe yourself a visit.

I first photographed the Barton-Leier acreage shortly after they moved there in 1994. At that time Grant had his studio in a small garden building and I've never gotten over the delirious clutter of the place. You can see how he underpainted his canvases on the floor, decorated their borders and then pinned them to the wall where, with an opaque projector, he later added dogs where appropriate.

Nixie Barton bubbles over with remarkable exuberance and the everlastingly blond and boyish Grant Leier is never far away. During the filming of a segment of the *Guerilla Gardener* at their place, Nixie did all the talking while Grant said he "stood in the background with spade and rubber boots nodding like a bobble-head doll." You wouldn't know it from that TV show, but he is in fact the articulate member of the pair.

Not every married couple seems to enjoy a companionship this close. Furthermore, these two have the uncanny ability to make me feel like the most important person in the world every time we meet.

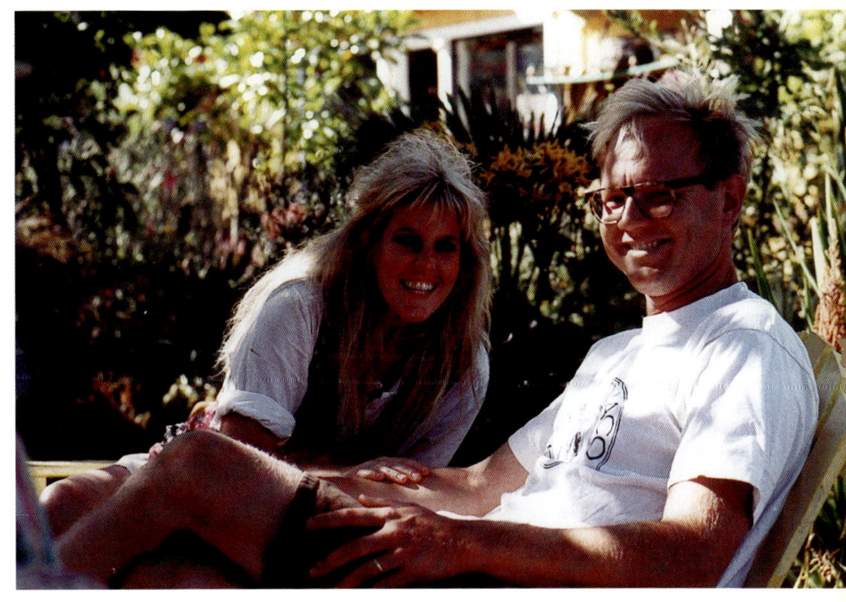

Nixie Barton and Grant Leier, July 27, 1997.

■ ■ ■ OLD CROW, NEW TRICKS, *Grant Leier, acrylic, 36 x 36 inches, 2007.*

Leier's first studio at Yellow Point was an outbuilding in the garden. He made clutter into a fine art.

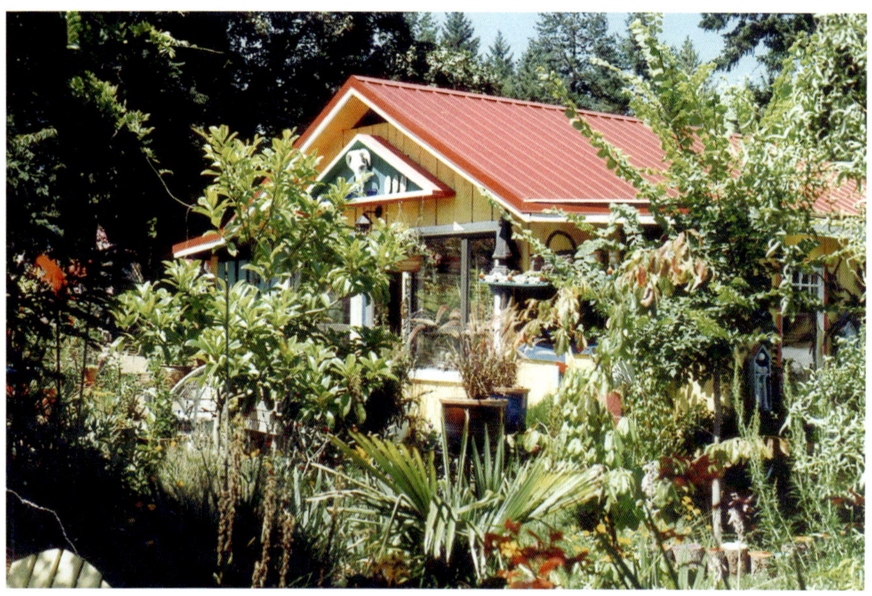

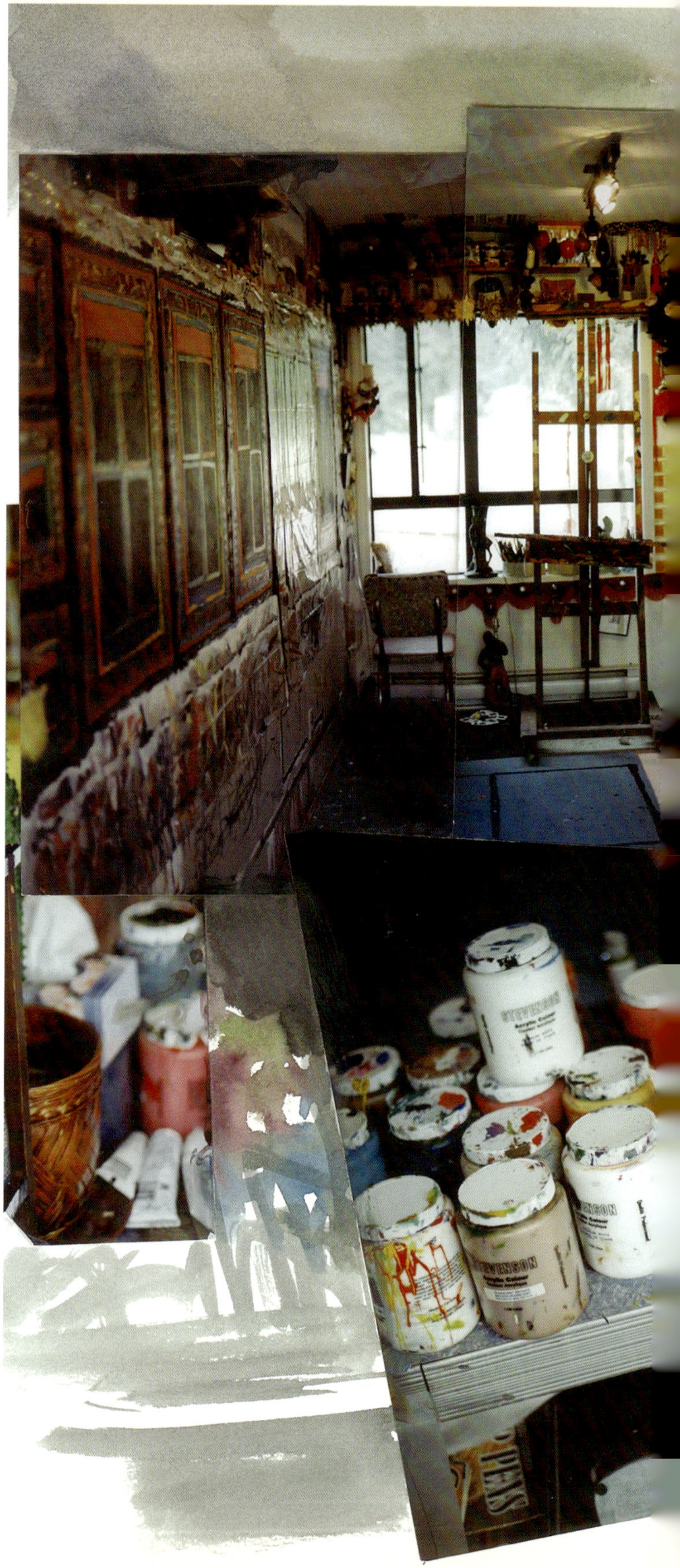

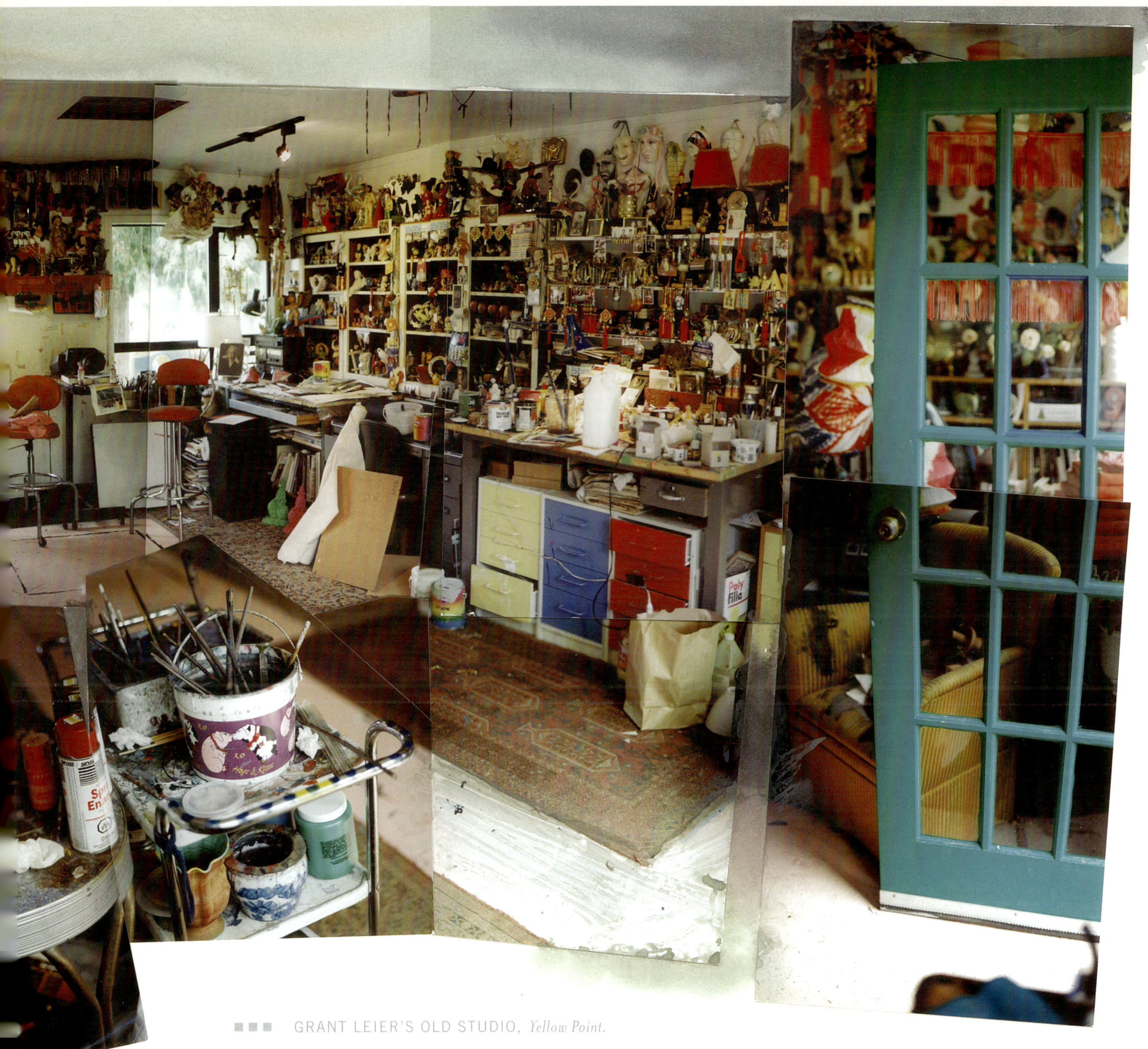

■ ■ ■ GRANT LEIER'S OLD STUDIO, *Yellow Point.*

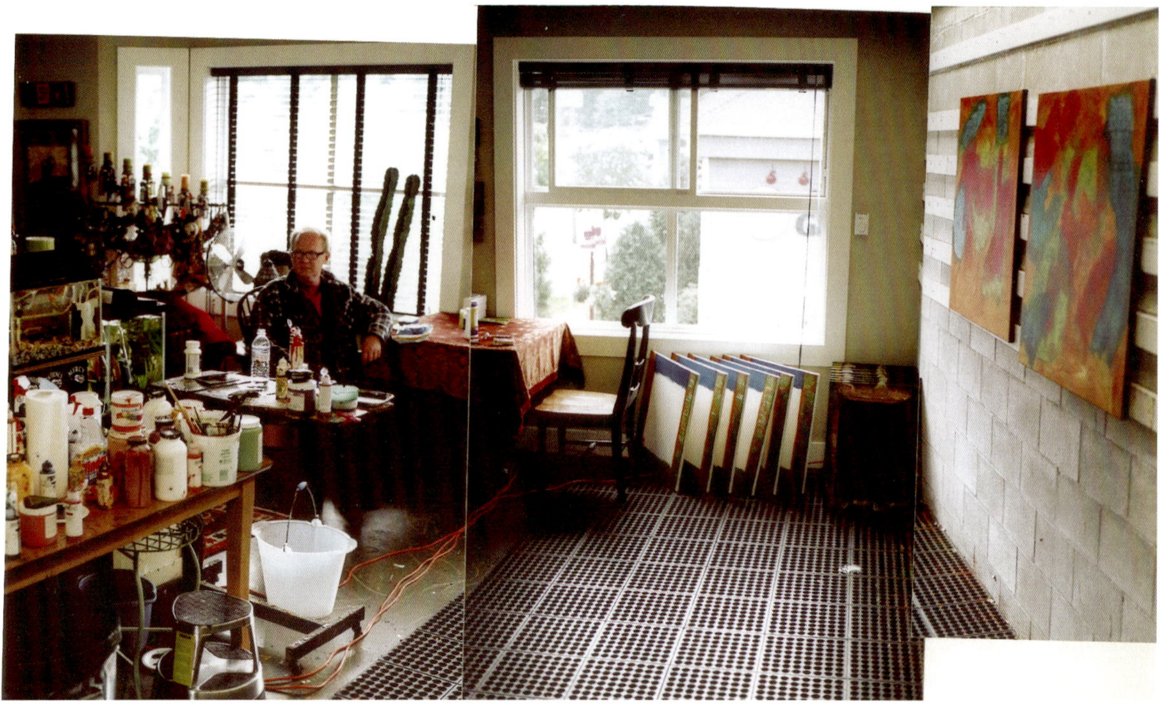

■ ■ ■ GRANT LEIER'S CURRENT STUDIO, *2006;*
the workspace is in a commercial block a few miles from his home.

Perhaps they make everyone feel this way.

Grant Leier was born in Lloydminster, Saskatchewan, in 1956. His schoolboy sketches of wildlife led to an early series of illustrative paintings featuring his sister grinning broadly. Next came many white ducks, an image that was eventually ensconced in three-dimensional shrines laden with Chinatown knick-knacks.

About the time of their marriage, Grant took Nixie's advice and switched from his illustration style to big brushes and unstretched canvas. In 1997 he began the continuing series he calls Romance. It came about by chance. "I had checked into a hotel and, in the room, there was a card advertising the hotel's room service with an impressionist painting of a tabletop, a wine bottle and wineglass. I really liked it," Grant concluded.

Who wouldn't? The imagery of a table for two, moonlight and roses seems to strike a chord with everyone. He went on to add olives and magnolias in huge Chinese jars. The romance continues...

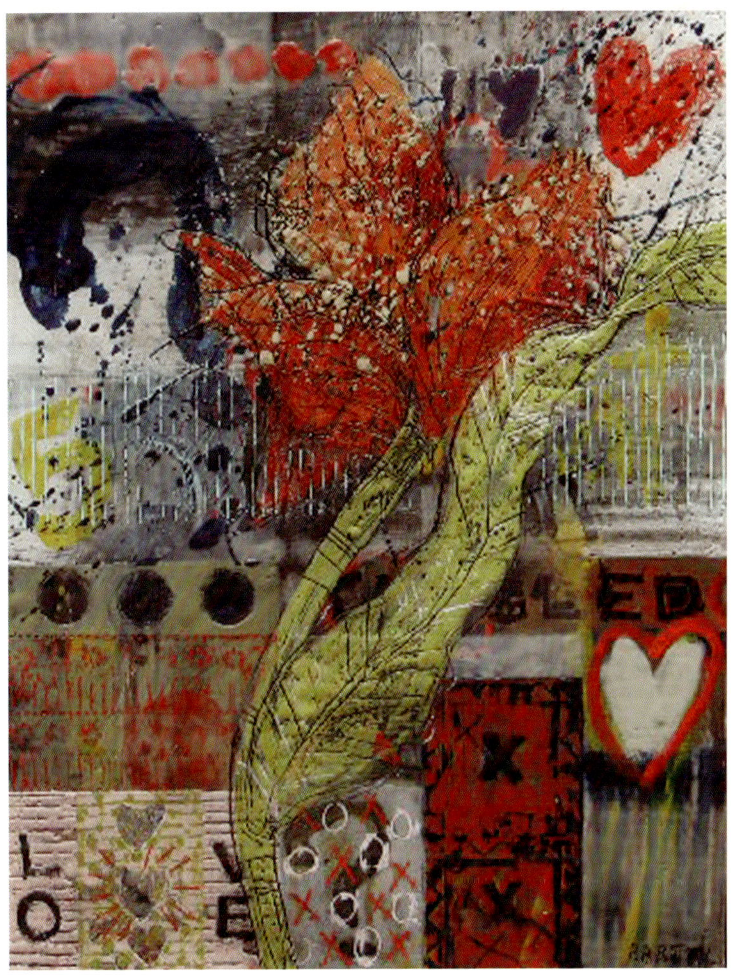

■ ■ ■ TANGLED, *Nixie Barton, encaustic, 18 x 24 inches, 2007.*

Nixie Barton was born in Vancouver in 1958 and grew up in Penticton and Nanaimo. Her artistic trajectory began with the nudes she painted in her school days at Malaspina College and the University of Victoria. Inspired by Matisse, she then focussed on tabletops with flowers and fruit. During the first years at Yellow Point, Nixie had her hands full raising their son, Grayson. Eventually, she began to decorate boards cut to the shape of icon paintings, gilded with gold leaf. Then she began creating brooding landscapes from her imagination, assembling numerous little canvases into larger compositions. At the time of my last visit she had built an elegant studio on the second floor of their home, totally devoted to the art of encaustic—working with molten wax invested with coloured pigments.

Inside their home, the floors and cupboard doors are treated as an extension of their canvases. The abundance of things—classical columns, plaster figurines, tropical fish, old packaging labels—runs rampant.

Outside, Barton and Leier treat their garden as another work of art. Grant's strategy is to buy a whole flat of plants at the nursery, rather than just one. Whatever survives his rough-and-ready approach to planting is welcome to grow big and show off its structure. Poured cement paths are embedded with marbles and kewpie dolls and plastic lizards. A row of posts is topped with bowling balls. A fake hippo surfaces on the pond. This chapter of the Barton-Leier saga is appropriately titled "Be the Brave Gardener."

Their garden and gallery have become so overwhelmingly popular that Grant recently rented a remote studio in a nondescript (though large and functional) space a few miles away. He's highly productive there. Though he has filled it with many tanks of tropical fish, it doesn't yet have the funky charm of the little studio in the garden that I photographed many years ago. ■

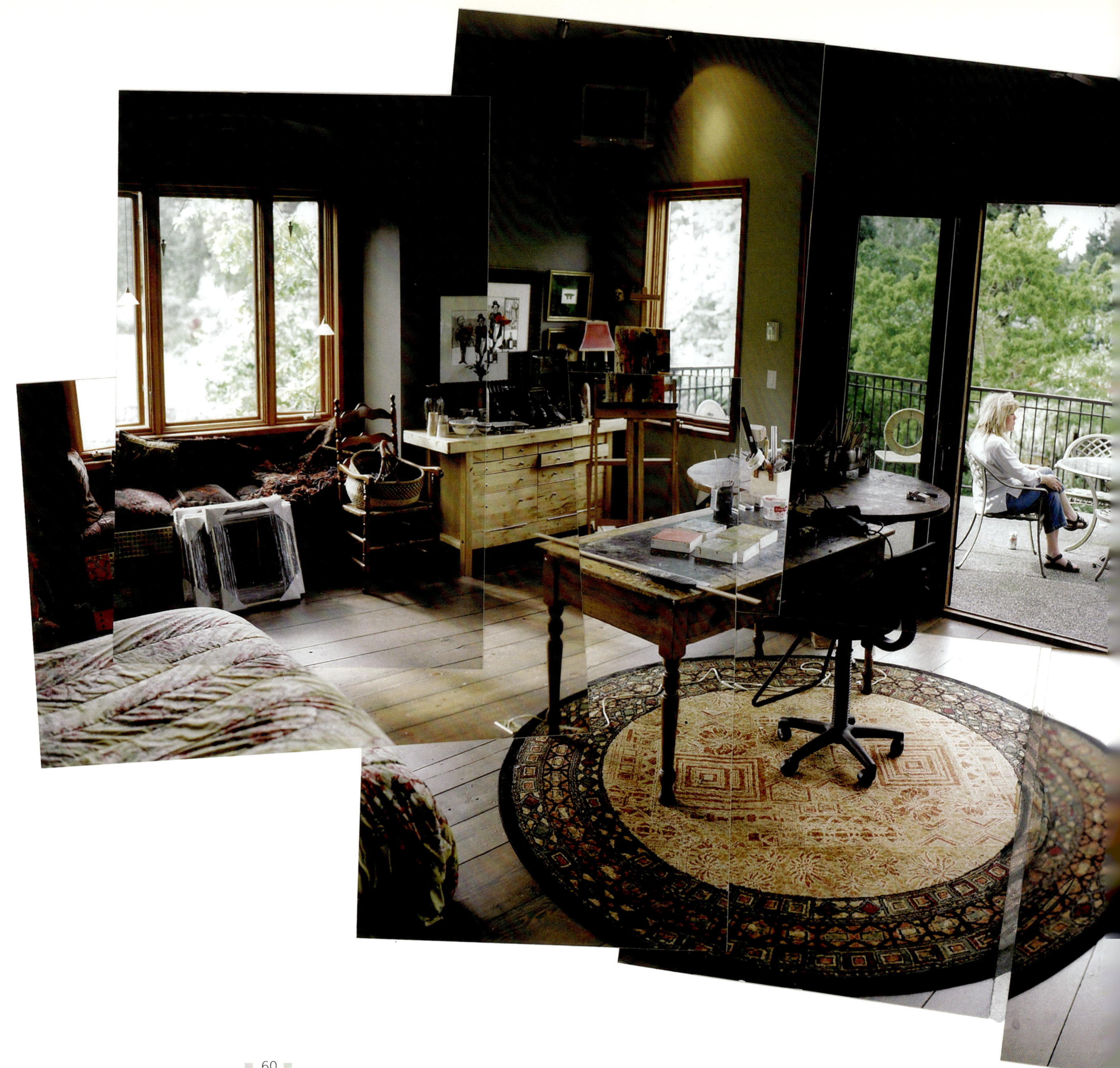

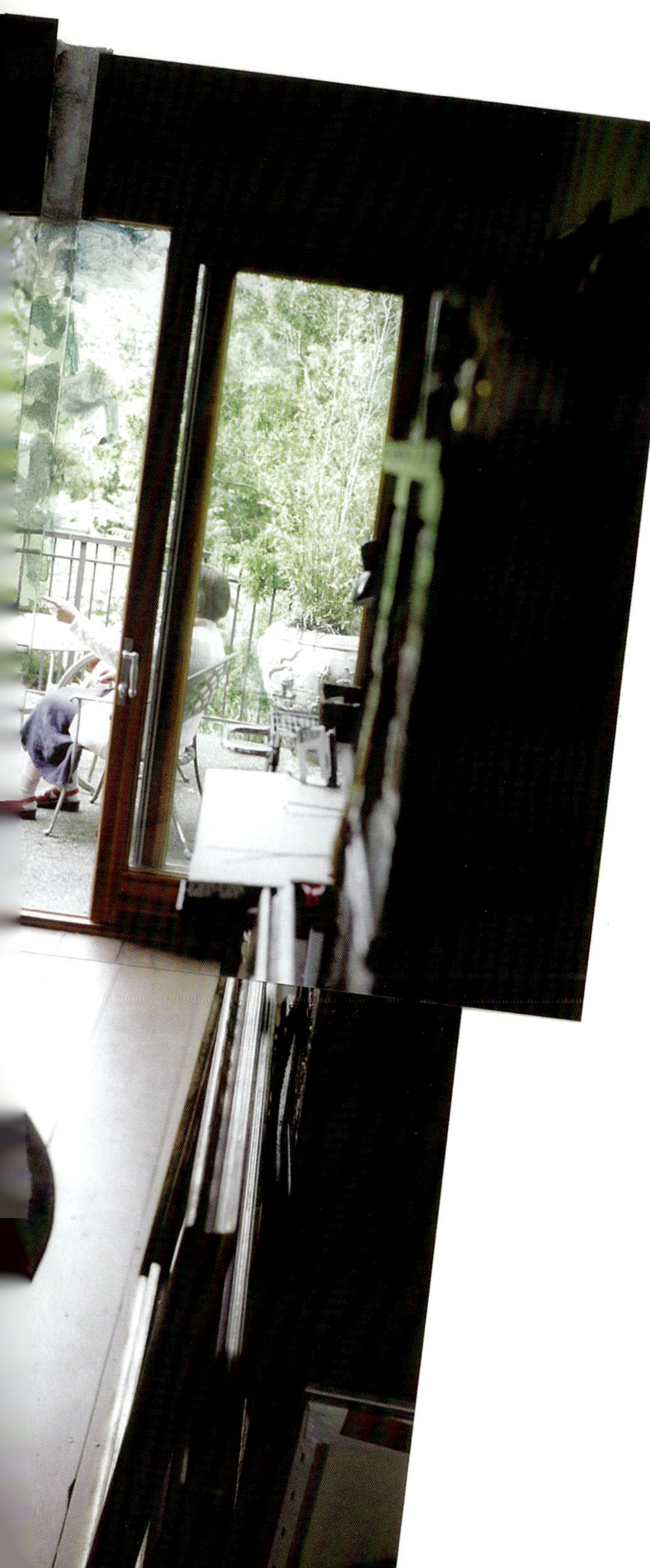

An electric frying pan and soldering iron are among the tools Barton uses to keep her coloured waxes flowing on the small wooden panels.

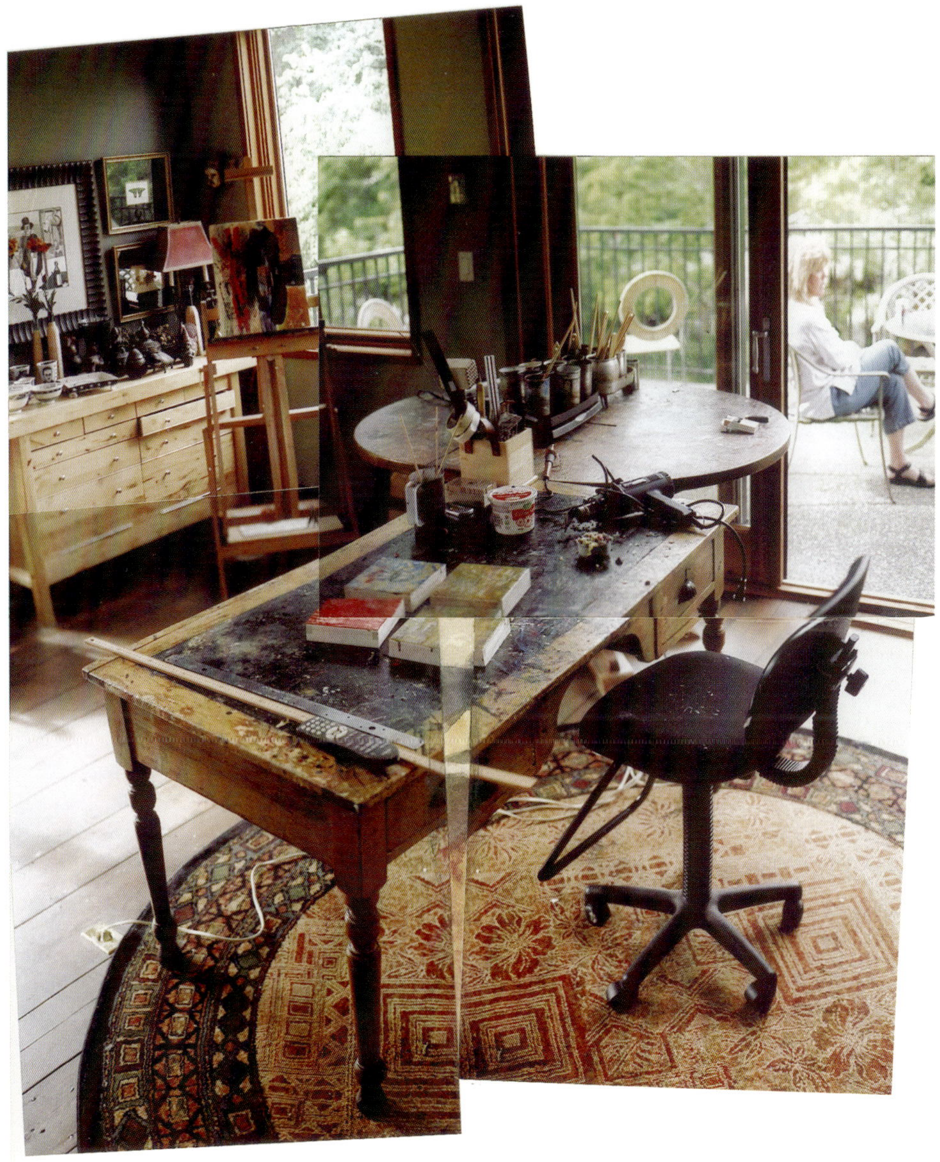

NIXIE BARTON'S STUDIO, *Yellow Point, 2006.*

MILES LOWRY

VICTORIA

I WENT TO VISIT MILES LOWRY IN THE LOFT APARTMENT HE SHARES WITH DAVID FERGUSON, A DANCER AND FELLOW ARTIST, IN AN OLD BRICK BUILDING IN DOWNTOWN VICTORIA.

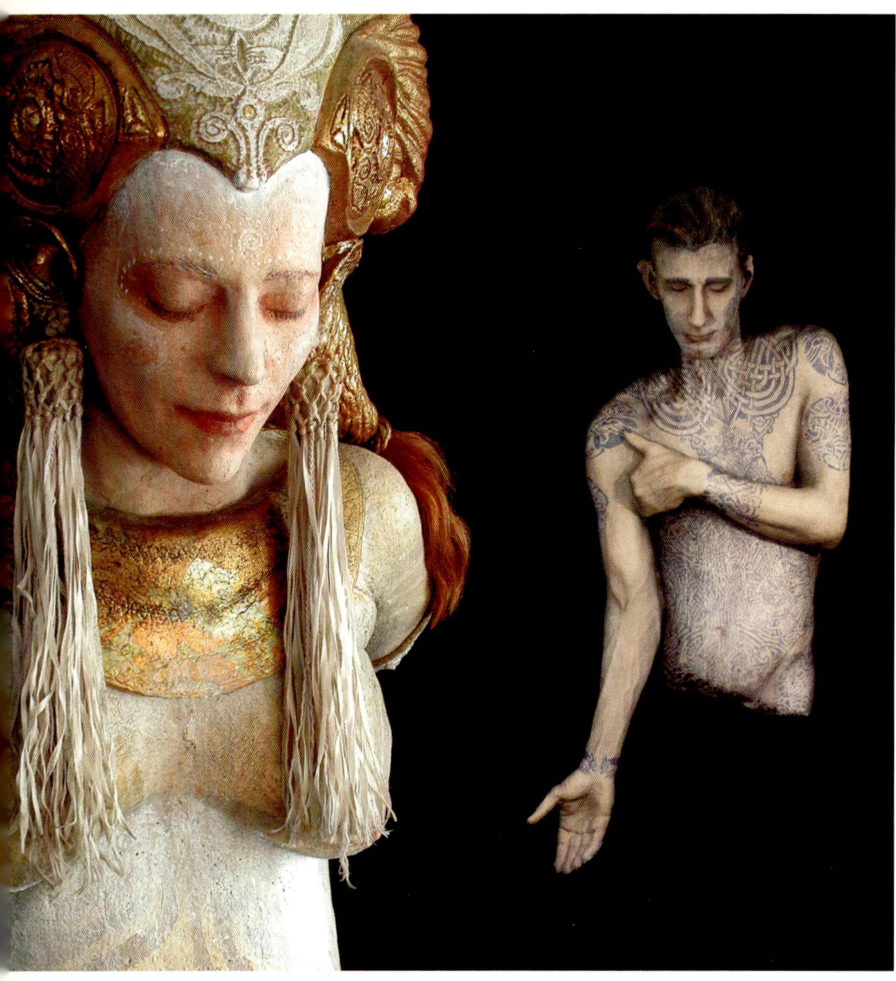

It was a hot summer day and, I confess, the sculptures hanging on the walls in the narrow entrance hall took me aback. Daunted, I proceeded into the creative ferment of their space.

With my back to the window over Government Street, I faced into their large room—brick walls, stained wooden floor. In the left corner a loft bed, raised six feet off the floor, was hidden behind a curtain, and the space under it was used for storage. In the centre a tiny kitchen could be glimpsed. Every other place in the flat was given over to art-making.

Animal skulls, sculptural glass, vases full of feathers and heaps of picture books crowded in. When I first met Miles years before, he was a teenager, making his way with airbrushed paintings of Celtic mythology—the Mabinogion and early Welsh tales—and the American Southwest. Later, he produced a series of paintings of people that I described at the time as "the essence of the soul floating imminent in a mysterious haze."

DANU ANCESTRESS *and* TATTOO,
Miles Lowry, cast paper and paint, life-size sculptures, 2006.

"It's still true," he confirmed recently. "I love that haze." His purpose was to draw the viewer in, rather than to make a decorative surface. Lowry's work has always been an art of suggestion.

From painting people, he moved to casting them. "I have created a process of capturing sculptural images from life and working with cast forms to express ideas about the human body as a vehicle for art," he has written. "The sculptures are cast in cotton fibre and infused with pigments and elements of the natural world."

These heads, busts and torsos—at once dreamlike and very particular—are decorated with Celtic knot-work painted on like tattoos, using a supple Chinese brush. He also embellishes them with bright feathers from tropical birds, and real hair.

A glance at the list of artworks that made up his recent show at the Simon Fraser University Art Gallery gives a hint of the breadth of Lowry's interests:

Wanderings in the Interior—a tableau of highly detailed cast figures based on Papuan Ceremonial Adornment;

Dissolve/Reveal—life-size figures dissolving into rust;

Powder—an exploration of female body-image; and

Clannad—a historical and magical interpretation of the artist's family as Tribal Celts.

As Lowry's partnership with David Ferguson has evolved, he has reached out into a world of performance. The Suddenly Dance Theatre, of which they are artistic co-directors, has given Lowry an opportunity to create in the realm of ritual and costume, dance and music. Clothing, set design, photographs, film and video have all come into play.

Among many other achievements, Lowry's cinematic poem, "Opium," based on the writing of French poet Jean Cocteau, was produced for Canadian television and selected for the 2007 Dance on Camera Festival at Lincoln Center in New York City. Recently, performances of Suddenly Dance Theatre, incorporating Lowry's film, were presented on stage with the Victoria Symphony as the final evening of their New Currents Festival. His latest book of poetry and paintings, entitled *Blood Orange*, was recently published by Ekstasis Editions.

Clearly, he has a philosophy and an overarching esthetic that he expresses in a surprising variety of media. This glance into his crowded studio gives some idea of the expanding world of Miles Lowry. ■

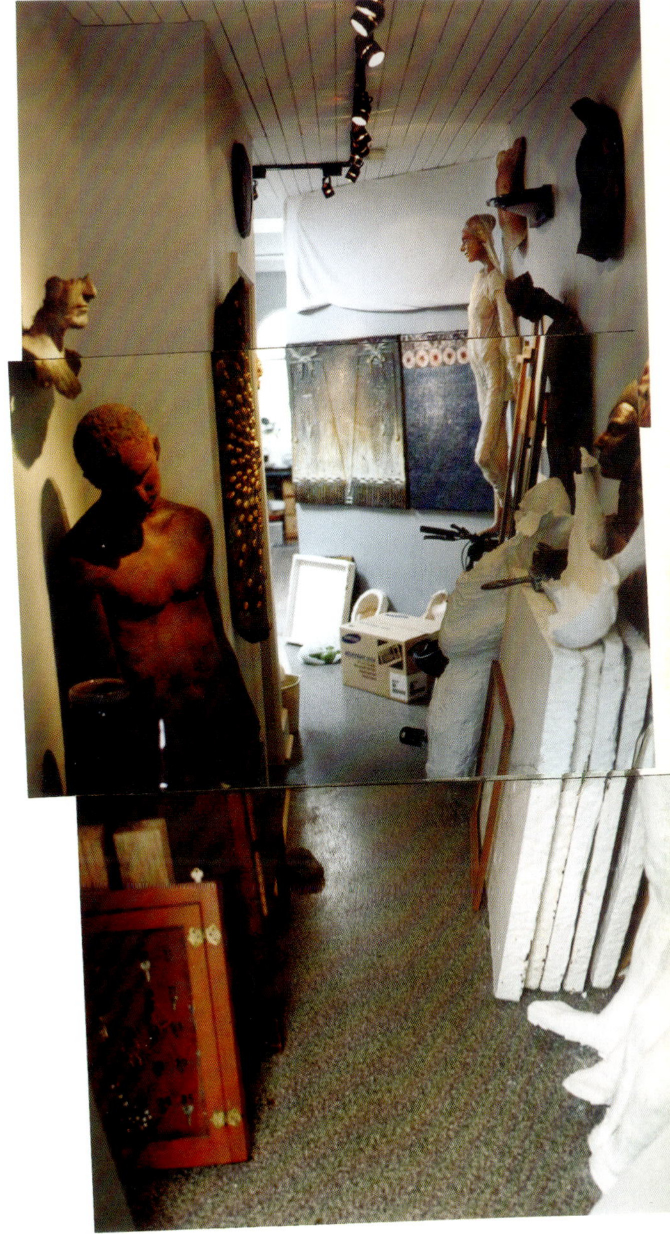

Entrance to Miles Lowry's apartment and studio, Victoria.

This 180-degree panorama can only begin to show the complexity of the Lowry live/workspace.

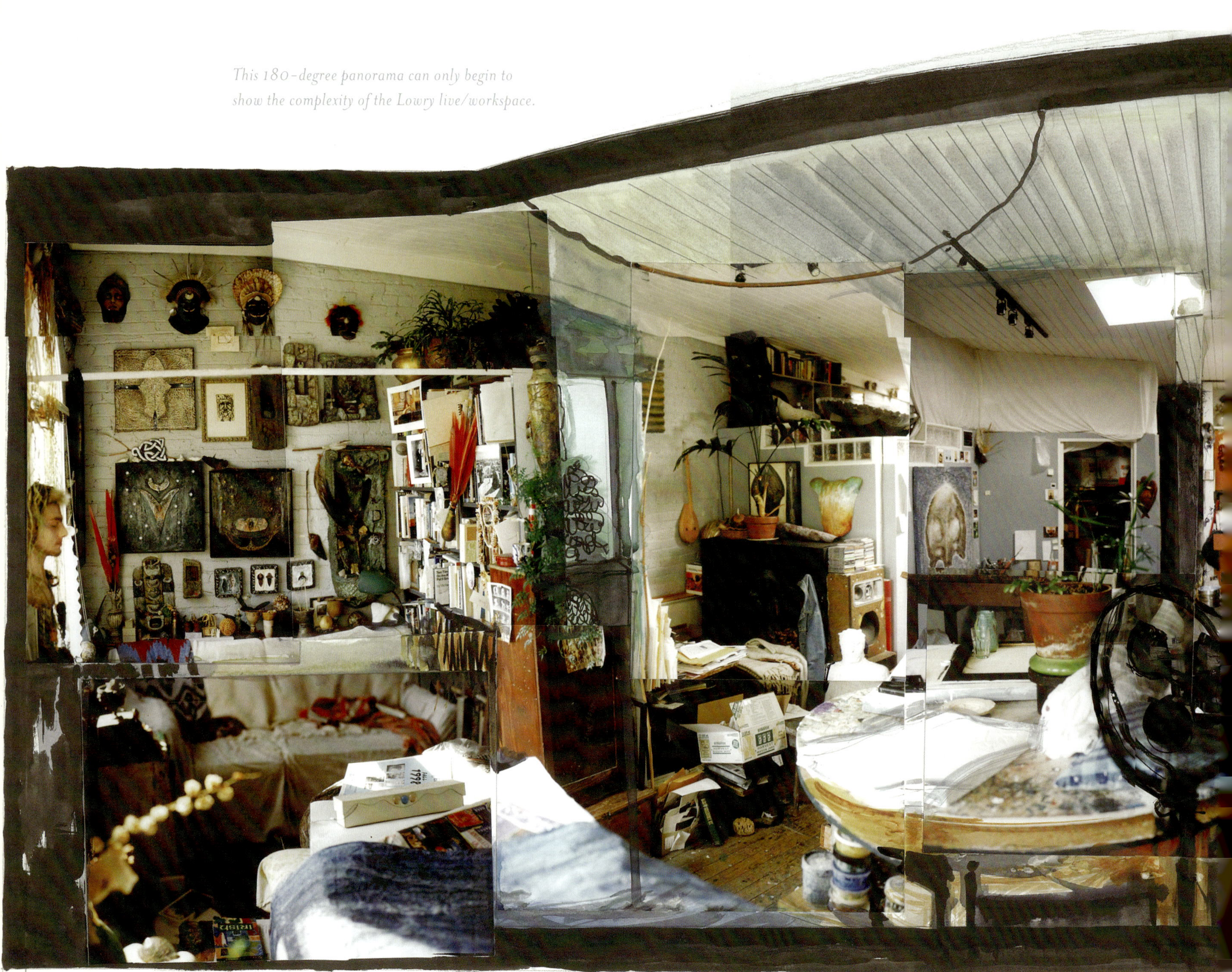

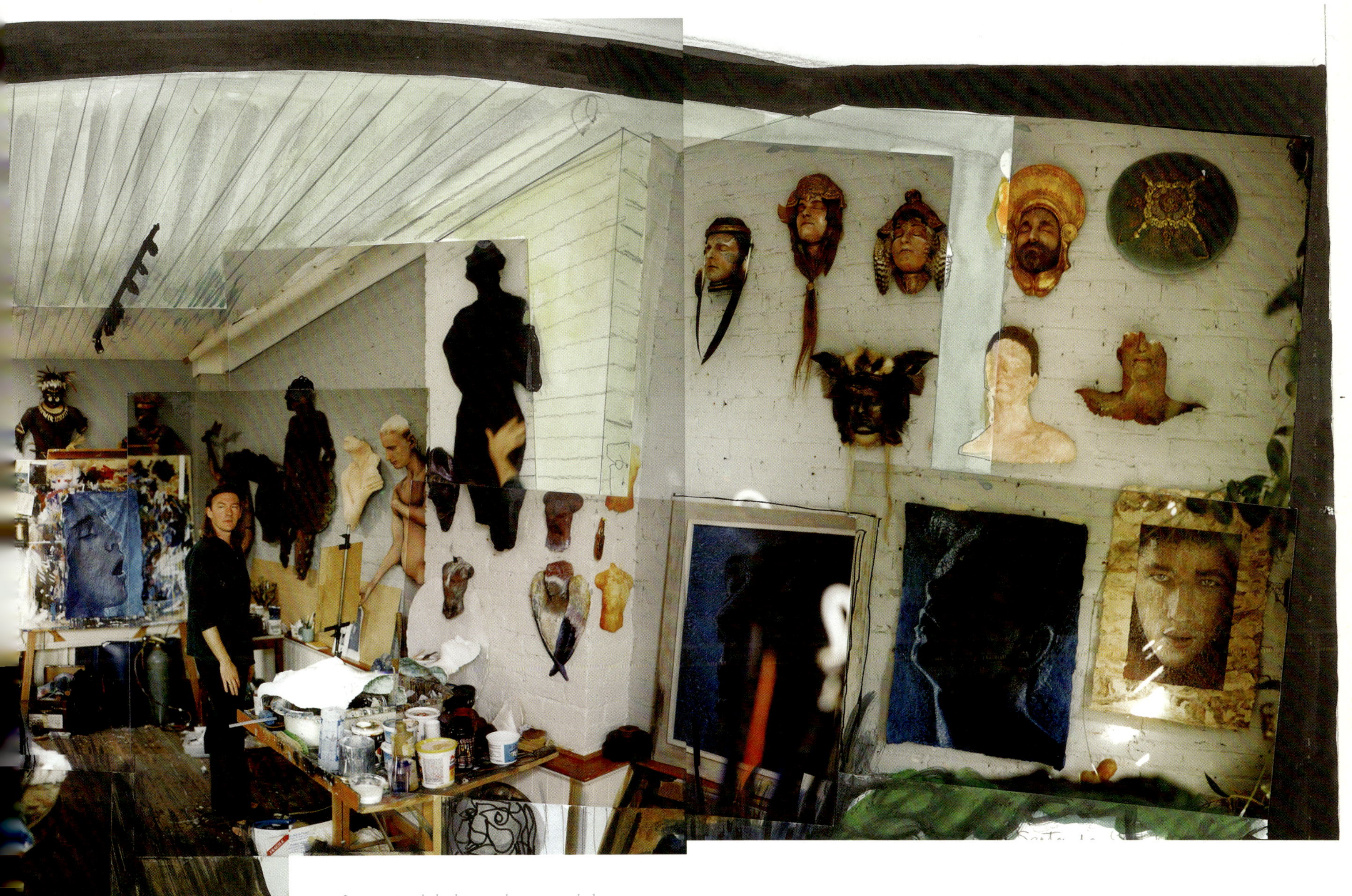

Lowry stands by his easel, surrounded by the spirits he conjures.

■ ■ ■ APARTMENT AND STUDIO OF MILES LOWRY, *Victoria, September 19, 1998.*

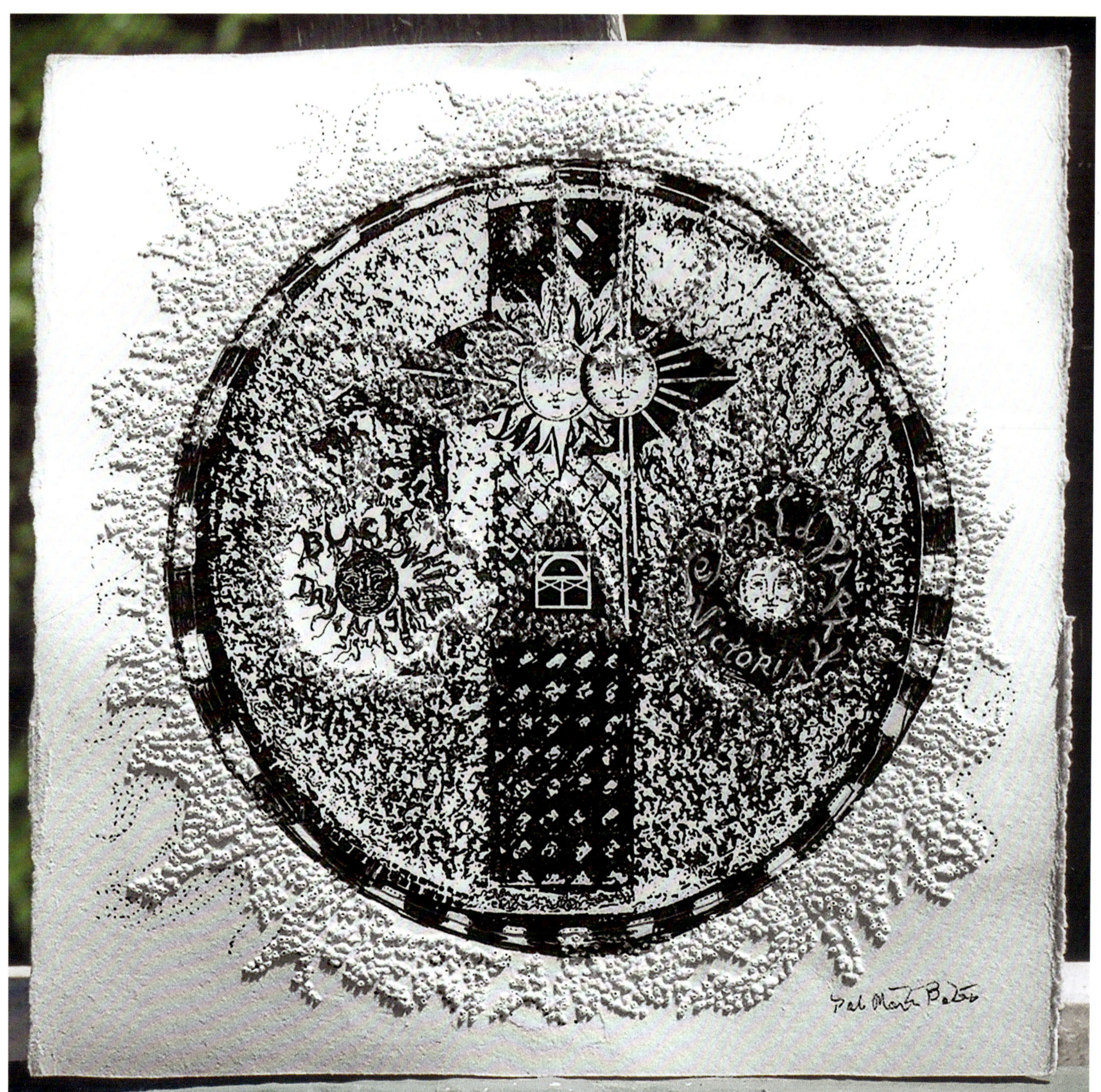
VICTORIA

PAT MARTIN BATES

VICTORIA

PAT MARTIN BATES IS AT THE CENTRE OF A SPRAWLING, GLOBAL NETWORK OF DYNAMIC INDIVIDUALS. VICTORIA WRITER YVONNE OWENS EXPRESSED IT WELL: "THE WORLD IS HER GARDEN, HER MEDIUM, HER PLAYGROUND, HER FRIEND."

In preparation for a presentation at Painter's Lodge, Pat and I spent two long afternoons in the sitting room of her spacious Oak Bay heritage home. There, she treated me to a rambling discourse on a dazzling range of information and experience: William Blake, Japanese papers, Yugoslavian refugees, the 13th-century mystic poet Rumi, cabaret songs, army bases, the spatial harmonies of Arab geometry; it was all part of the mix. To simplify Pat Martin Bates is to miss the chaotic richness of her life.

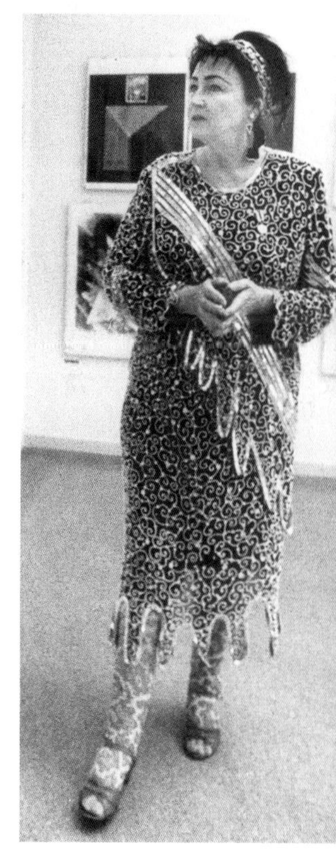

Pat Martin was born in Saint John, New Brunswick, on June 5, 1927. She studied at Mount Allison University with Stanley Royle and went on to graduate from the Académie des Beaux Arts in Belgium in 1957. Her first professional show was in Ottawa in 1962. Two days before the opening, a fire in the gallery destroyed all the paintings. She set to work immediately to replace them with new work—predominantly painted in reds!

In that year her husband Al Bates (a paymaster in the Canadian Forces, whom she had married in 1948) was posted to the wintry fastness of Wainwright, Alberta. Martin Bates' palette turned white shortly after she arrived, a whiteness she explained also as the result of a childhood experience. When she was eight her beloved father died and she was brought up by her great aunts, who lived in an old parsonage. There, the small windows scarcely lit the dim interior and young Pat sat and looked out on areas of winter snow, filtered by heavy lace curtains, stained glass and ivory fans. The impression stayed with her.

In 1963 the Bates family (they have two children) came to Victoria to live. Here she introduced black as a major element in her work. She says this black was a result of falling down a coal chute when she was a child, after which she was bedridden for six months.

■■■ TEA WORLD PARTY VICTORIA, *Pat Martin Bates, estampille print, 7 x 7 inches, 2004.*

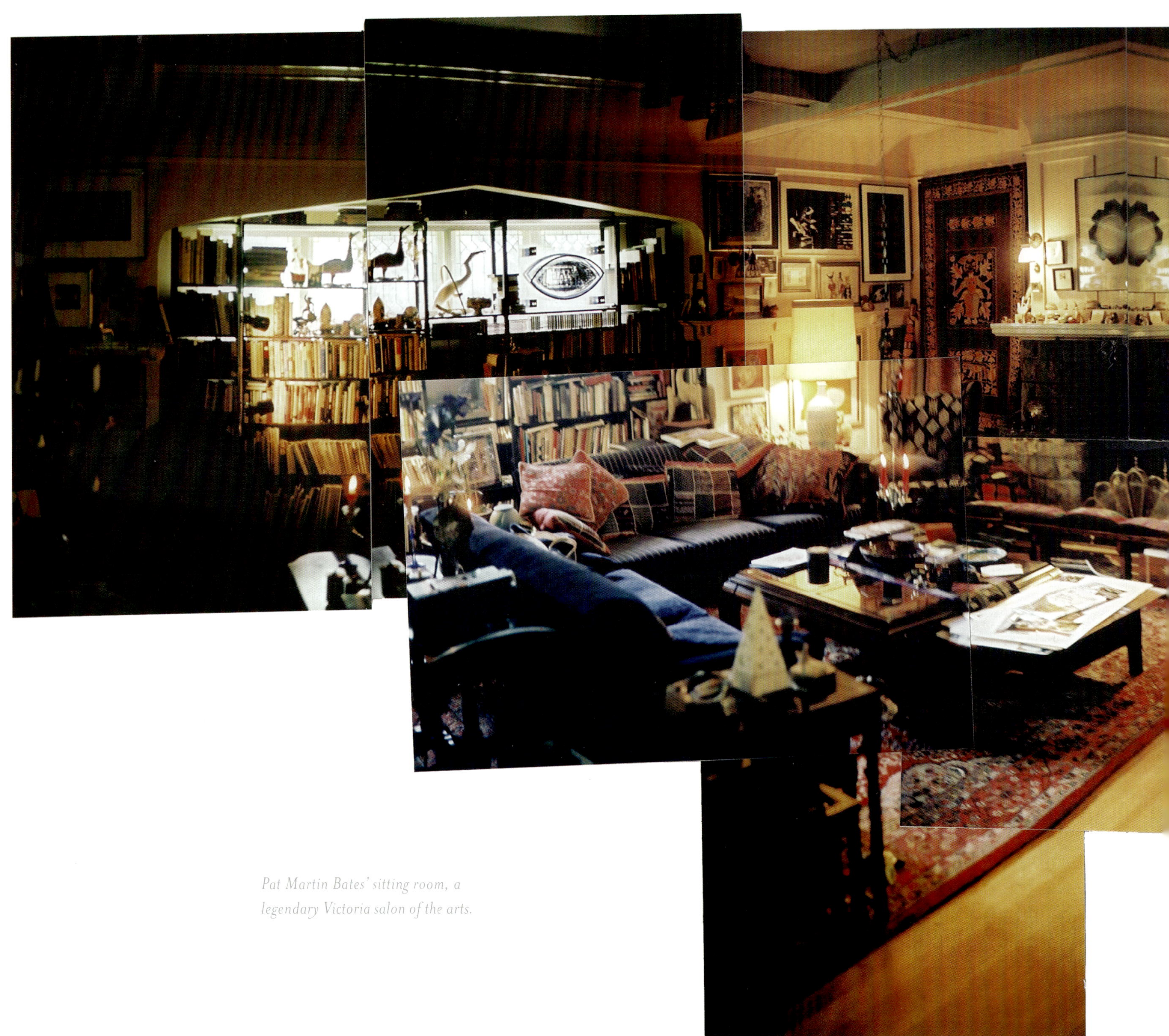

Pat Martin Bates' sitting room, a legendary Victoria salon of the arts.

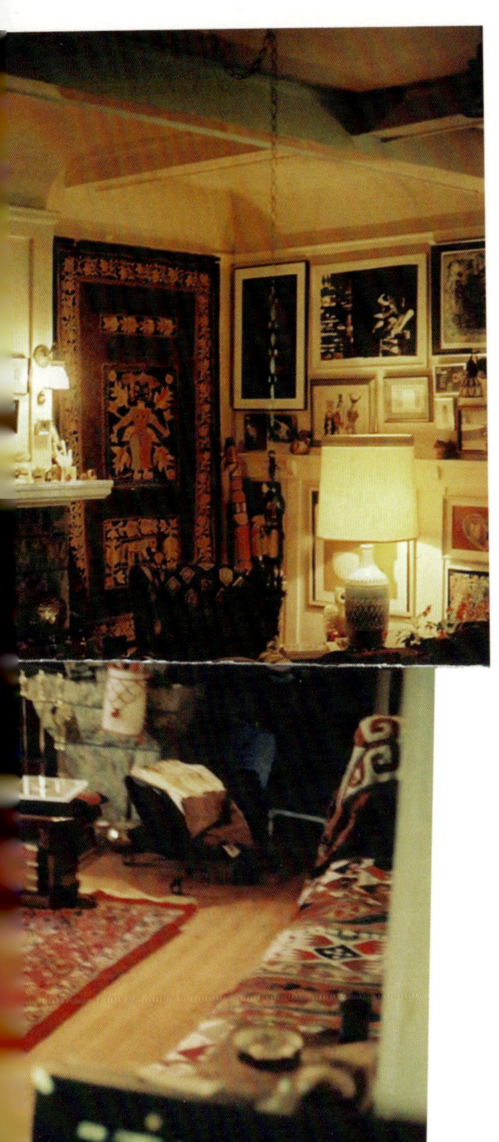

"Black, for PMB, does not represent darkness," Alma de Chantal wrote in *Vie des Arts* magazine. "Still less death. On the contrary, it symbolizes rather a passageway opening on light, wisdom, knowledge."

Martin Bates is a printmaker but her approach to printmaking does not involve the reproduction of drawings. It's more like making footprints in the snow. There are no multiple editions of a single image. Each print is for her an opportunity to form a unique impression, an embossed low-relief sculpture in paper, created with a printing press.

As interesting as these surfaces can be, they are for this artist the visible membrane between ourselves and the ineffable. With her grandmother's big hatpin, she pokes thousands of holes in the paper. In this way she perforates the silence and lets the inner light shine forth. "Pierce the mystery," she has said, "and discover what is on the other side of blackness."

She places her perforated prints before a window or in a light-box, and that homely illumination becomes a sufficient substitute for cosmic brilliance. Or, to put it more effusively, she creates a dazzling, winking landscape of black and white and silver.

Pinpoints of light dance in patterns approved by mystics (hexagram, circle, mandala, triangle) and by Mother Nature herself (solar flare, spiral, star). Grommets and tiny gold wires make visible the gravity that draws the planets together, while Martin Bates' independent playfulness represents the chaotic randomness that keeps the stars apart.

These "estampille" print assemblages are a pleasure to create. "I don't look forward to being rewarded," she has explained. "Art and the doing of it are their own rewards. Art for me is a bridge to another level—a silent communication—a nutrient."

I was not sure exactly where in her rambling house to find her studio. The dining room is always richly layered with her artworks so I made my photocollage there on an overcast afternoon while standing precariously on a chair. Using no flash and no tripod, I made some very long exposures. The results, like the artist, are a bit mysterious. Martin Bates is slightly visible at the right edge.

Martin Bates later gave me a photograph of herself in a favourite dress. It was taken at the Norwegian International Print Triennale in 1989 in Fredrikstad where she was awarded the Gold Medal. "You have no idea how thrilled I was to receive that medal," Martin Bates told me. The only other woman to win had been Bridget Riley and no other Canadian had been so honoured.

"Wonderful memories—shrimp and beer on boats, wild Viking dances, hunting for sacred standing stones... so long ago. Well, you get the picture," she continued, her singsong voice carrying over from the next room where, by now, she was pursuing something different. "It was a beautiful dream time."

Upon her retirement in 1994, Pat Martin Bates stopped keeping her vast curriculum up to date but still devotes herself to creative pursuits. ■

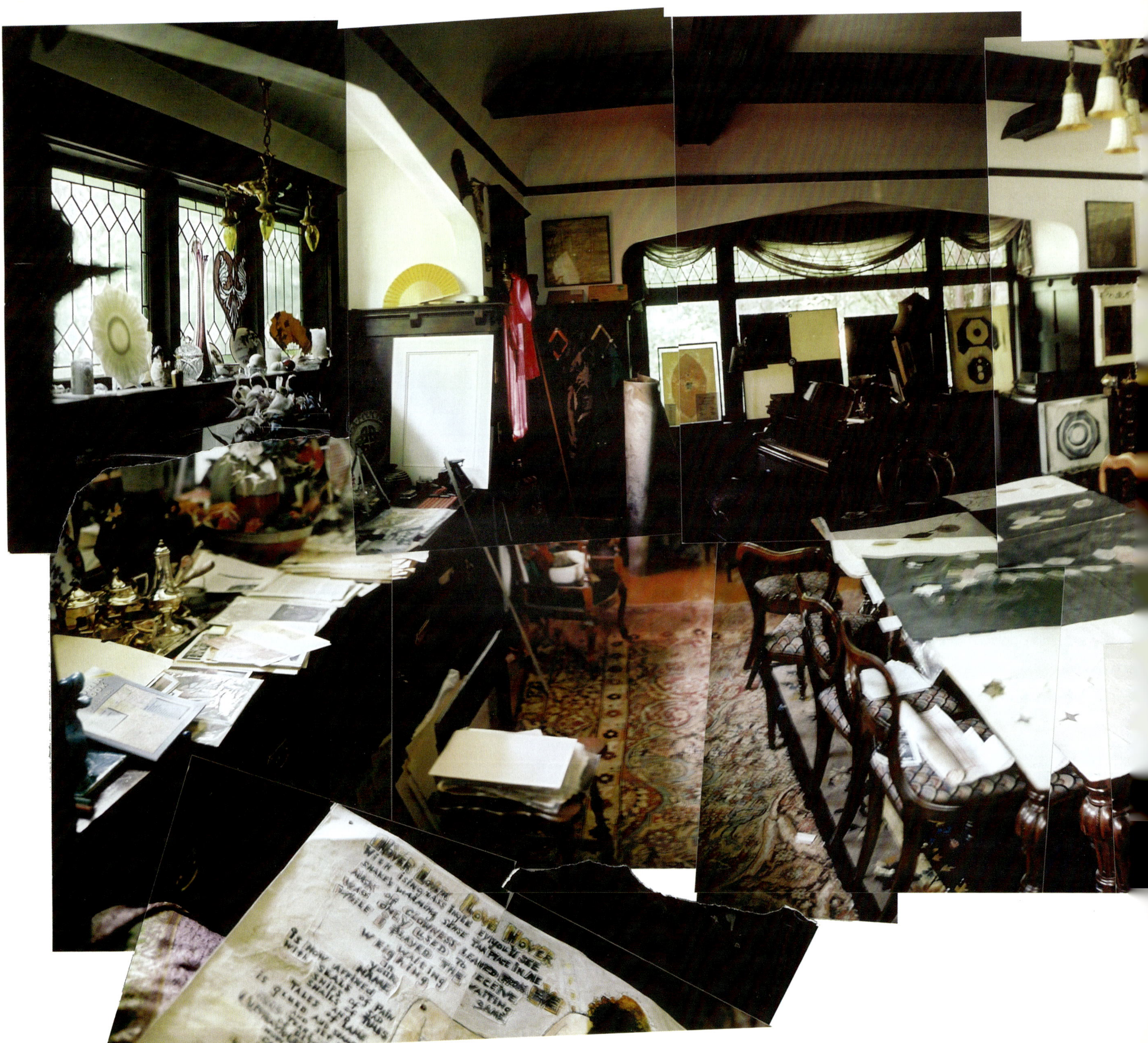

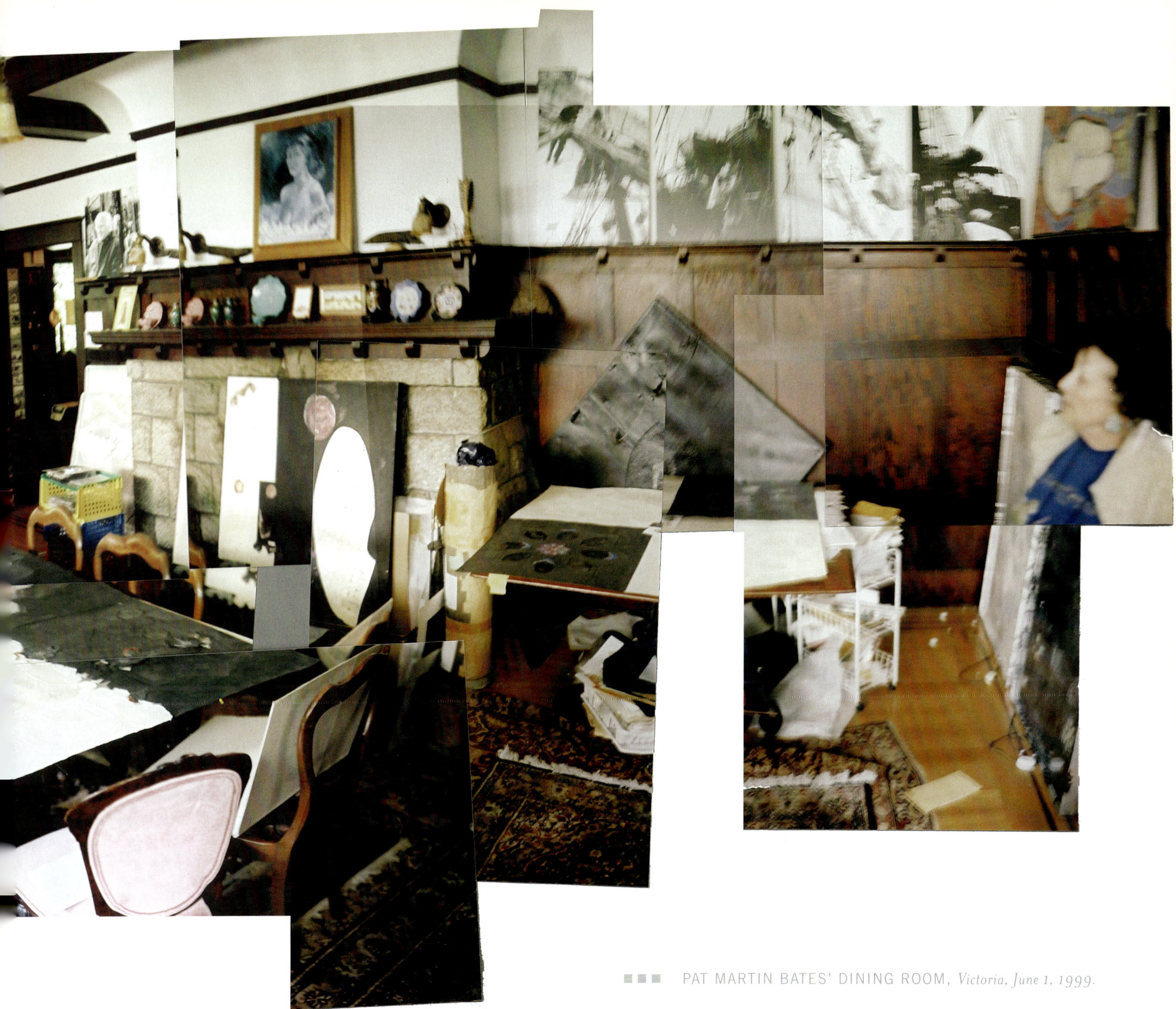

PAT MARTIN BATES' DINING ROOM, *Victoria, June 1, 1999.*

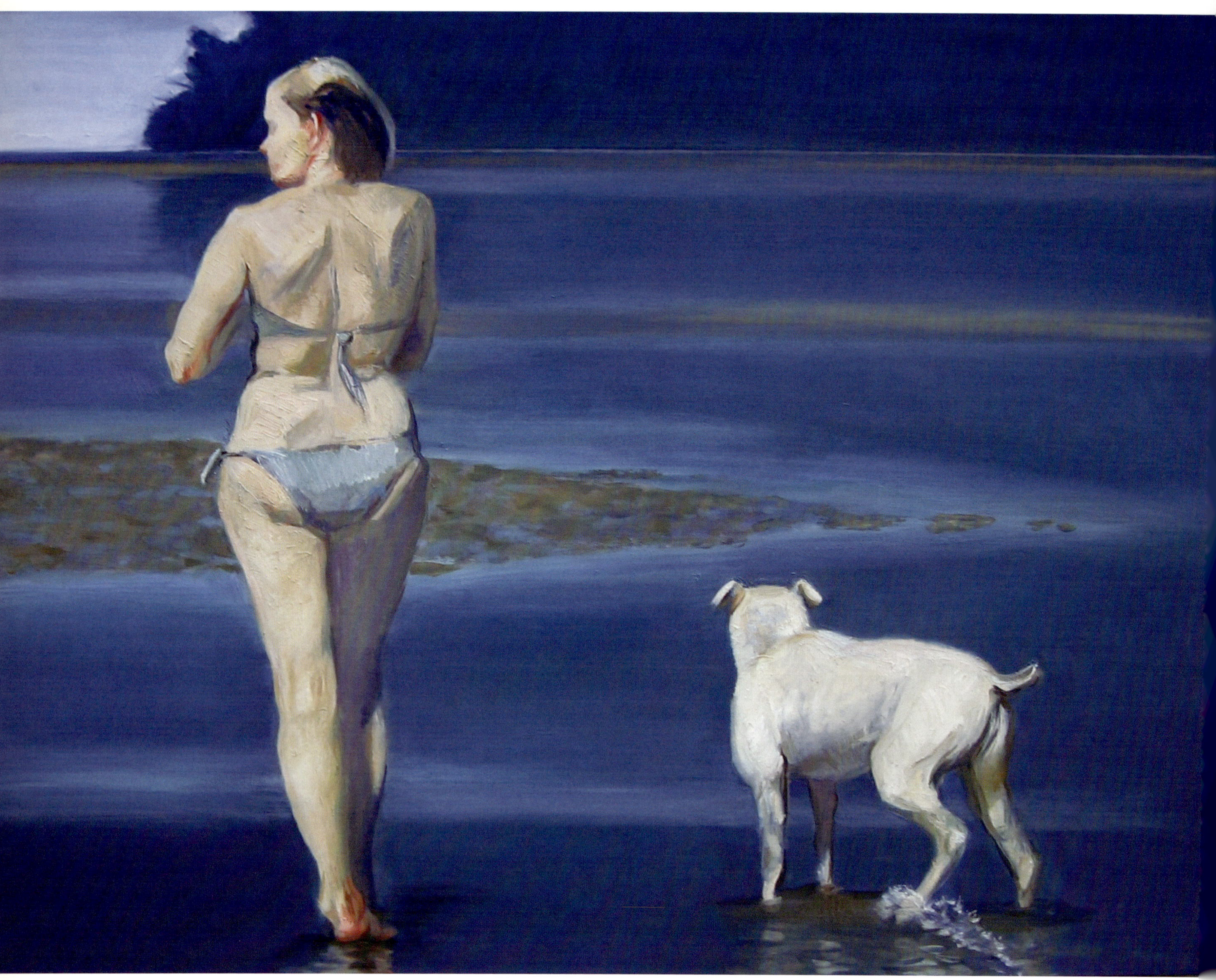

JUDY McLAREN

NORTH SAANICH

JUDY MCLAREN HAS A STUDIO THAT HER HUSBAND CREATED FOR HER IN A SPACIOUS BUILDING BEHIND THEIR HOME. SHE CAN RETREAT TO IT, LEAVE THE CARES OF WIFE AND MOTHER BEHIND AND TAKE UP THE ROLE SHE WAS TRAINED FOR: SHE IS AN ARTIST.

McLaren graduated from the Ontario College of Art in Toronto in 1983. "Hugh McKenzie was definitely my favourite teacher," she noted, recalling some of the worthwhile things he taught her—how to prime canvas, the difference between lead and zinc white, and why you might limit your palette. "We learned to appreciate painting as a craft. It is so important to feel proud of your work, from the inside out."

After a stint in the Civilian Artist Program of the Canadian Forces (she was an honorary captain, though she never learned how to salute) she worked for three years at the Royal Ontario Museum. During her time there, McLaren drew whatever was required—dioramas, maps, biological specimens, cartoons. Her superior at the museum was "definitely Old School. He taught me how to draw with scientific accuracy."

Later, she married "a sailor from Victoria" and they soon moved west. They raised two children in Victoria and McLaren illustrated a number of children's books. She feels it is a field of great vitality. "This is definitely the golden age of book illustration," she asserted. While people fondly recall the masters like Arthur Rackham and N.C. Wyeth, there have never been as many good illustrators at work as we see now.

McLaren enjoys working on specific projects. "Having discipline imposed on an artist is a very healthy thing," she reminded me. "It's a shame that patronage is a thing of the past." Not only are artists finding it hard to generate income, but they have lost that contact between the patron who had the original idea and the artist who brought it to life.

"The artist used to have a very important position in society. But these days the artist is cut off, left with his own belly button for inspiration," she sighed. Working with a patron brings focus to the work.

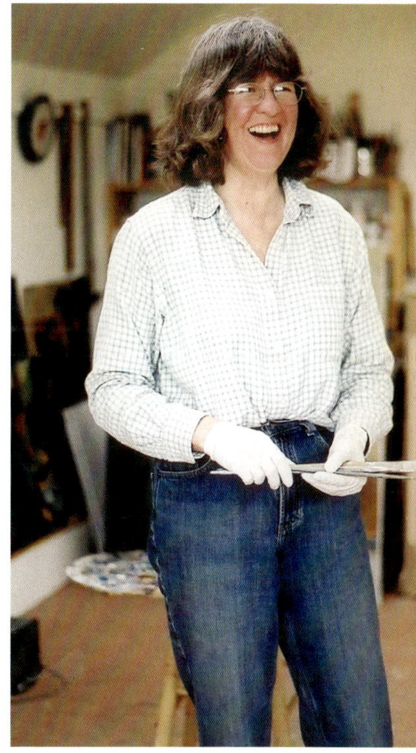

Judy McLaren.

■■■ WOMAN AND DOG, *Judy McLaren, oil on canvas, 36 x 48 inches, 2007.*

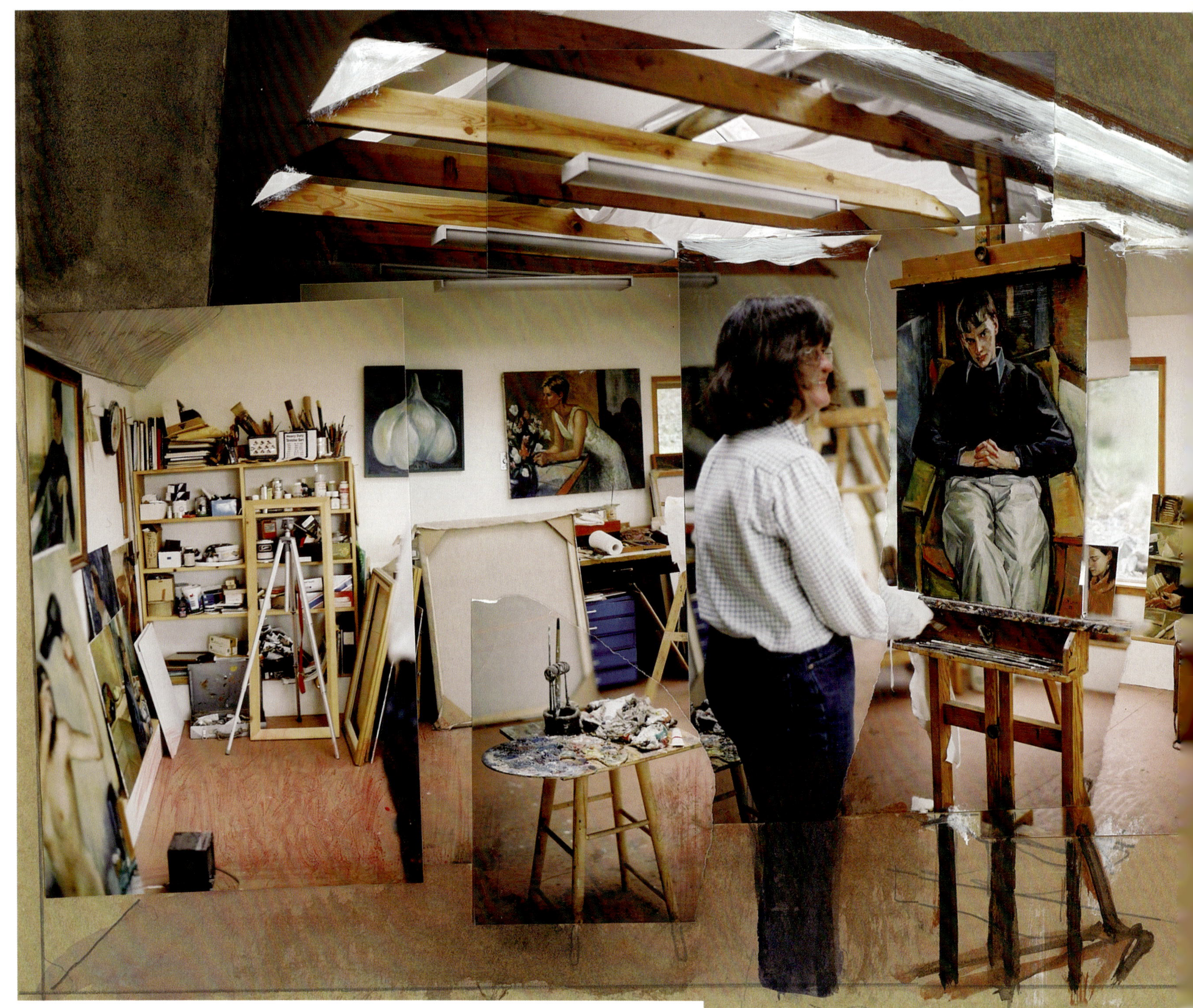

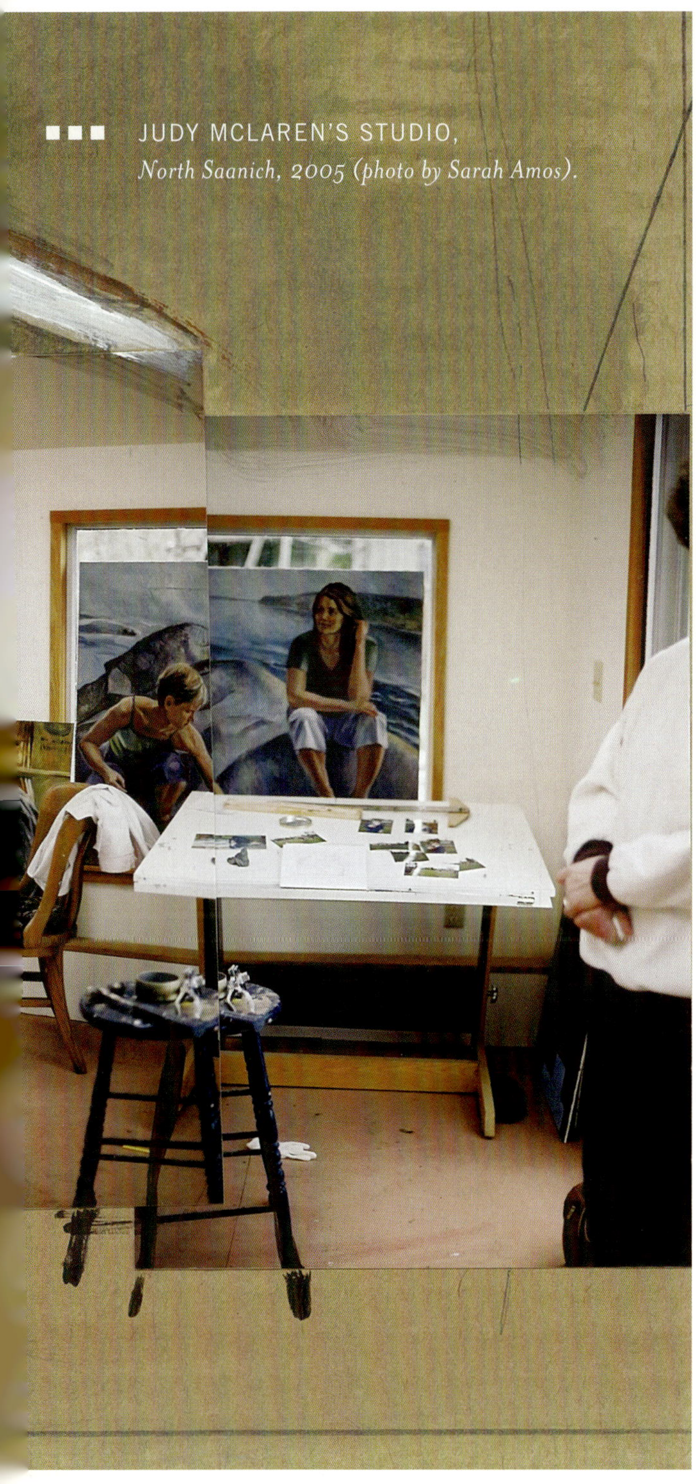

JUDY MCLAREN'S STUDIO, *North Saanich, 2005 (photo by Sarah Amos).*

The artist must "accept certain limitations and material constraints, but within these you can extract the essence from the set subject and push it to a higher level. You're sharing your artistry with your viewers, turning the mundane into something precious. That's what life is all about!"

These days McLaren usually works on commissions. Her oil paintings are surprisingly consistent. The subject is frequently a person, often an adolescent, in a moment of reflection. Her colours emerge from a considered palette, with rich harmonies playing off against neutral backgrounds. The brush marks—not too big, not too small—offer an insight into her fascination with Impressionism.

"I am very confident about my work now," she commented. "I couldn't have said that 5 or 10 years ago. But I seem to have reached a synthesis, an understanding of what I want to do." And what is that? "I don't think of myself as a portrait painter. I think of myself as an artist who paints portraits. I am using the subject for my own purposes. I am not necessarily always going for a likeness. I am interested in human character."

She doesn't try to tell a story about the characters, with the details of their lives articulated by complex background detail. She doesn't use the paintings as a pretext to get her own psychological insights into view. She doesn't use the character as an excuse for experiments in painterly technique. She just paints people in a straightforward way.

While the likeness is undoubtedly there, her message is more forcefully conveyed by the pose, the composition, the quiet and respectful space that she allows her subjects to inhabit. Perhaps parenting is a useful analogy. Like a good mother, she gives her models their privacy and independence, but is close by to help them reveal their own character. "I am attempting to distill the essence of something mundane and raise it to a new level."

The adolescents she often depicts come across as tender, sensitive and vulnerable people. "I am trying not to be sentimental," she admitted. Her subjects often seem to be turned inward and, when I said that, she seized on the idea. "Last year when I was teaching on Saltspring Island a man came to me and said, 'So, you're the person who paints people who think.' That's exactly what interests me. When the outward form manifests that sensation, when they are alive enough to show that they are *thinking*, then I know I'm done."

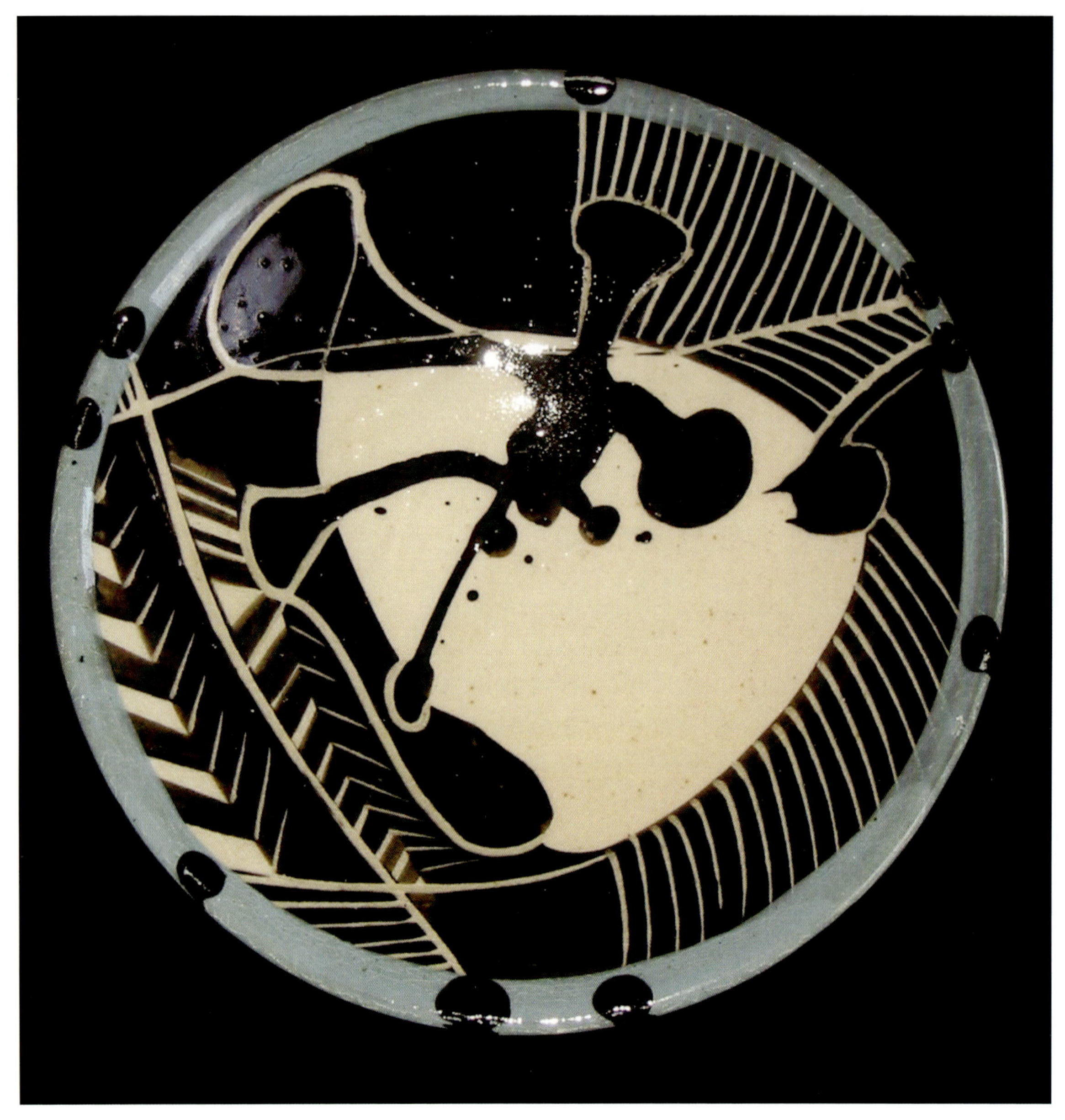

■■■ BOWL, *Wayne Ngan, ceramic, 9 inches in diameter, 1985.*

WAYNE NGAN

HORNBY ISLAND

WAYNE NGAN'S POTTERY STUDIO IS ON THE NORTHERN EDGE OF HORNBY ISLAND, ABOVE A SWERVE OF BAY, OVERLOOKING A SAND-STONE SHORELINE THAT'S PITTED AND POOLED.

When I sought Ngan out I entered his workshop and confronted a sleeping dragon, the huge wood-fired kiln surrounded by hundreds of pots, jars, plates and bowls. Beyond, sitting beside the large lily pond in his garden, Ngan was patiently at home.

Wayne Ngan is a winner of Canada's most prestigious prize for craftsmen, the Saidye Bronfman Award, with which he was presented in 1983. He is the only potter to be given a one-man show at the Vancouver Art Gallery and his works are frequently presented by our government to visiting heads of state. A collection of his pots is part of the permanent display at the Canadian Museum of Civilization in Ottawa.

Born in China in 1937, Ngan came to Vancouver in 1951. His training at the Vancouver School of Art set him on a course of modernism, but his love of clay has kept him grounded in tradition. With a wispy beard and workmanlike clothing, he looks the ancient sage, but his wit and legendary business sense mark him as a modern man.

Working with the simplest forms—cylinders, spheres, cones—Ngan has created memorable and unique expressions. His clay bodies are finely made, with crisp rims and a bright, ringing tone. The forms are simple, never fussy.

With his permission I visited the separate studio where he throws the pottery. Ranked on shelves around his wheel are plates and pots, sculptural forms and moulds from which he could make many more. In China or Japan, an artist of his stature would have a team of apprentices turning out work from these moulds. With regret, he told me that Canadians aren't willing to devote the years of hard physical effort required to become a good apprentice.

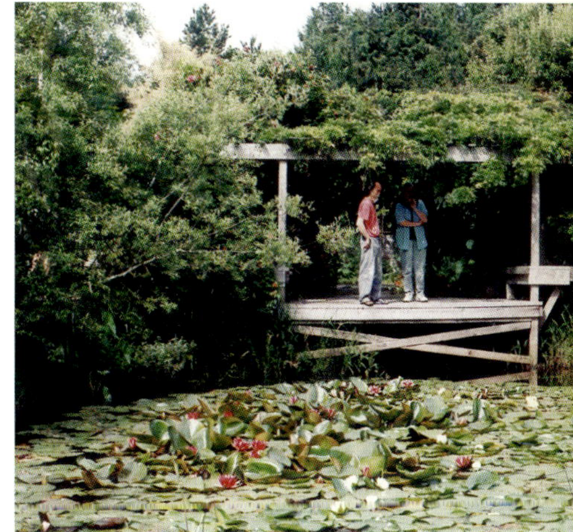

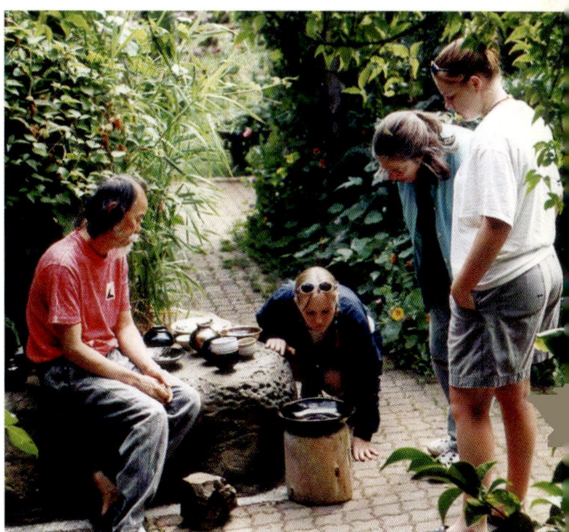

Wayne Ngan's garden, and the artist with visitors, 2000.

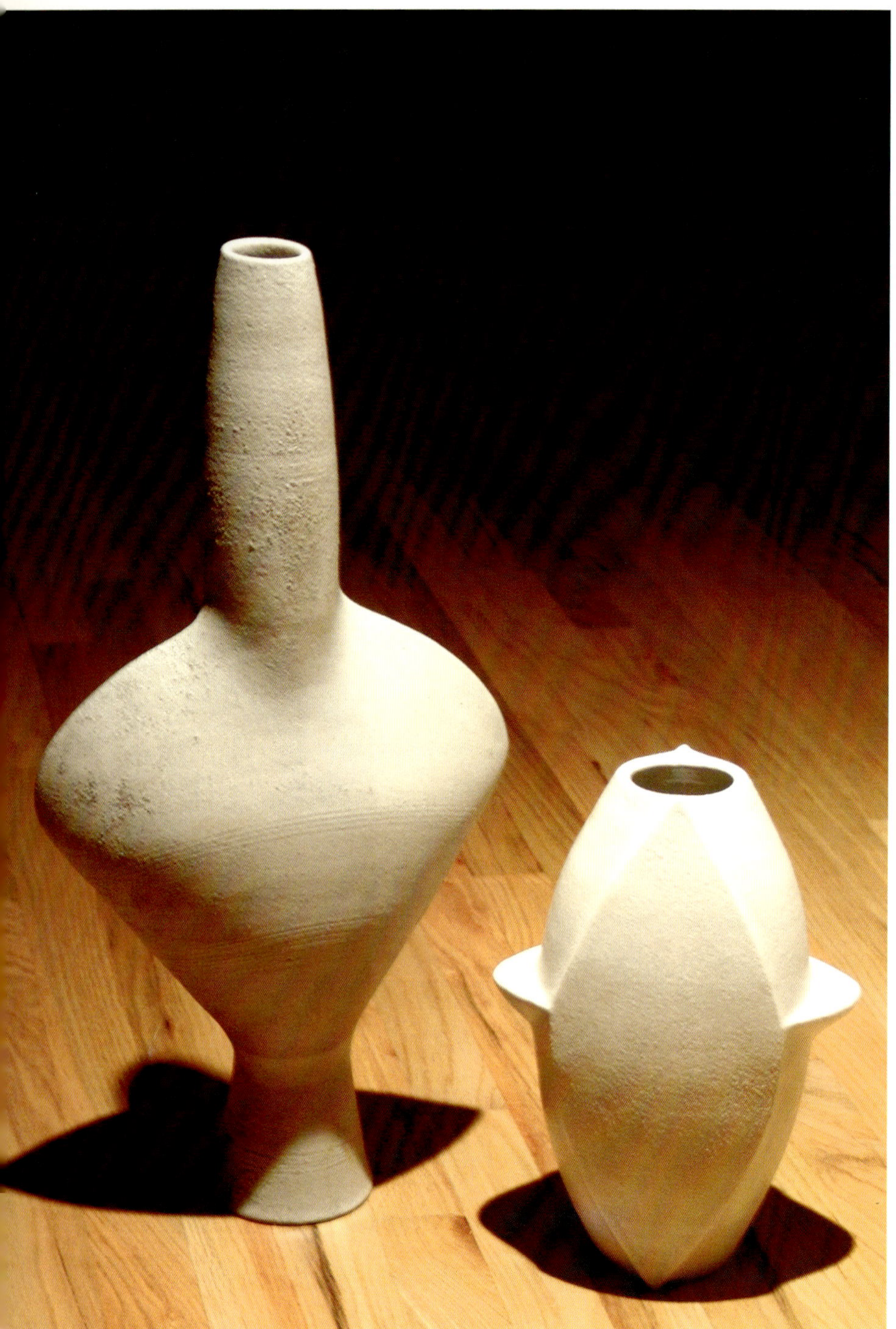

Exploring his garden, I came across a bronze sculpture as big as a refrigerator. He was delighted to encourage my interest; he drew my wife and me into his home and immediately began opening the cupboards. He brought out a tiny Venus, that ancient mother goddess of Willendorf. A gift from an admirer, this talisman inspired Ngan to create numerous little models of his own. Cast in bronze, they rested on a low shelf with larger bronzes that bore reference to bones and skulls and dried gourds.

On he led us, into a large storage cupboard full of shelf after shelf of his pottery. We passed two ceramic models for a studio he never built, shaped like folded birds' wings. Tea bowls in nubbly salt glaze nestled within "oil spot" classics, and white ones were pitted like orange peel. Some were decorated with *hakeme*—broad swaths of slip stroked on. Others were painted up like Picasso's pictures.

Ngan always achieves an integration between pot and surface, and the apparently plain "colours"—black, white, buff—are not colours at all but complex interactions of minerals. Consider one of his large globular vases, glazed a glossy black. To show us what he was trying to achieve, he brought out a basket of glaze tests—dozens of them. From the windowsill nearby he picked up a petrified shark's tooth. As he rubbed it, the oil from his hands polished it to a translucent darkness. Then he began matching it with the glaze-test tiles.

On an all-too-quick pass through the kitchen we had a glance at pots he puts to use, for storage, cooking, serving. I wanted to linger, but he was already in the bedroom. On the floor: a futon on the *tatami* and his clothes. On the

VASES, *Wayne Ngan, ceramic, 22 inches and 11 inches tall.*

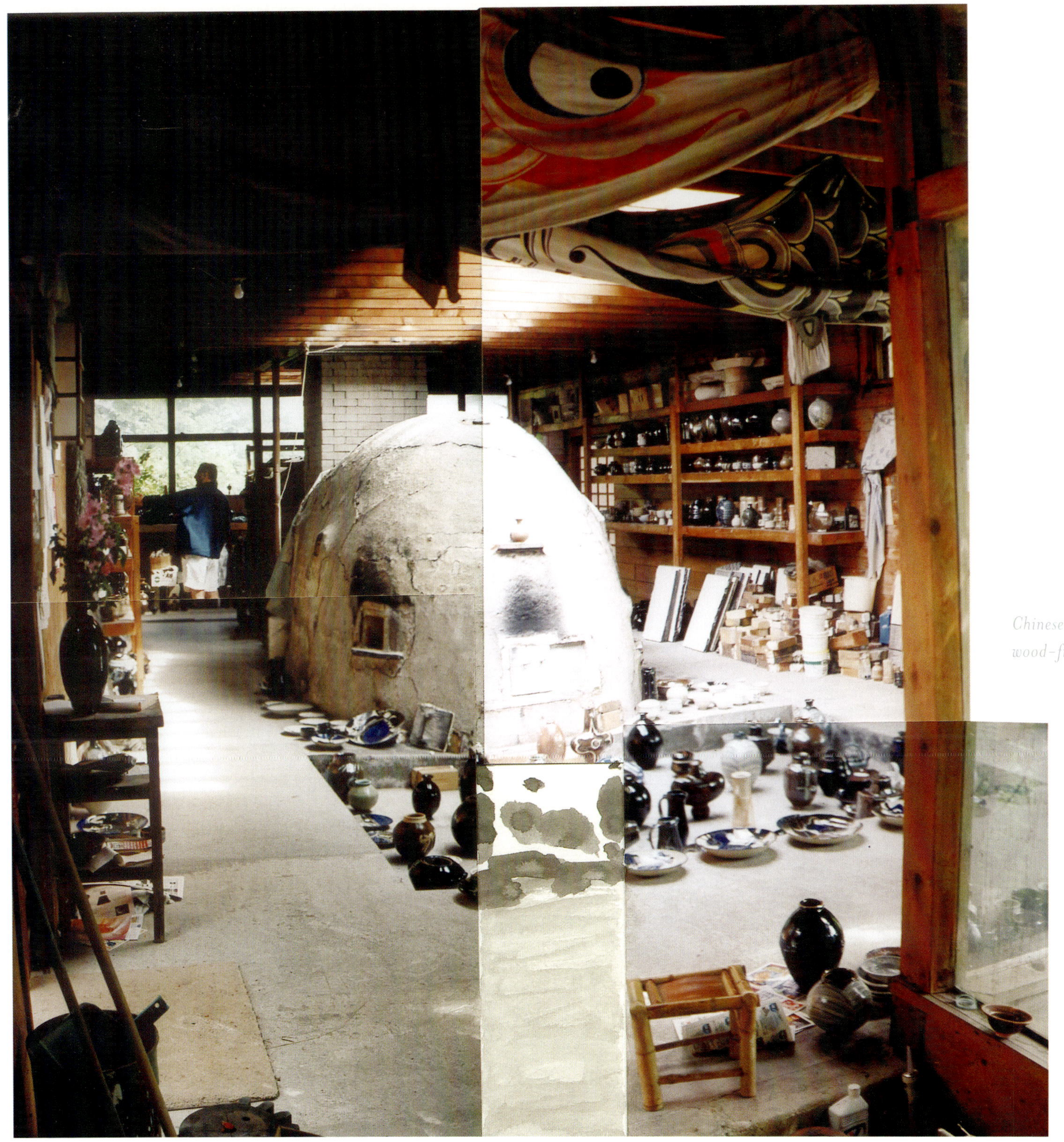

Chinese-style wood-fired kiln.

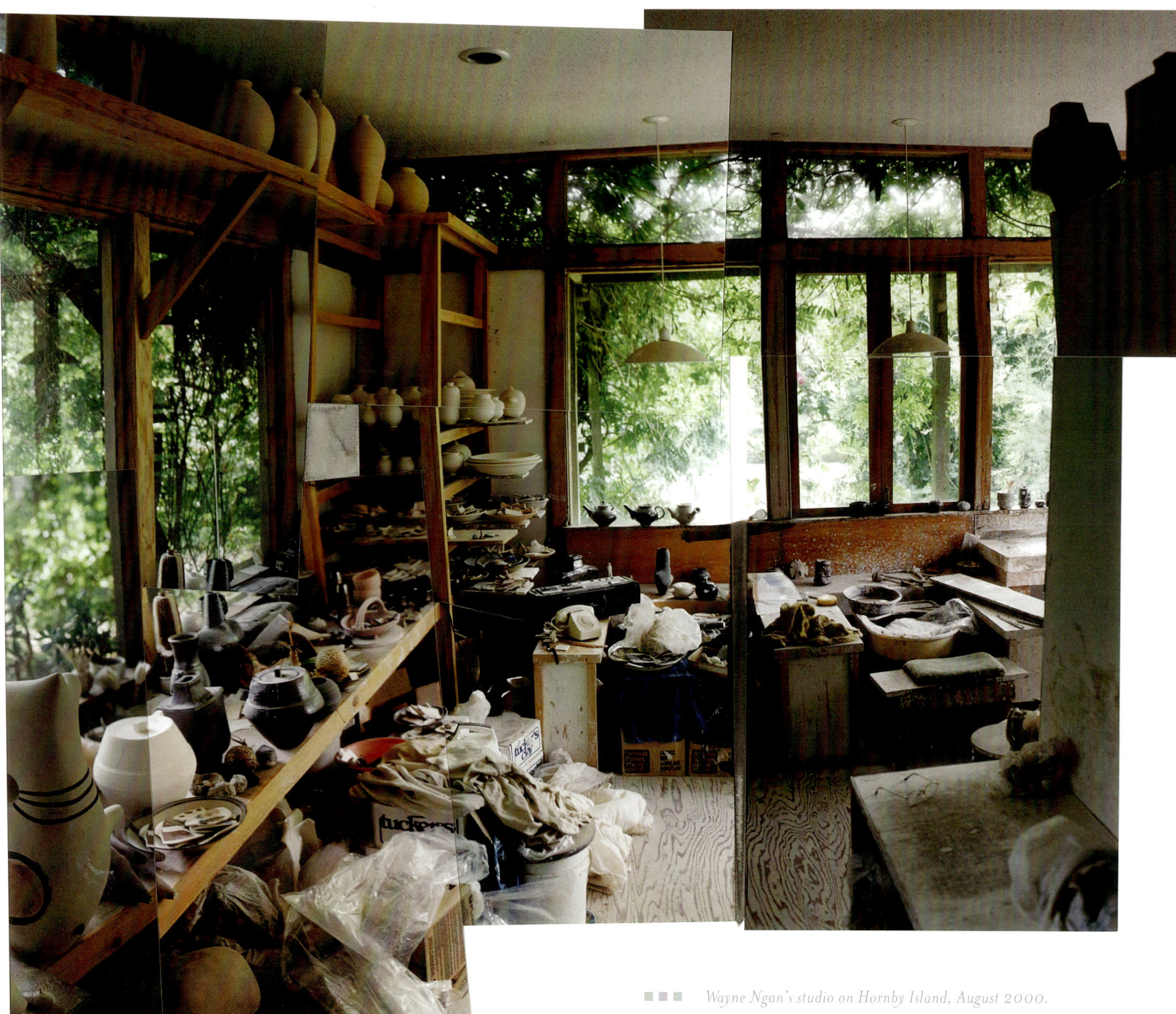

Wayne Ngan's studio on Hornby Island, August 2000.

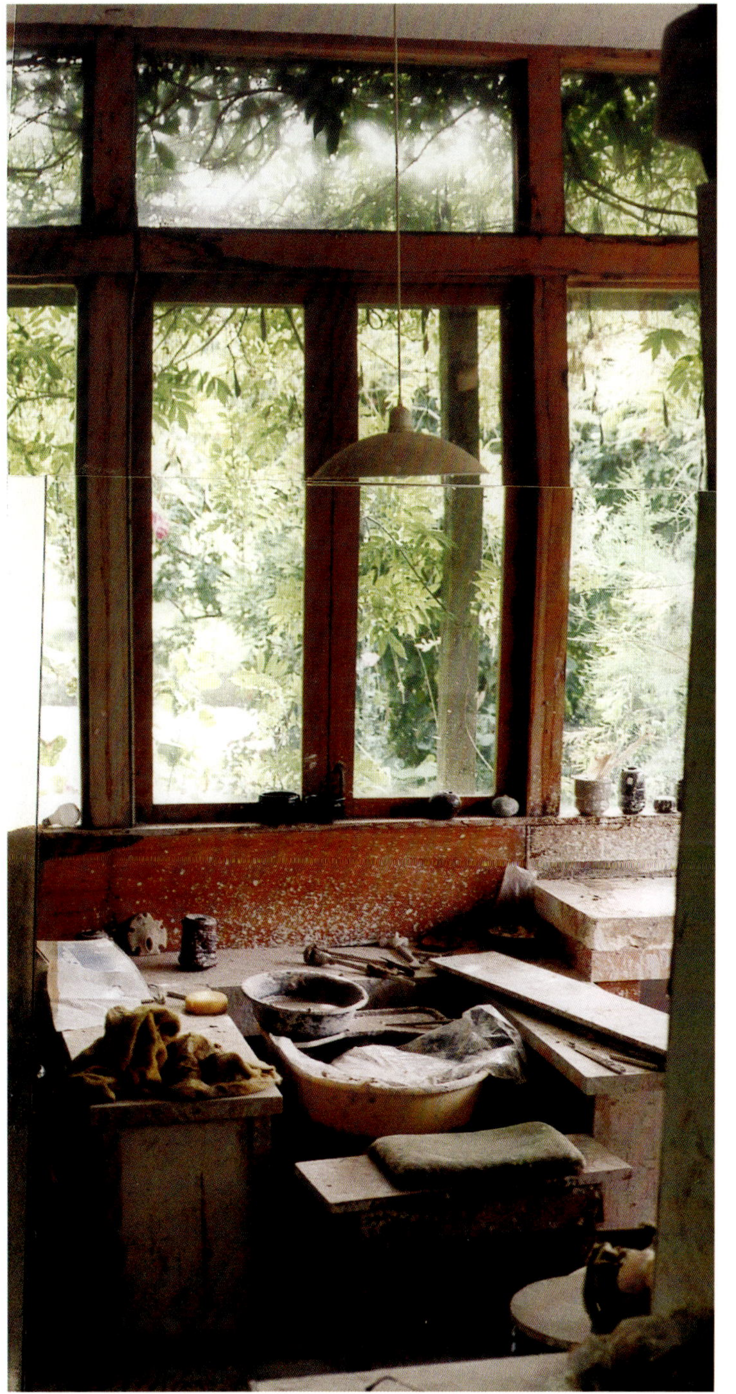

Bisque-fired wares of all shapes await decoration in Wayne Ngan's pottery studio (far left). Sitting on a simple bench, Ngan can look out over his potter's wheel and consider the view of his lily pond. A tape player and old telephone keep him company during the long winter hours.

wall: his ink painting of a songbird on a branch. In the cupboard: one little Japanese jacket ... and more pots.

For the next half hour we sprawled on the *tatami* mats handling the choicest of the choice. Many of these pots are not dramatic, but when the potter directed my gaze to the texture, the fire marks and the proportions, his revelation of elemental principles of earth and fire became wonderfully obvious. He glazes his pots with a complex of geology, chemistry and thermodynamics, and then causes this intricate alchemical dance to rise up into the air and sing. I can see why he has kept these pieces.

There was more to show but, acknowledging the press of visitors, he eventually resumed his position by the lily pond—he'd spent more than an hour and a half with us. We walked away, newly sensitized to the forms and colours of the world, and of the bowl we were carrying. ■

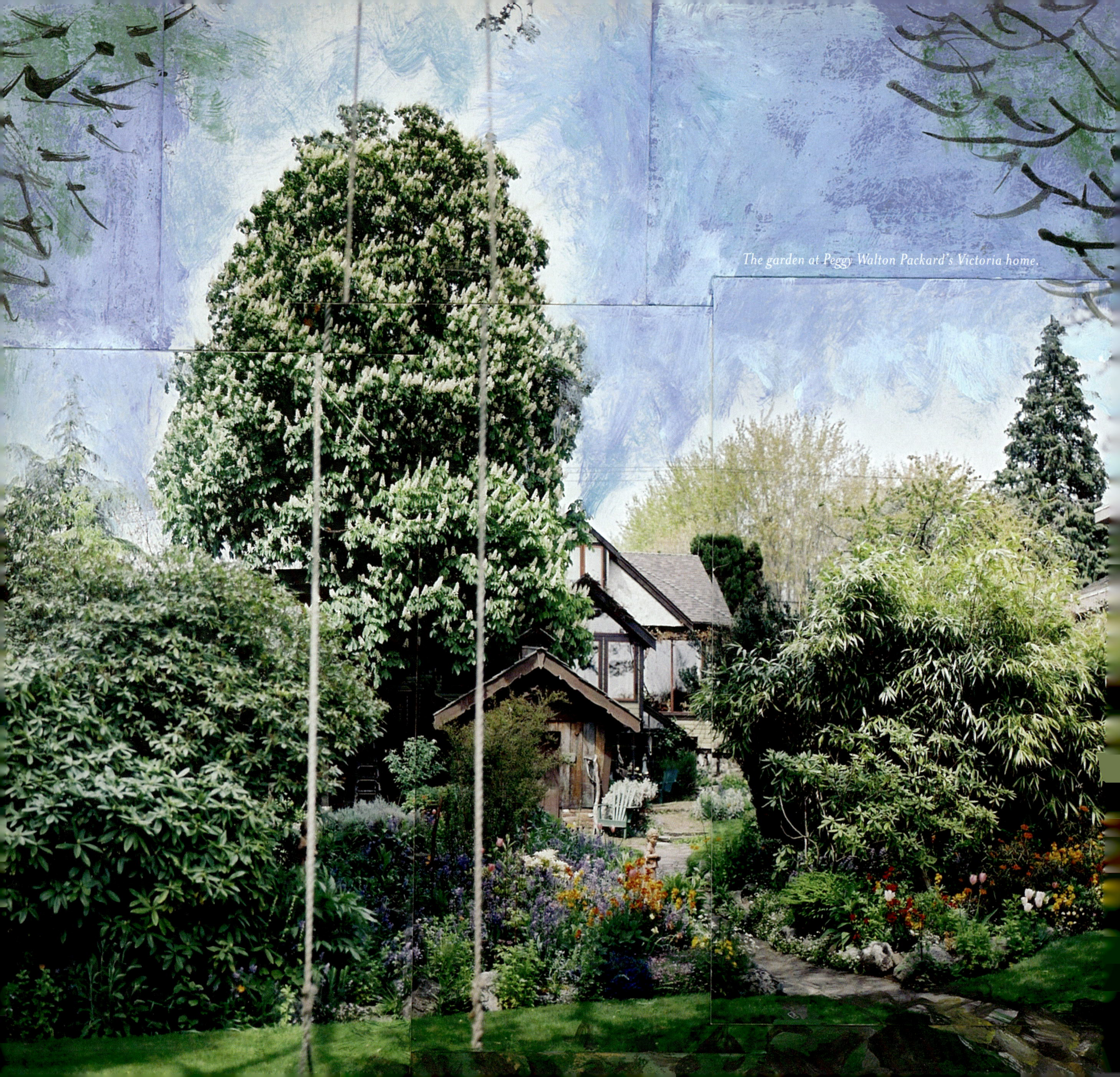

The garden at Peggy Walton Packard's Victoria home.

PEGGY WALTON PACKARD

VICTORIA

I PARKED AT THE BOTTOM OF THE GARDEN ON A QUIET VICTORIA STREET AND, AS I ENTERED THE GATE, THE ENCHANTMENT BEGAN. RAMBLING TERRACES WITH GENEROUS FLOWER BEDS ROSE UP TO THE HOUSE.

Stone paths curved past a number of attractive ponds, overarched by ancient trees. The largest, a Garry oak, had a swing big enough for even the biggest child.

Set about the garden with an unerring sense of placement were a number of sculpted figures. A sprite looked out from beneath the bird bath. A pensive lute player considered a melody from his pedestal among the bamboo. Hansel and Gretel, mounted on a stump, clung to one another as they gazed at a faraway horizon. Near the house, a stone stage set the scene for life as a performance, the furniture cobbled together from driftwood. For all their rustic naturalness, these seats were surprisingly sturdy and comfortable. Peggy Walton Packard knows how to arrange the elements of life.

Peggy Packard has lived her life in Victoria, enriching local culture with her talent for music and theatre, teaching and sculpture. Her true artistic legacy involves figurative sculptures, mostly of children. Curiously, her most public sculpture is perhaps her least typical, a bust-length portrait of Queen Elizabeth in Beacon Hill Park.

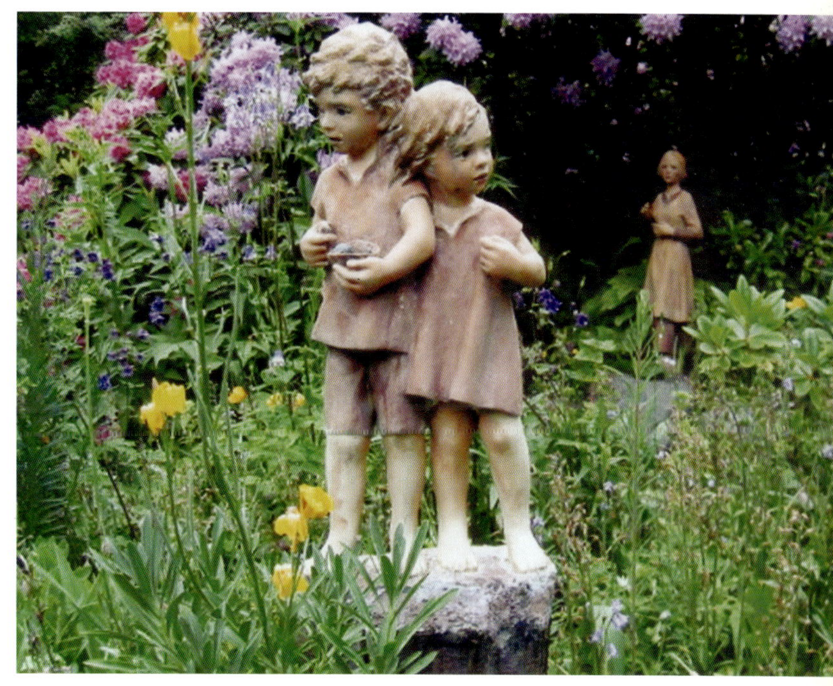

Sculpture in the artist's garden, painted ceramic, 22 inches tall.

Born in 1914, Peggy Packard grew up on her father's acreage high on the Lansdowne slope overlooking Oak Bay and the Olympics. The property has been much reduced, but is still home to Packard and her sister. Even the old swing in the garden remains.

As a talented and ambitious young woman, Packard decamped for Philadelphia and the Pennsylvania Academy of Fine Arts, studying sculpture under the esteemed Paul Manship, and, simultaneously, she also trained at the famed Juilliard School of Music in New York. Her stay in Philadelphia and New York lasted five years.

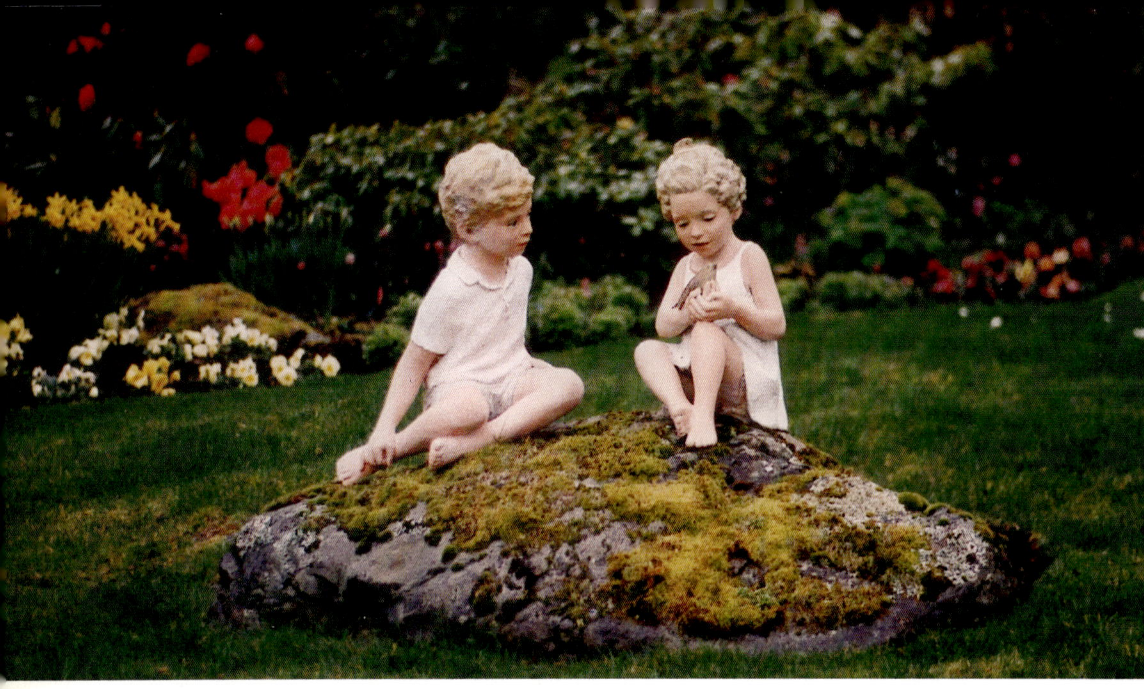

(left) Painted ceramic sculpture, 24 inches tall.

(right) The artist's home and studio, Victoria, April 1999.

She then returned to Victoria with a husband and two children. Before long, the couple divorced, and Packard and her family were left to make the best of things. Living as an artist in Victoria in the 1930s was a desperate undertaking. At the request of Victoria's Montague Bridgeman china shop she sculpted Cathy and Heathcliff of *Wuthering Heights*, one of her many subjects that was offered to Wedgwood Potteries in England. The design was satisfactory but Wedgwood, due to the war, was backed up for years with unmade models.

Packard went on pursuing matters in a modest and local way, though her talents are world class. In the beginning she successfully drew portraits in pastels but, with another talented portraitist in the city, she decided to concentrate on sculpture.

In the glassed-in anteroom of her studio I discovered dozens of sculptures lining the shelves. A little girl in old-fashioned sleepers; a svelte and sinuous nude woman; noble heads; two dachshunds and much more. On the floor were the ghostly forms of moulds used for casting some of the figurines.

Lifting the latch of a big red wooden door, I entered the stone foundation of what was once the family's barn. There, where the stalls had been, I met the artist. The walls were whitewashed; work tables were surrounded by shelves where, thick with dust, plaster figurines harkened back to her days at the Pennsylvania Academy. Packard covered her latest clay project with a plastic bag so it wouldn't dry out, and then led me up a steep flight of steps. With her head she pushed open a trapdoor.

Upstairs, we entered the main part of the old barn, a large space that had housed her father's cars—a Model T and a Cole. At one end a small stage supported a grand piano and musical scores. The walls were covered with paintings.

Clear of mind, able of hearing, informed and animated, Packard is a delight in conversation. She has a distinctive turn of phrase, describing herself as "chewed up" about a bad review,

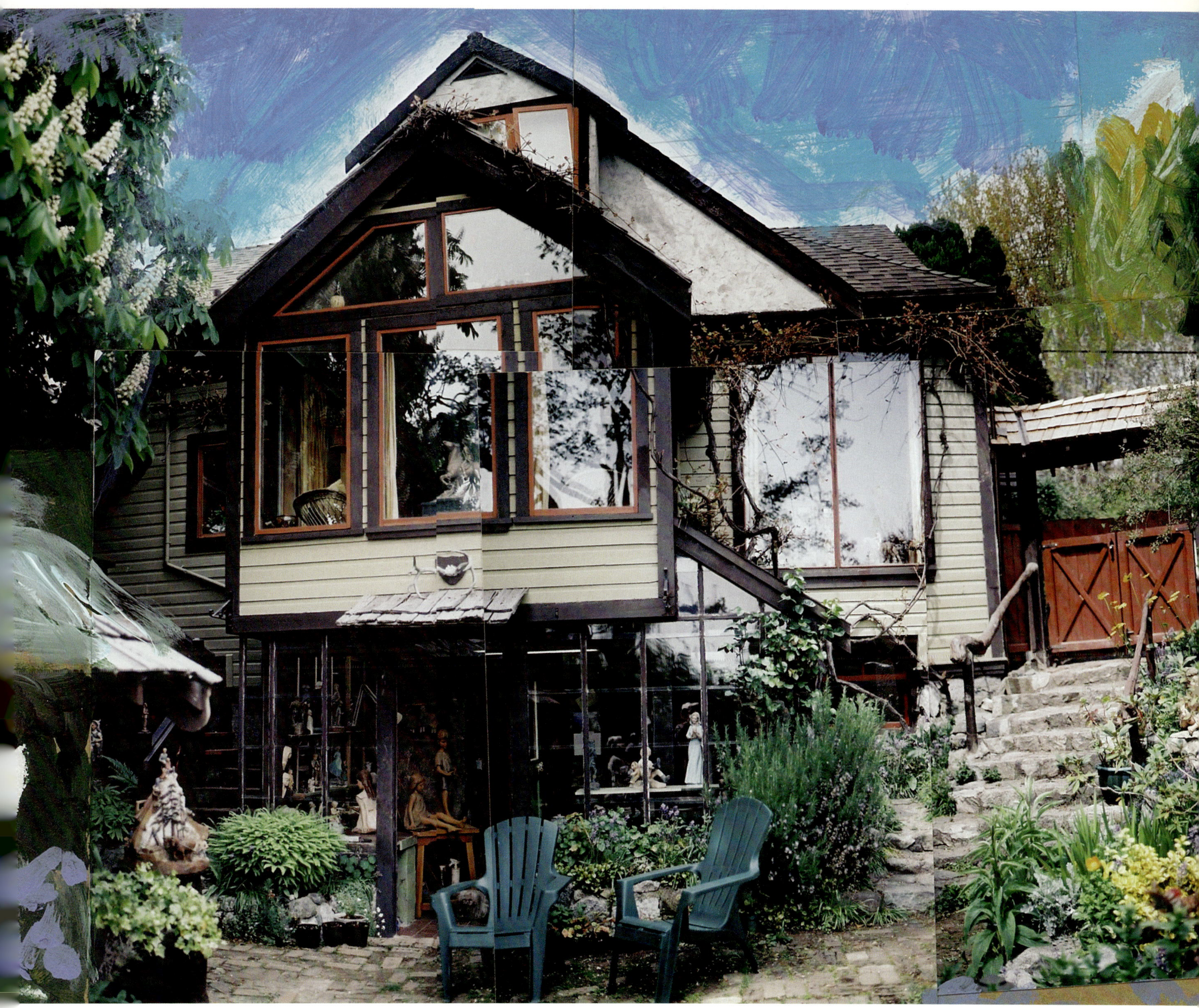

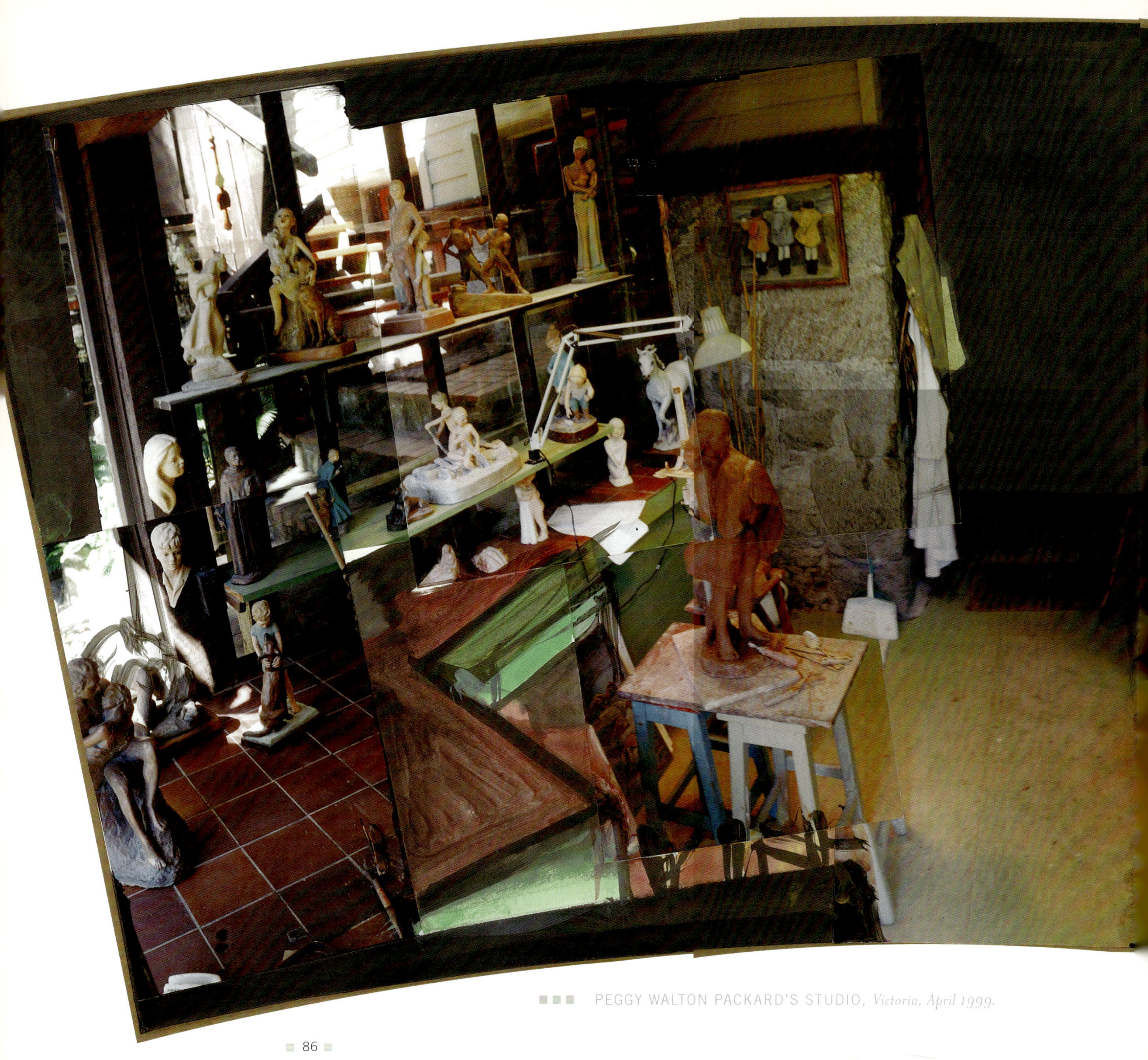

■■■ PEGGY WALTON PACKARD'S STUDIO, *Victoria, April 1999.*

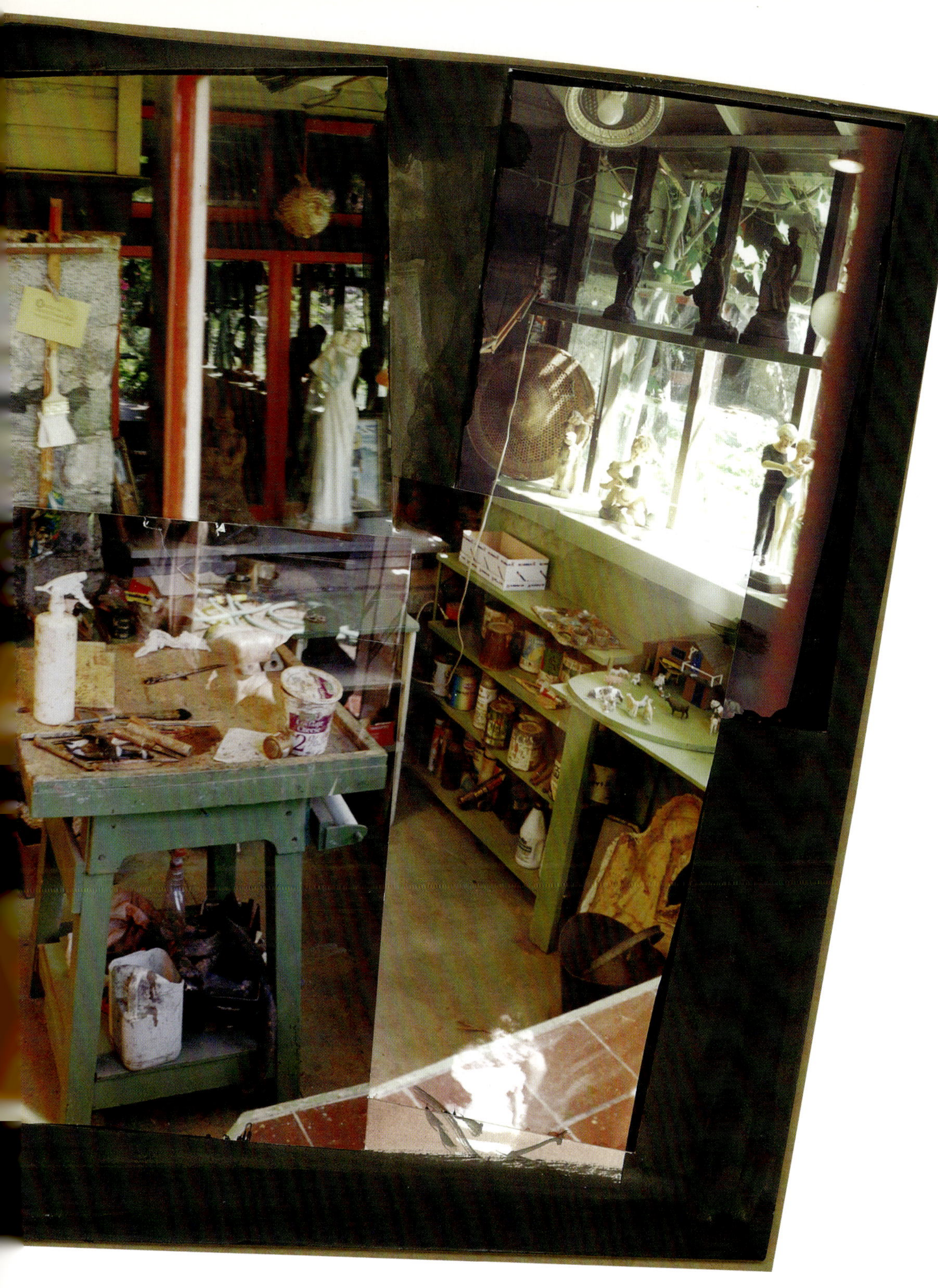

or how she would feel "like a chump" to accept money for her work—making sculpture takes so much time and trouble. She is well aware that her work could be construed as "Pollyanna-ish."

It is difficult to make a model of a person, for each of us knows what people look like. More difficult still is to make one that expresses an emotion. Almost impossible these days is to make a figurative sculpture showing a positive and loving emotion, without its being ironic or saccharine. To do all these things with not just one figure but with a number of figures interacting is enormously complex. To come unexpectedly across such a group, enacting their myth in a secluded corner of a garden, is magical, more affecting than the anticipated experience we look for in an art gallery.

I asked Packard about the sources of her subjects. When a beautiful youth dips his toes into a garden pool has he become Narcissus? Elsewhere, two figures on horseback rode swiftly away across the garden. Packard sang a few stanzas of Schubert's song "The Earl King" to complete the scene.

A visit to the sculpture garden of Peggy Packard is a journey to a better world. ■

RON PARKER

VICTORIA

IT'S A SURPRISE TO FIND THAT RON PARKER'S SPACIOUS LANDSCAPES ARE CREATED IN A JAM-PACKED SECOND-FLOOR BEDROOM IN HIS FAMILY'S HOME. PACKED, MAYBE, BUT ALSO CAREFULLY ORDERED.

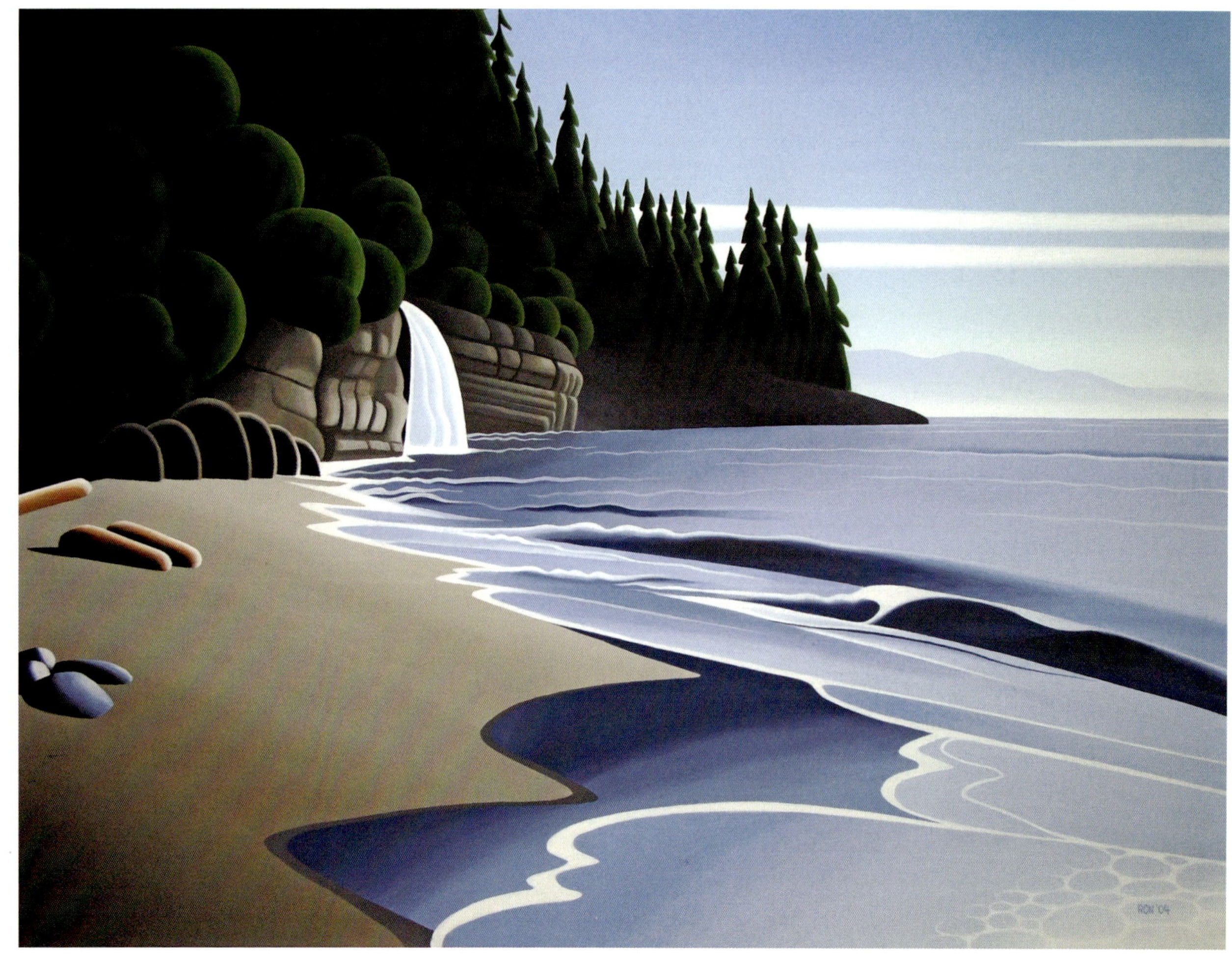

MYSTIC FALLS,
Ron Parker,
acrylic,
30 x 40 inches, 2006.

In the photocollage you can see his camera, photo files and rear-view projection screen close to his drawing table.

When I first interviewed Parker in 1986 he had just released the latest of his three books of high realist paintings of Rocky Mountain wildlife. His accomplishments as a wildlife artist are exceptional, and many editions of his prints were sold through the famous Mill Pond Press. A decade later I caught up with him at Goward House in Victoria where he presented exquisitely rendered studies of women. In recent years Parker has allowed himself a forthright evolution to a new, simpler style.

Many artists—especially the successful ones—are timid when considering changing styles. How did Parker come to terms with his developing vision?

"It's pretty simple," according to the artist. Canadian decathlon champion in 1966, Parker has been coaching track-and-field athletes for the past 40 years, with 16 young people under his tutelage at present. "A number of them came to the gallery for the show. And it came to me that painting is similar to coaching. Get rid of the stuff that doesn't matter."

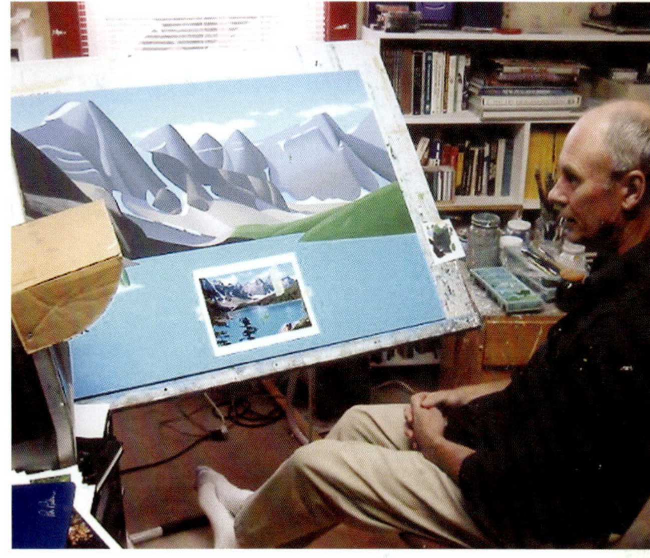

Ron Parker in his studio.

When Parker stripped away the fussy detail—every hair on the wolf, each leaf on the tree—he was left with elementary shapes, significant colours and the rhythms that carry energy through each image.

How does a painter achieve rhythm? "Take one shape," he told me, "and make sure it is mirrored in everything, repeating the shapes so that they give a rhythm to the painting."

Parker is methodical and pragmatic. Even so, his pictures breathe a spiritual air. Where does he get his inspiration? "I hike by myself a lot, backpacking. I remember one day I was at Sentinel Pass, the highest hiking pass in the Rockies. I had a 360-degree view—mountains, mountains, mountains receding into the distance on every side. All I could hear was my pulse, beating in my ear. I get that same feeling sometimes when I finish a painting."

Parker's recent paintings are often compared to those of Lawren Harris. Harris's later paintings—of mountains, of icebergs, of pure abstract shapes—were actually based on his understanding of Theosophy. And Parker? "I don't try to make a statement," he said. "It's about a mood, a feeling, calmness, serenity..." His paintings reveal that he has succeeded in creating a palpable atmosphere of peace.

This minimalism isn't altogether new to Parker. While his wildlife work was highly detailed, he told me that at that time, his sketches were quite simple: "Exactly the same—except that now there are no animals. I went for a balance of light and dark and an interesting-enough design which would flow through."

To get that flow-through, he takes something from the foreground and "pulls it through" the painting. Emily Carr was a strong advocate for grasping the big movement in a landscape, typically using the forest fronds and sweeping clouds to express her larger purpose. To create Parker's broad rhythmic force on the canvas, "waves are great," he acknowledged.

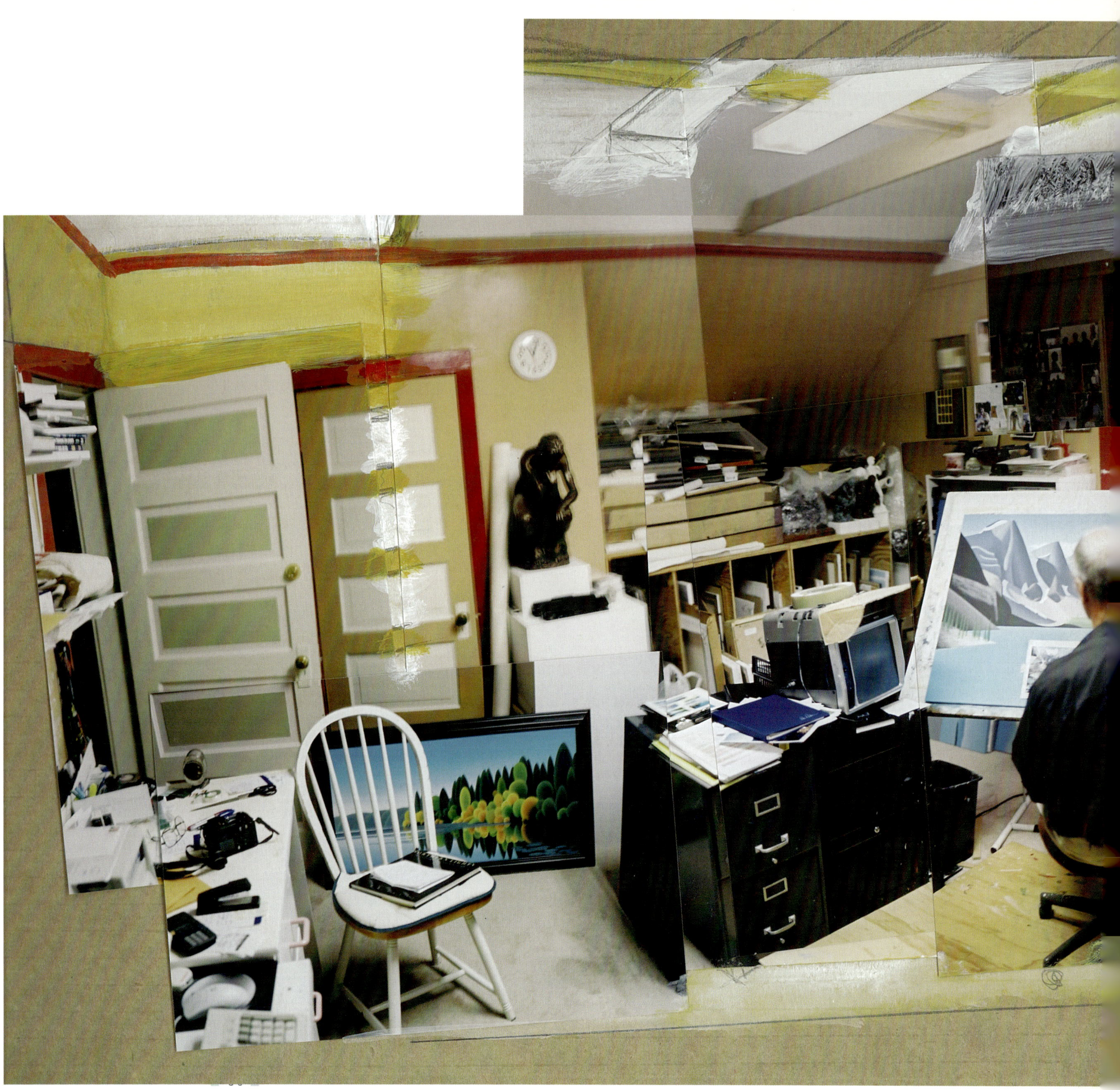

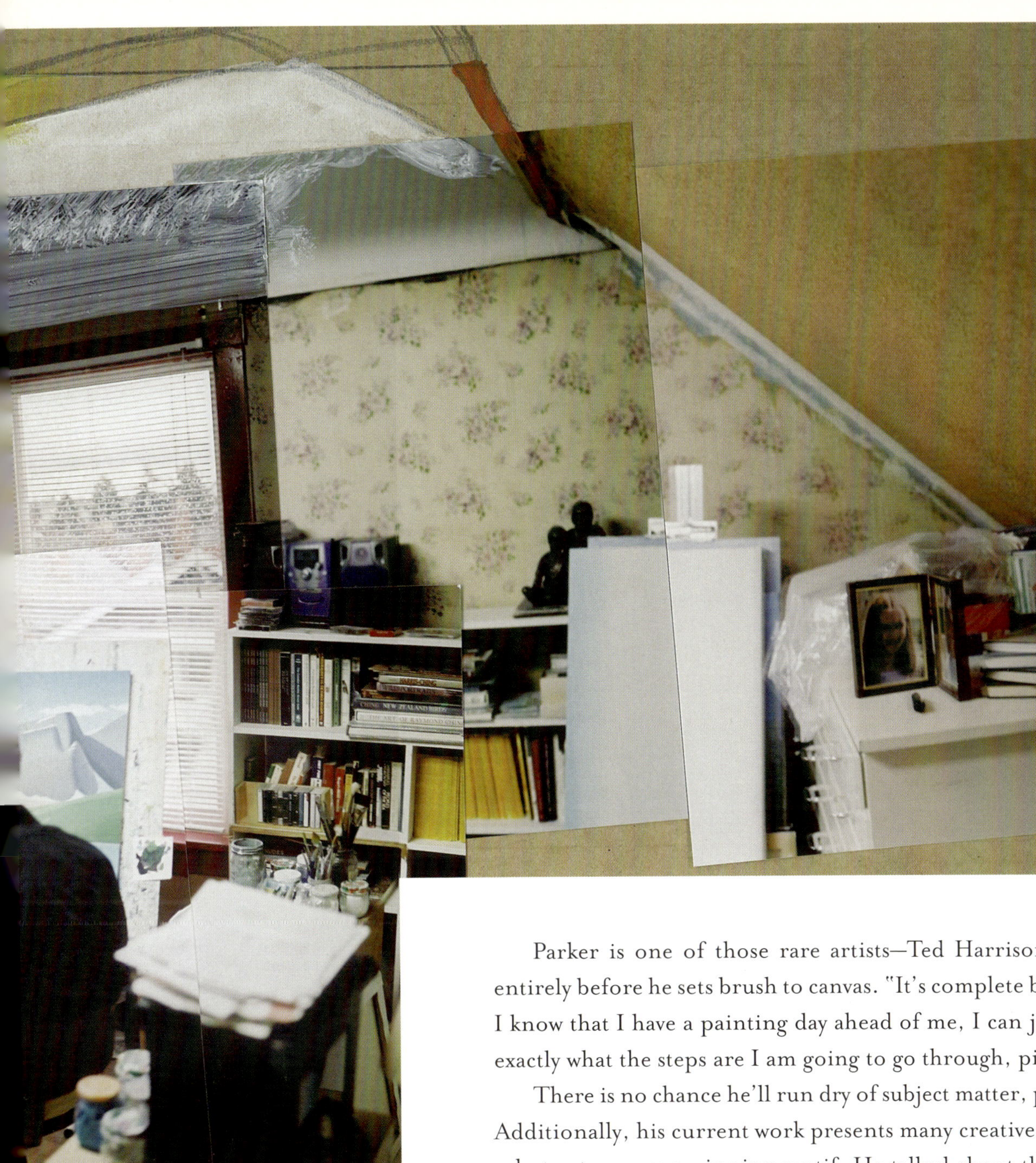

RON PARKER'S STUDIO,
Victoria, November 2004.

Parker is one of those rare artists—Ted Harrison is another—who visualizes his paintings entirely before he sets brush to canvas. "It's complete before I do anything," he explained. "When I know that I have a painting day ahead of me, I can just lie in bed in the morning and imagine exactly what the steps are I am going to go through, piece by piece."

There is no chance he'll run dry of subject matter, painting views of the straits around Victoria. Additionally, his current work presents many creative openings for his artistic progress. Parker's arbutus trees are a winning motif. He talked about the challenge of Garry oaks. What is the essence of their form, without the leaves? Snow on the mountains, with its calm shapes and shadows, is a natural for him. He's also making inroads into the rolling rhythms of the foothills.

In this master's hands, the glowing gradation of tones and the precision of Parker's compositions convey a message of space and tranquillity.

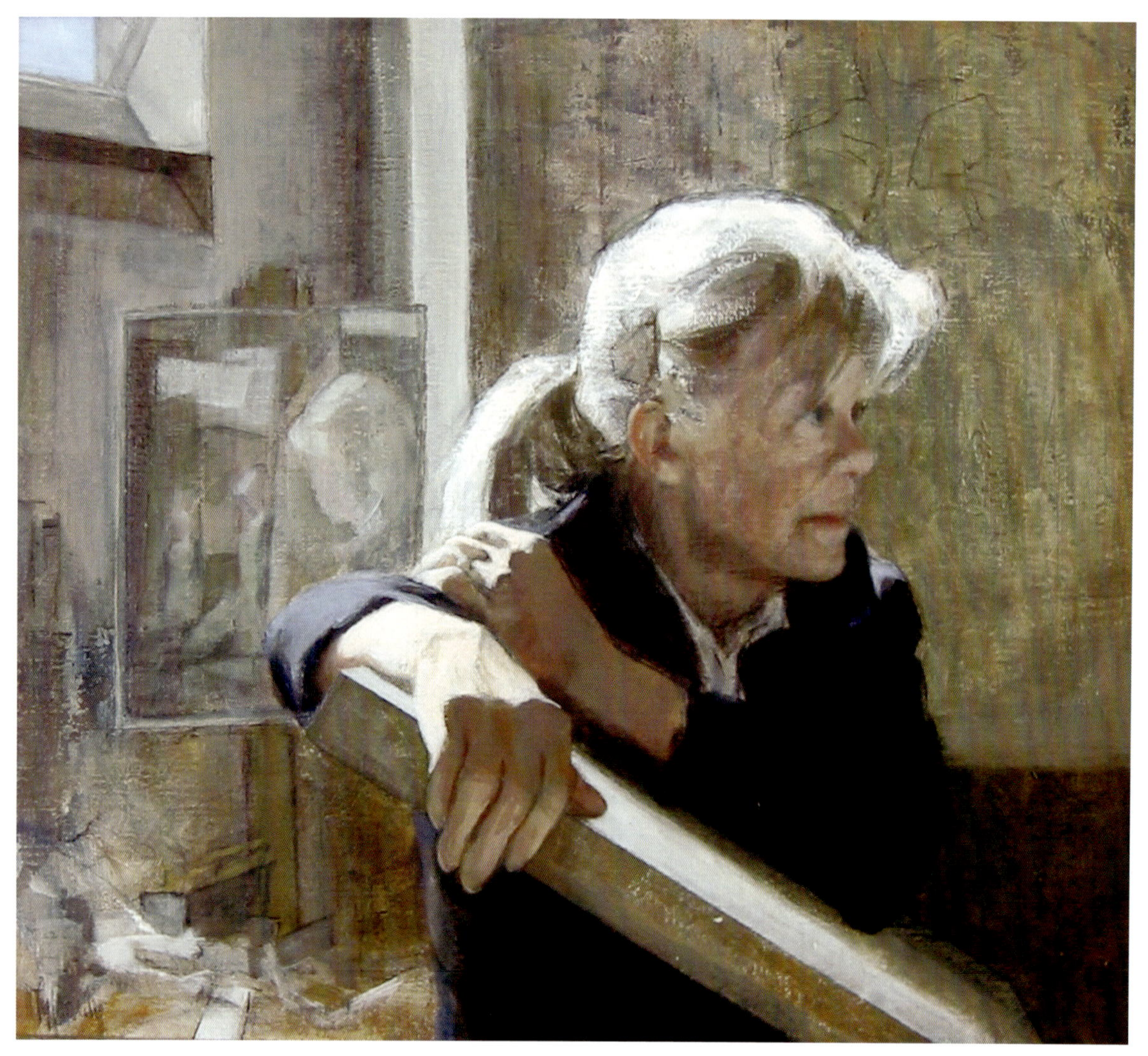

■ ■ ■ SELF PORTRAIT, *Myfanwy Pavelic, acrylic on canvas, 18 x 24 inches, 1989.*

MYFANWY PAVELIC

NORTH SAANICH

MYFANWY PAVELIC'S STUDIO IS A LARGE AND DRAMATIC SPACE UNDER A CATHEDRAL CEILING. ON THE DAY I VISITED TO TAKE THESE PHOTOS, SIR YEHUDI MENUHIN WAS EXPECTED.

He was coming to conduct a concert at the University of Victoria; it was his own idea, as a way of thanking Pavelic for her contributions to his music schools, his causes and his own image over the years.

Pavelic wanted to make the most of his visit, so she decided to have a show and sale of her paintings, and to donate the proceeds to Menuhin's schools. She'd prepared something new. In a "somewhat depressed mood" the previous winter she found herself driving about the Saanich Peninsula. At the end of a country road she came to a stop. There she found no greenery, no sunshine: just a bit of slushy snow melting between the furrows of a farmer's field. And something spoke to her. The resulting landscapes can be seen in the paintings hanging on her walls in my photographs.

Pavelic is known as one of Canada's premier portrait painters, though she eschews that description. That afternoon, in pony-tail and big, horn-rimmed glasses, she was perfectly at ease. On camera, she is quite a bit like her friend Katherine Hepburn. Candid, good-humoured and immensely talented, she invited me warmly into her world, a place where Hepburn, Menuhin and Pierre Trudeau have felt at home.

Myfanwy Spencer was born on April 27, 1916, the daughter of the owner of Spencer's, Victoria's first department store. The Spencer family owned the *Victoria Daily Times* as well, though both these assets passed out of the family after the death of Myfanwy's father in 1946. Her childhood was enriched by trips to Europe and the best schooling—in Victoria, at Norfolk House, and in Montreal, at Miss Edgar and Miss Cramp's School. Music and art were the passions of this young and precocious Canadian. In 1937, she was living in London and was "presented at court." Back home in Victoria in 1938, she helped Emily Carr catalogue the paintings in Miss Carr's studio.

By 1940, Myfanwy had visited Lawren Harris's charmed circle in Vancouver. With the coming of the war, she travelled across the country, drawing portraits for the Red Cross, and personally raised $10,000. Then she moved to New York and took up residence in the famed Algonquin Hotel. With private tutors in both music and art, she lived in a rich cultural world. Eventually, her music studies were sidelined by wrist problems so she set aside her dreams of becoming a concert pianist and concentrated on art.

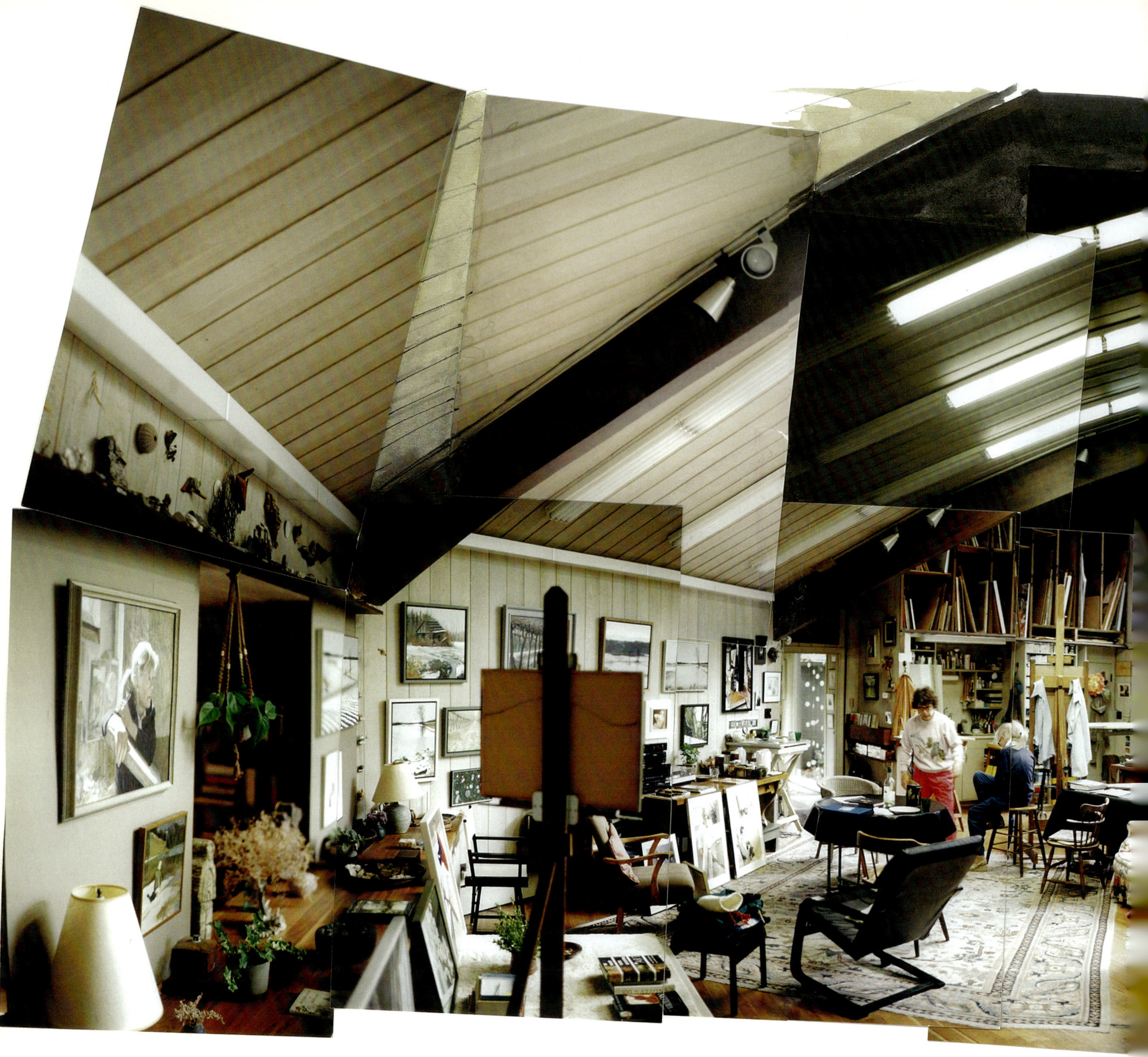

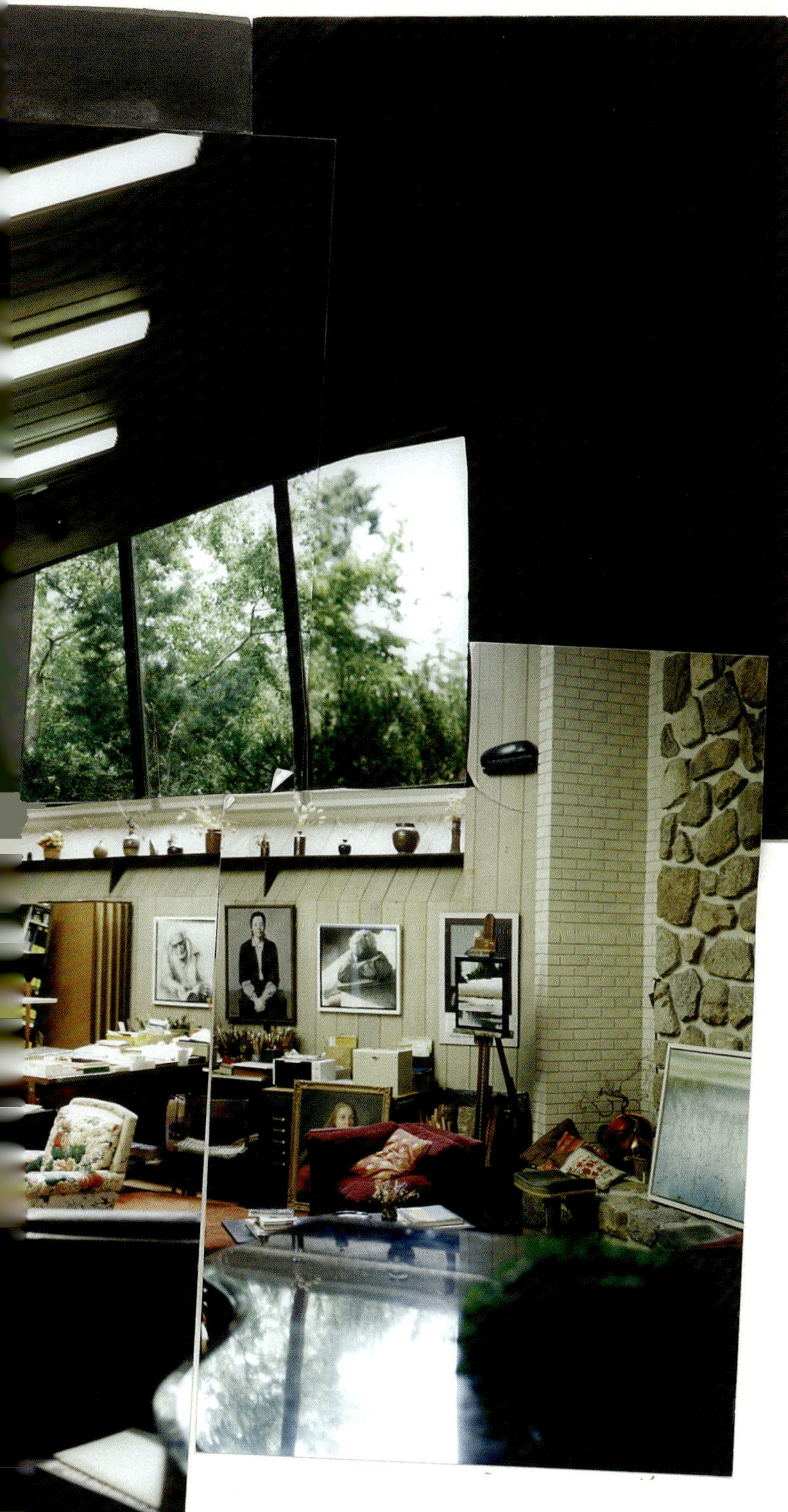

In 1948, she married Nikola Pavelic, a Zagreb-born Croatian who had graduated from the Sorbonne with a Doctor of Law degree. Myfanwy and Niki returned to Victoria in 1950 for the birth of their daughter, Tessa.

The three Pavelics then divided their time between summers in Victoria and the rest of the year in New York for Tessa's education. It was in 1969 that they all returned permanently to what had been the Spencer family's summer home in Saanich. There Myfanwy built her superb studio, which immediately became the setting for events of legendary status in the local arts community. The studio has soaring ceilings, a beach-stone fireplace, a grand piano and Myfanwy's painting equipment. Its fine acoustics were an essential part of the design.

Pavelic's efforts have been crowned with great success. In 1976, she was elected to the Royal Canadian Academy of the Arts. In 1983, she was commissioned to paint Sir Yehudi Menuhin's portrait for the National Portrait Gallery in London, the first by a Canadian artist. In 1990, she was chosen to paint the official portrait of former prime minister Pierre Trudeau that now hangs in the Parliament Buildings in Ottawa. The University of Victoria awarded her an honorary doctorate and she has donated more than 250 of her own works to that university. She is a member of the Order of Canada.

Of course, it's not all been a bed of roses. Her time has been claimed by motherhood; from childhood she has been dogged by pain and damage to her knees, wrists and back. But somehow she has put in the long hours of meticulous labour necessary to create thousands of superb paintings and drawings, and has given many of them away in support of causes she favours.

In conversation, Pavelic seems sincerely interested in the doings of everyone around her. Yet she cherishes her aloneness and, when the interview is over, she retires into her world as a private person. "The universe of Myfanwy Pavelic," as the poet Robin Skelton has written, "is a universe of separate tables."

MYFANWY PAVELIC'S STUDIO, *September 9, 1996.*

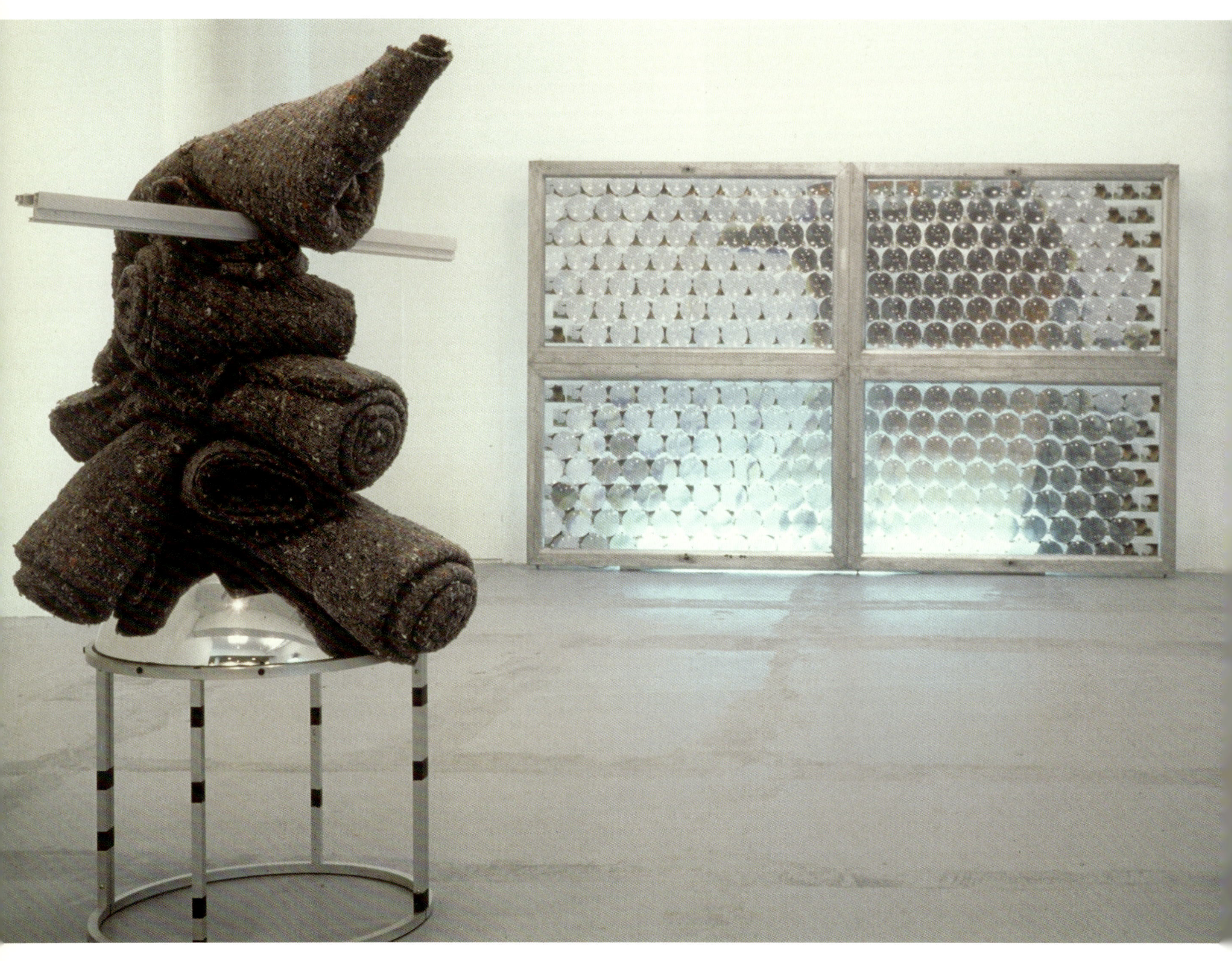

JERRY PETHICK

HORNBY ISLAND

JERRY PETHICK WAS BORN IN LONDON, ONTARIO, IN 1935. HIS ARTISTIC EDUCATION TOOK PLACE IN LONDON, ENGLAND, AT THE CHELSEA COLLEGE OF ART AND THE ROYAL COLLEGE OF ART.

In 1967 he saw his first hologram and became a pioneer in the field of holography in San Francisco. In 1975, Jerry, his wife, Margaret, and their son, Yana, moved to Hornby Island. To visit Pethick and sit at their picnic table under the apple tree was an unforgettable experience, like sharing home-brew and speculative philosophy with Confucius or Socrates. His art has been the subject of serious investigation by the major galleries in this country and many abroad.

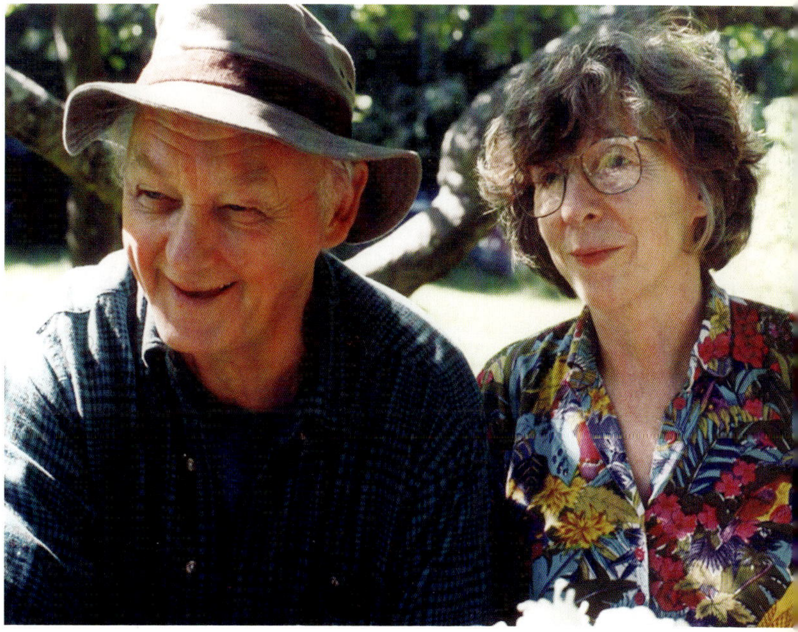

Pethick's friend Jamie Reid has said, "Although he was a great artist, there was nothing of the great man about him except for his total dedication to his work and the absolute energy and confidence with which he pursued his artistic aims."

Pethick's essential message was that the world is not divided into "I and thou," but is, in fact, a unity. He showed us that our usual perception of space, which constructs a distance between each of us, is an illusion. He demonstrated this by creatively reinventing space as material for his sculpture. Not clay or bronze or even glass and silicone—space.

Our mindset is woefully limited. "We learn to make choices *between*; we don't perceive *among*," Pethick told Vancouver curator Scott Watson. "Instead of the real, we deal with models of the real... language itself has come to rest on a bipolar metaphor so that it is almost impossible to locate my concerns in language."

Pethick went beyond making sculpture from painted plaster at the Chelsea College of Art and moved on to

Jerry and Margaret Pethick, Hornby Island, August 2000 (photo by Sarah Amos).

■ ■ ■ OUT OF THE CORNER OF AN EYE, *Jerry Pethick, aluminum, glass, felt, photos, lenses, mirror, plastic spokes, 287 x 366 x 222 cm, 1990.*

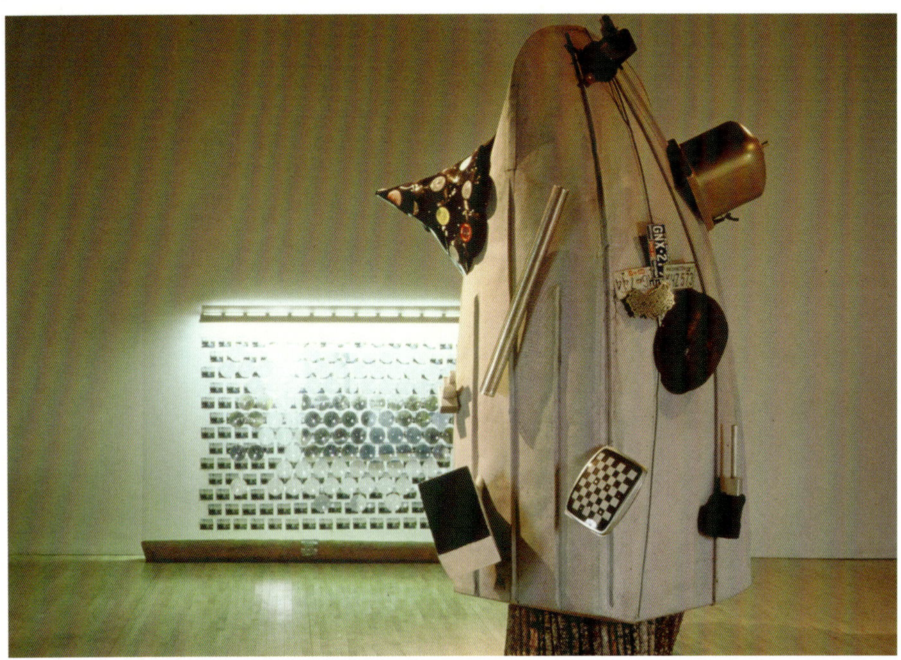

HOMESHIP/FAUX TERRAIN, *Jerry Pethick, wood, photos, lenses, coal, TV, aluminum, foam, records, steel, rope, 460 x 425 x 510 centimetres, 1990/92.*

plastic, which has colour within it, not on it. When he was shown the first holograms by their inventor, Dennis Gabor, he said to Gabor, "Maybe you've made sculpture obsolete!"

"I hope so," the inventor replied.

Pethick pursued holography in the United States where, at that time, it was in the hands of the military. He devised and patented the fundamental methods of simple sand-table technology, effectively giving holography to artists, and he was a founder of the San Francisco School of Holography in 1971.

Eventually, Pethick saw no point in working in darkened rooms. With the family's move to Hornby he emerged into the daylight. Pethick's materials now consisted of what he could find at the co-op store or the legendary Hornby Island recycling depot. From odd bits, he cobbled together silent projectors of luminous metaphor.

Aluminum, glass, silicone, enamel, mirror—all silica—made a perfect foil to show the dazzling optical tapestries blazing forth from the diffraction grading of the Spectrafoil (a reflective material used for fishing lures). Here is richness of colour such as painters Tom Thomson and Cornelius Krieghoff never dreamed of. Pethick's enigmatic and playful sculptures function as a counterpoint: tangible indicators of another, virtual space that this artist opened to us.

In 1909, Gabriel Lippmann, the French psychiatrist who created the first colour photographic plate, proposed, as a model of sight, the multiple-lens arrangement of a fly's eye. An array of lenses could provide information that the brain would process in a way entirely different from the camera (which is monocular) or our normal two-eye (binocular) vision. As the viewer changed position before the field of dozens—even hundreds—of lenses, "reality" would change too. It was only a theory. But with profound understanding and irrepressible wit, Pethick

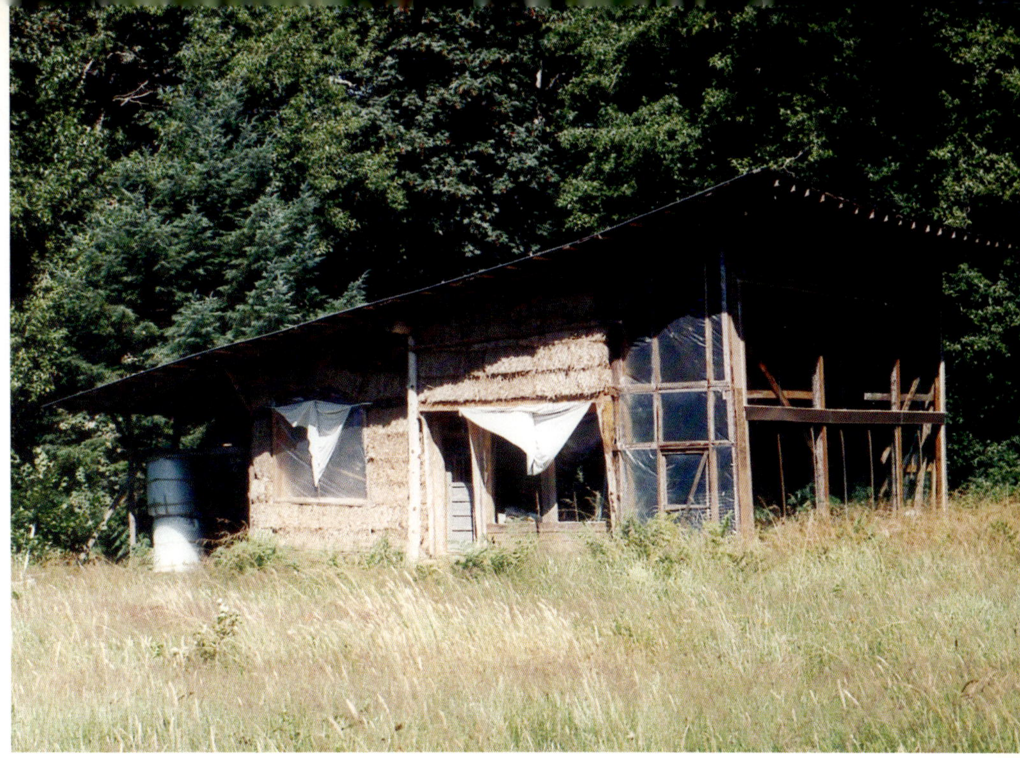

Jerry Pethick's straw-bale studio.

built the necessary "bias arrays." Many, slightly varied photos of a scene are positioned on a wall, with a Fresnel lens mounted in front of each.

When we look at the array of lenses in an "out of focus" way, a virtual space appears before our eyes, and we recognize it as a world of our dreaming. We move around, come nearer or go farther back from the array, and the image responds and moves with us. The old certainties of objective scientific observation are shown to be no longer relevant. As our brains process this information, we learn to inhabit a new spatial awareness. A different model of the universe takes place within our senses, and it is a revelation.

In the photo of Pethick's artwork, a bias array titled *Faux Terrain* stands next to *Homeship*, which offers some old-fashioned, three-dimensional reality. *Homeship* is a space exploration of a different sort, an engaging monolith garnished with objects of interest visually, sculpturally, materially and conceptually. It's a four-metre hulk, aptly compared to a breaching whale, made with two aluminum boat hulls, which rises up out of the gallery floor on thrusting afterburners made of firewood.

What does it all mean? Under questioning, Pethick elucidated the Buck Rogers theme of *Homeship* and the objects stuck onto it. The barrel of chocolate is what he'd like to take with him into outer space. The broom is to "sweep away the cobwebs from the sky." And the washing machine drum? "You've got to have some way to wash your clothes," Pethick said.

Jerry Pethick died in 2003. For these sculptures, and much more, he will be remembered. ■

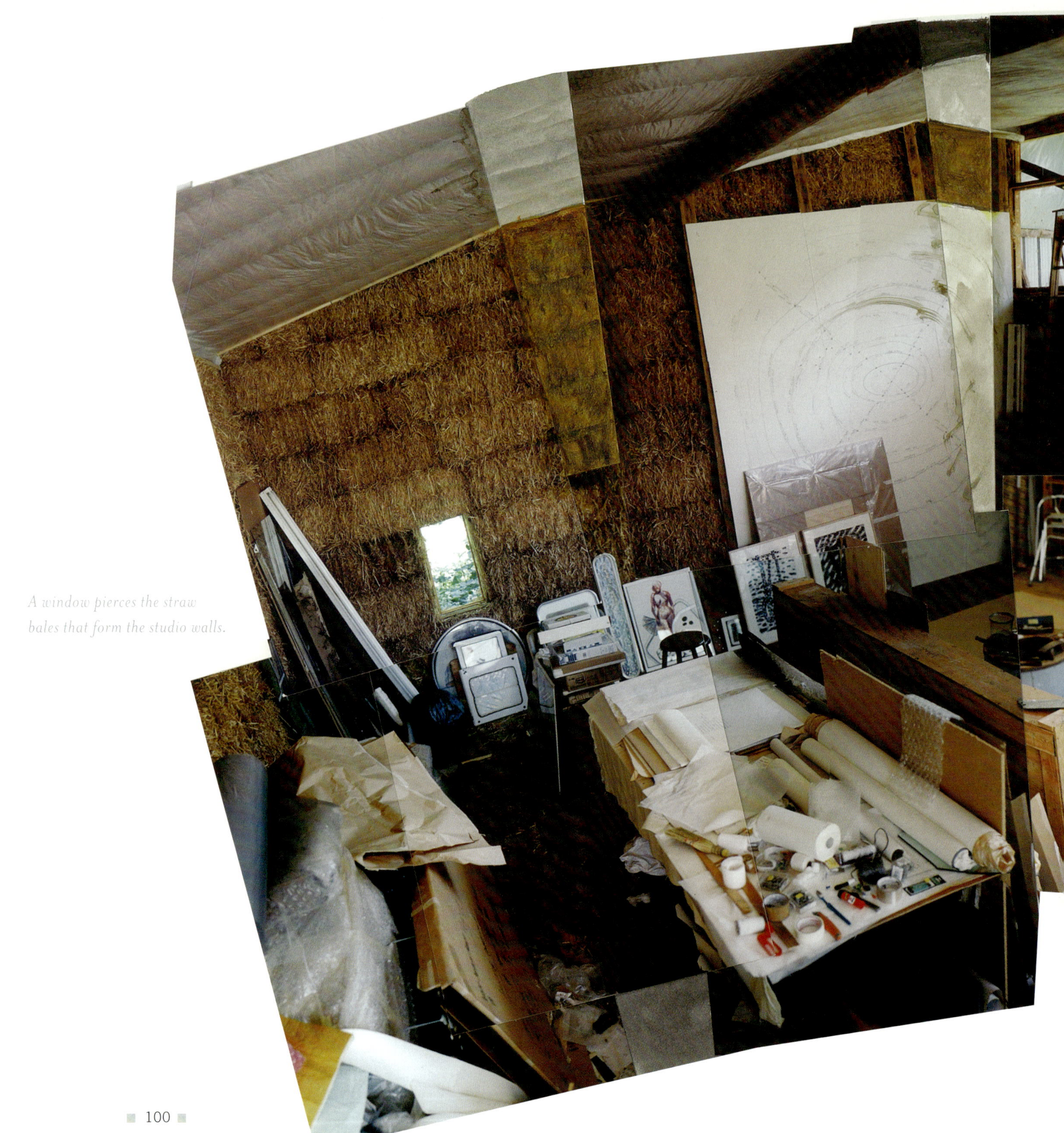

A window pierces the straw bales that form the studio walls.

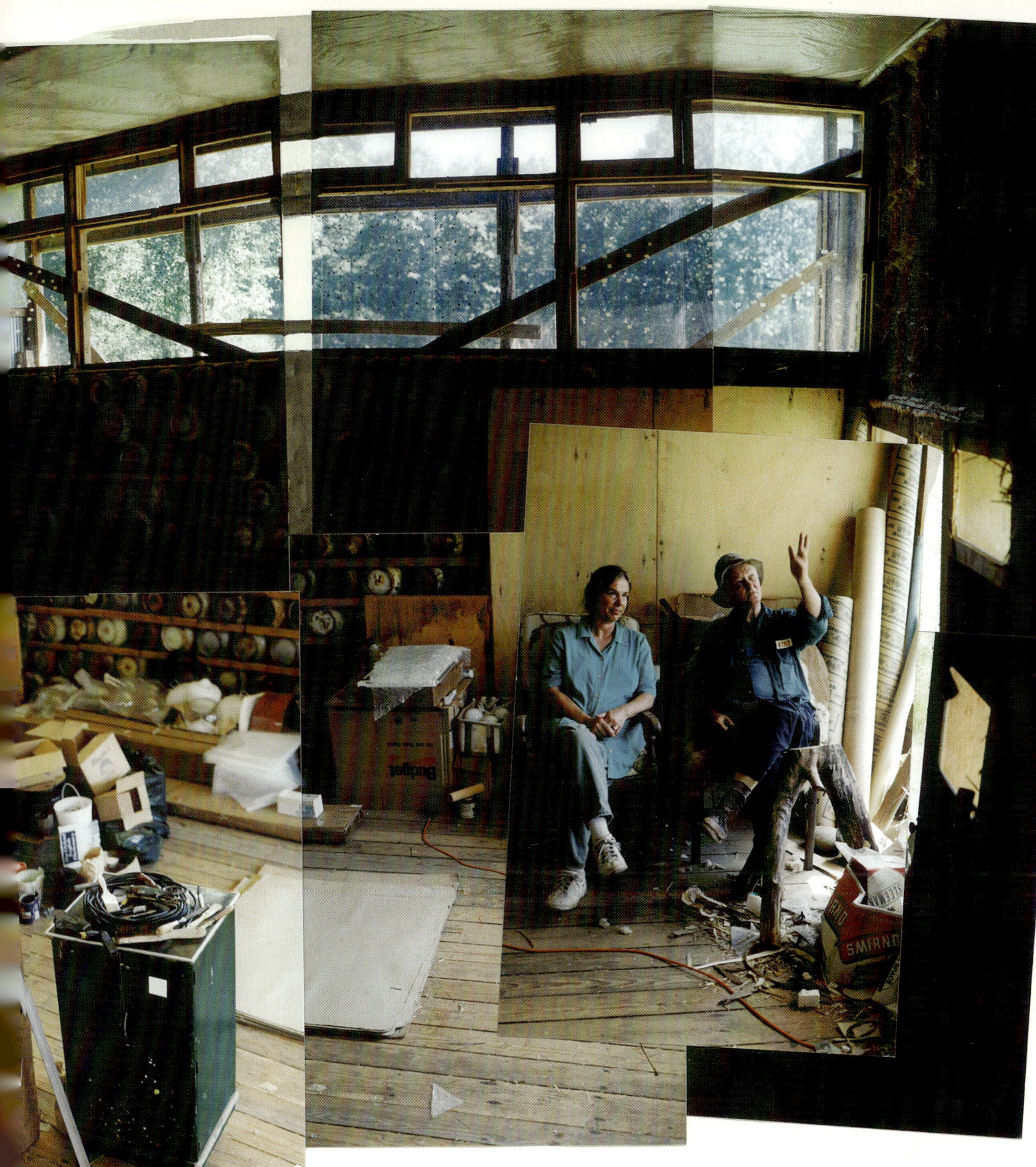

Stacks of propane tanks filled with water make up a solar-heat collector at the south edge of the studio. Pethick is with artist Sarah Amos.

JERRY PETHICK'S STUDIO, *Hornby Island, 2000.*

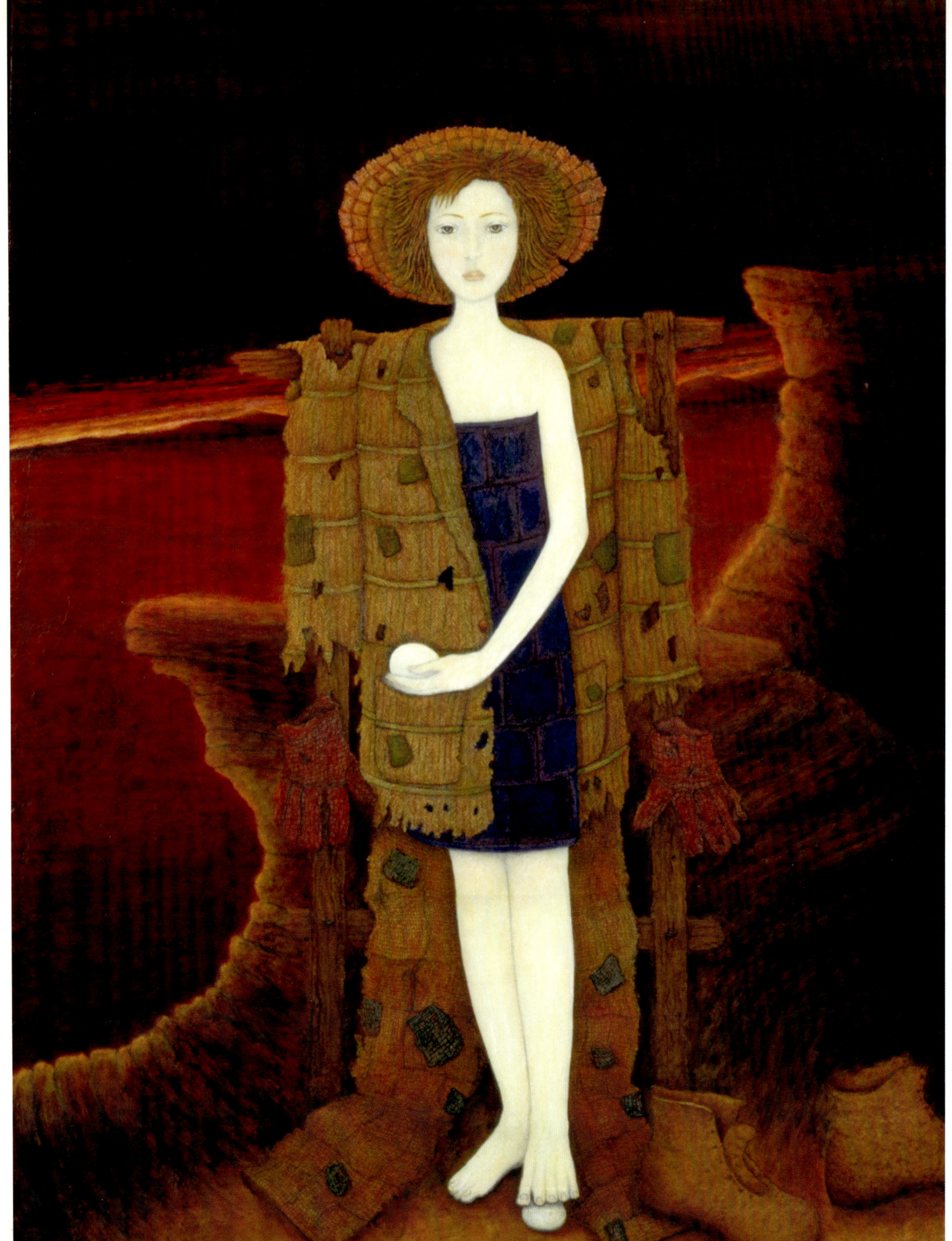

DUNCAN REGEHR

VICTORIA

DUNCAN REGEHR AND HIS WIFE, CATHERINE, LIVE IN A SECLUDED WOODLAND OUTSIDE VICTORIA. THEIR DRAMATIC LOG HOME SEEMS APPROPRIATE FOR THEIR ARTISTIC LIFESTYLE.

It looks out over a little pond with willow trees; on the far side, the old barn has been transformed into an efficient and attractive studio. It is a perfect retreat for this artist, to let his dreams emerge.

Regehr seems larger than life. He's taller than average, and carries himself with the confident deportment born of his successful career on stage and screen. Working from his homes in Santa Monica and Shawnigan Lake, he exhibits his art in galleries in California, New York and Scotland. His success is due in equal parts to his innate ability and the diligence with which he pursues his art.

Regehr was born in Alberta and raised in Victoria. His Russian-Mennonite immigrant father, Peter Regehr, was a microbiologist whose lifelong passion for painting had an influence on his son. In 1969 Duncan was plucked from teenage anonymity by Dr. Ralph Allen of the Victoria Fair Theatre Company, and he discovered the stage.

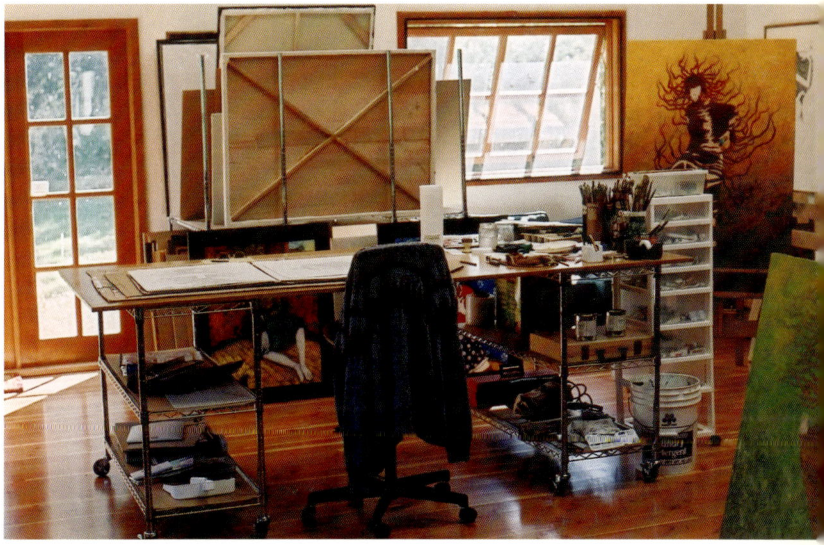

A sense of order and geometry pervades the quiet of Regehr's country studio. Materials are prepared in multiple units, and much of the furniture is on wheels.

Regehr later moved to Ontario where he pursued his theatrical career—first at Stratford and in Toronto and then, in 1980, on stage and in films in California. Simultaneously, he also pursued his passion for painting and poetry.

In California he starred in made-for-TV movies, notably as Errol Flynn in *My Wicked, Wicked Ways* in 1985 and in the title role of the TV series *Zorro* in 1993. As an artist, during this time he created numerous series of paintings inspired by standing stones in Britain, minimalist geological landscapes and the inner life of Los Angeles.

In one of Regehr's earlier publications, he describes his pictures succinctly: "Highly focused compositions

GENESIS I, *Duncan Regehr, oil on canvas, 40 x 30 inches, 2001.*

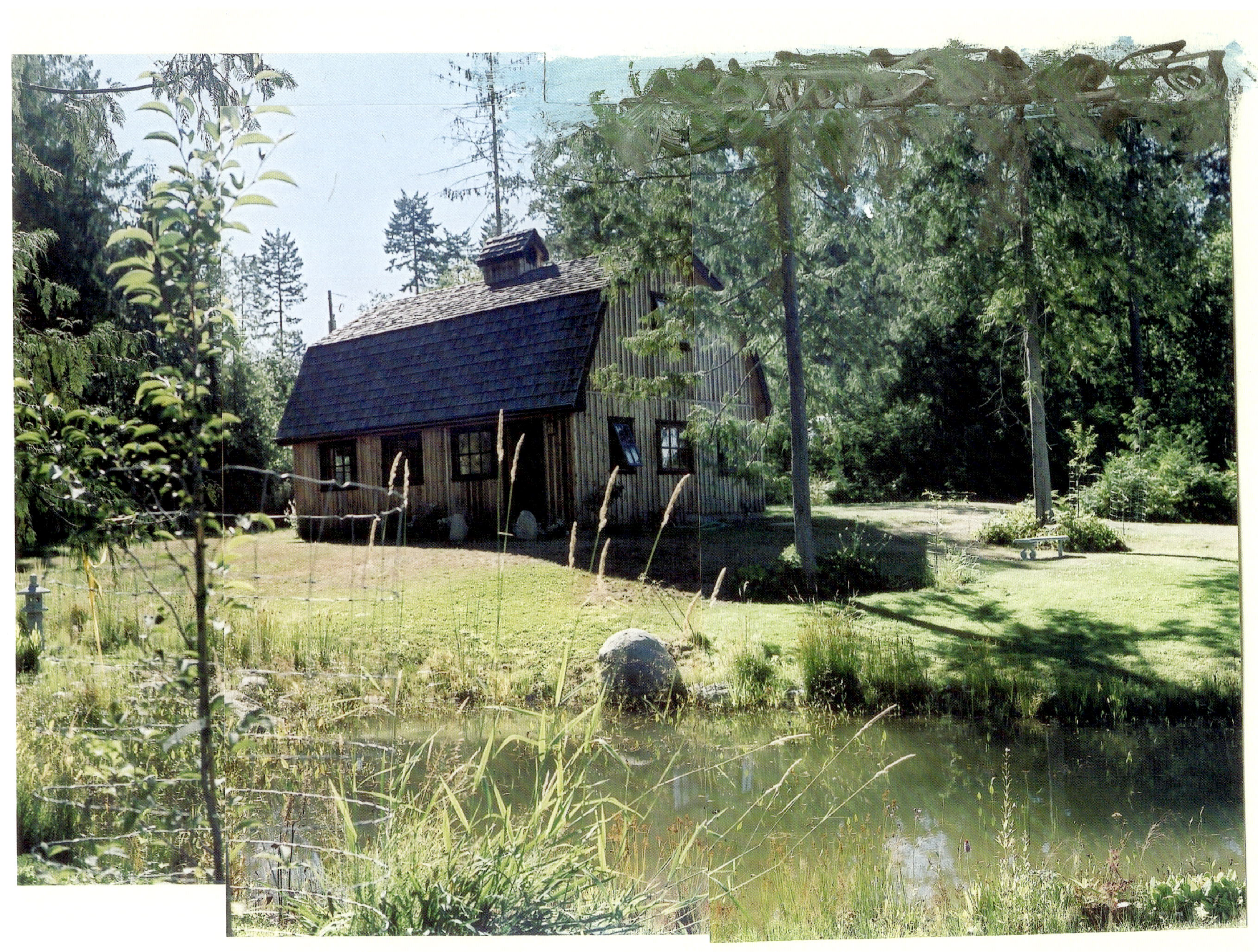

View of Duncan Regehr's studio, from his home.

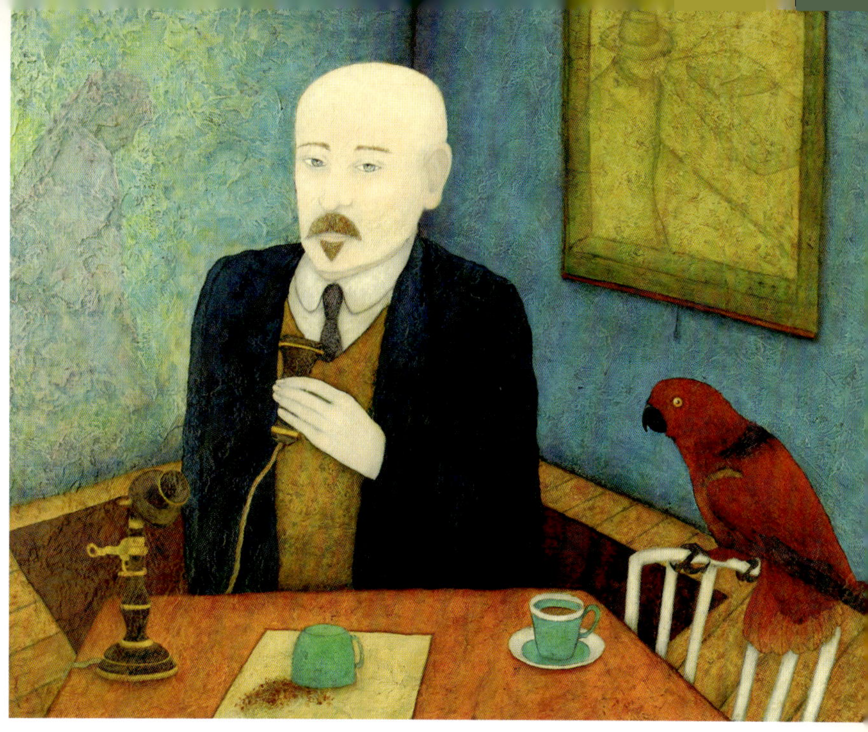

THE PSYCHIC,
Duncan Regehr,
oil on canvas,
24 x 30 inches,
2005.

situate one or more persons in a close, yet colourful space that is often shared with a variety of thematically related objects."

The artist's theatrical background informs these compositions, emphasizing character and relationships. Though these pictures may remind you of somewhere, it's not an external reality. There is always an imaginative narrative at work, setting up relationships between the parts, which carries the viewer deep into the characters' thoughts and situations. These are symbolic paintings.

Regehr patiently develops his potent imagery, circling in on it through drawing, painting and lots of poetry. His themes are presented in the accompanying words but, as he wrote in one of his books, "A verbal or literal attempt at illumination is likely to confuse, oversimplify or miss the mark altogether."

Regehr's technique is impressive—and obsessive. Perhaps the willingness to spend hours with a pen fits neatly into the actor's life—many hours of waiting in the trailer or dressing room. The large ink drawings of crows are masterpieces of Regehr's distinctive and elegant line.

Each bird seems to be made more of leaves and straw than of feathers, and the crow itself becomes a scarecrow. The crows seem transfixed as if in a timeless sunset on Mars. The scarecrows, and the people who seem to be within them, wait for something in this lowering emptiness. Minutely scratched renderings of straw, feathers, wood grain and the tattered weaving of worn-out clothes yield to glimpses of the smooth, opalescent glow of flesh.

It's impossible to get all the way around Regehr's work in words, and it may come as a surprise to his audience to discover that the often dark and complex images are born in a tidy, light-filled country studio. Perhaps contradictions are an integral part of the art of Duncan Regehr.

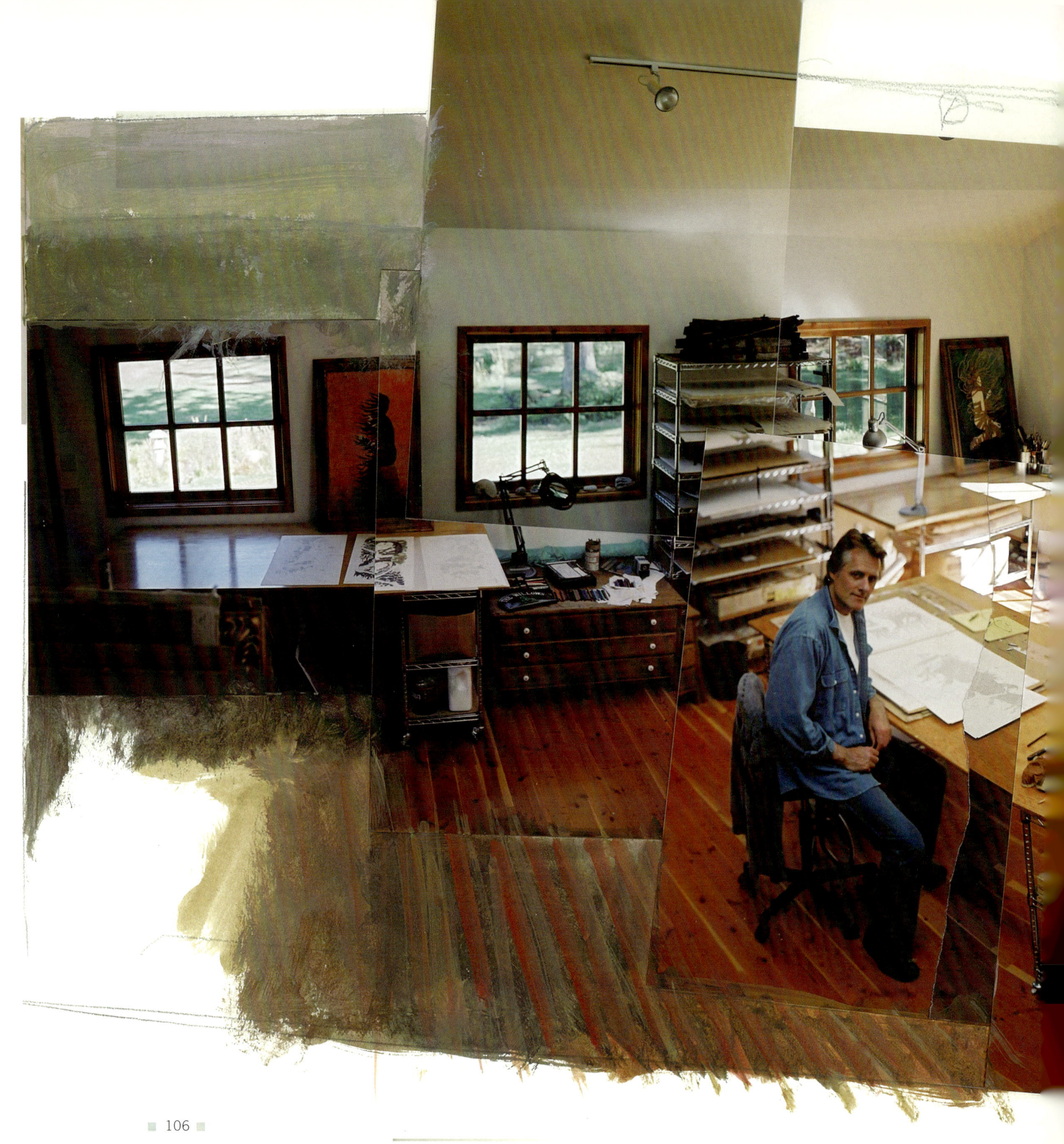

■ ■ ■ DUNCAN REGEHR IN HIS STUDIO, *Shawnigan Lake, September 2006.*

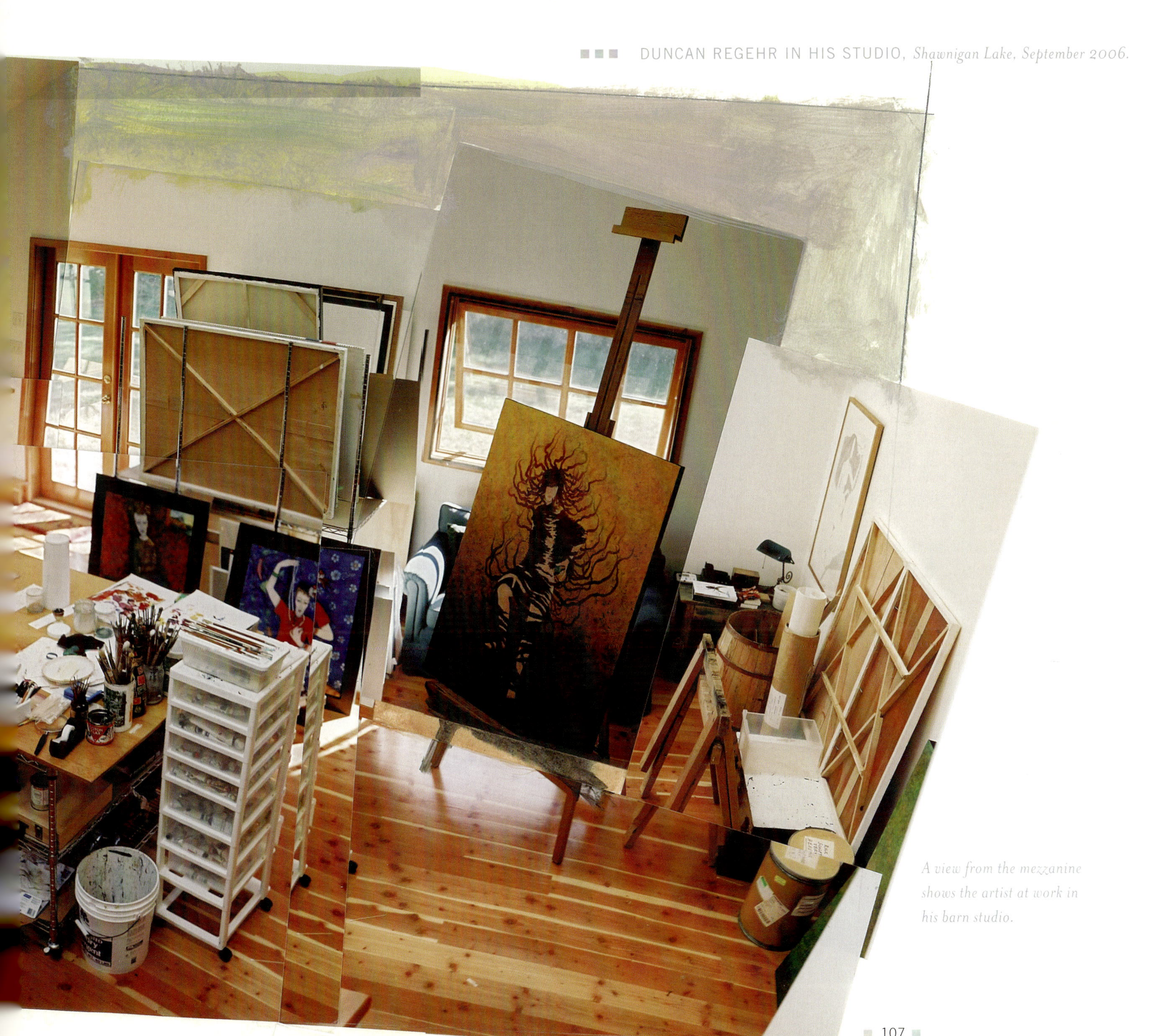

A view from the mezzanine shows the artist at work in his barn studio.

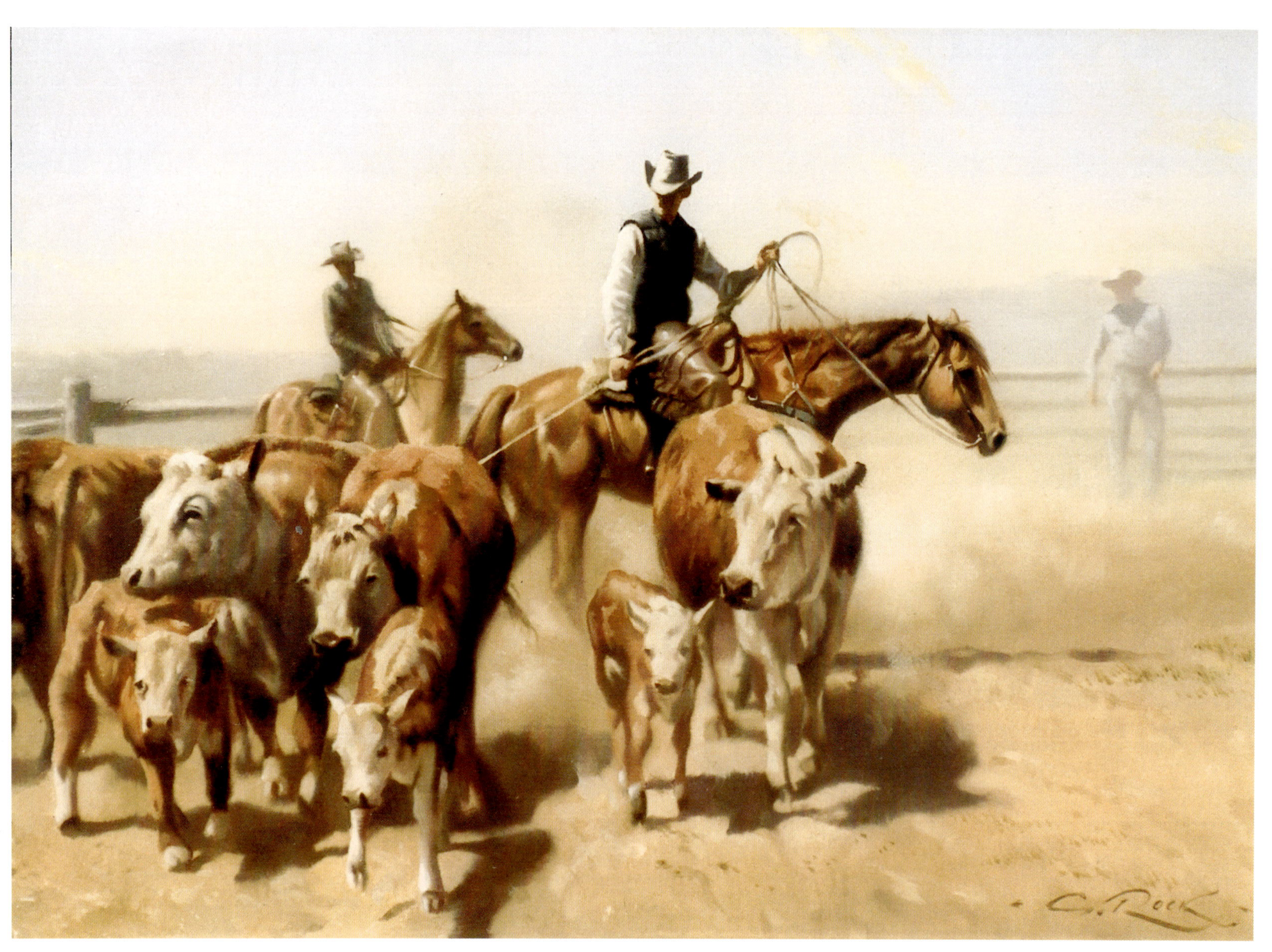

■■■ BRANDING SCENE, DOUGLAS LAKE RANCH, B.C., *Geoffrey Rock, oil, 14 x 10 inches, not dated.*

GEOFFREY ROCK

VICTORIA

WHEN I LAST VISITED THEM, GEOFFREY AND JOAN ROCK WERE LIVING IN A MODERN, OPEN-PLAN HOME AT THE WATER'S EDGE ON THE TIP OF VICTORIA'S TEN MILE POINT.

Their children had grown and left, and Rock took over the spare bedroom upstairs. It had a single north window to the left of his easel, the ideal light for an artist. This practical advantage was enhanced by the window's idyllic view of the blue water of Haro Strait.

This studio made a change from Rock's first home "studio." Joan Rock remembered that, at the end of World War II, her husband was kept busy painting portraits of the military and royalty in the kitchen of their tiny London flat, where he worked as the understudy for Sir James Gunn, president of the Royal Society of Portrait Artists.

Born in 1923 in Birmingham, England, Rock was the illegitimate child of a 17-year-old girl. Two strikes against him, as he pointed out. Following studies at the Birmingham School of Art, he trained in London. "It was a year before we were allowed to touch a brush," he recalls, "and three years before we moved from plaster casts to life drawing."

Geoffrey Rock married Joan, his vivacious wife, in the war years and she was his unfailing support. Arriving penniless in Canada in 1956, the Rocks built a life for themselves in Montreal and then in rural Ontario. Coldwater flats, ramshackle farmhouses and laundry tubs full of diapers came and went. They raised a family and renovated a home and together they soldiered on.

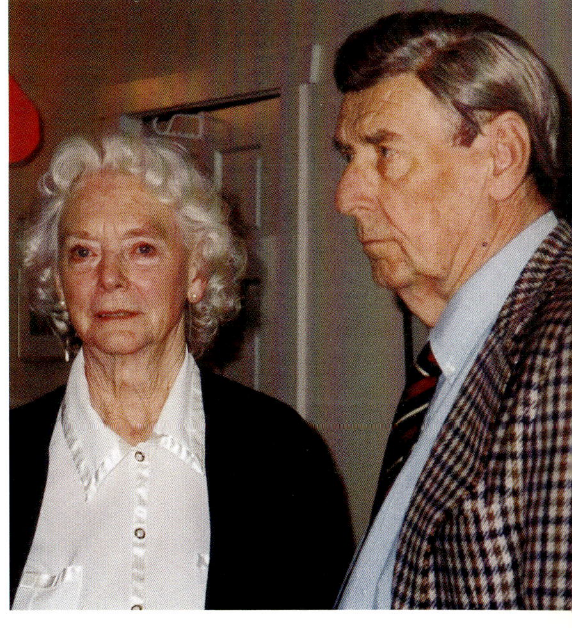

Joan and Geoffrey Rock, February 1999.

In 1963 a lucky break came along and Rock was introduced to Toronto's famous Laing Galleries. Favourable reviews, prestigious exhibitions and clients of unimaginable wealth made their appearance in the artist's life. From his rural home in Cheltenham, Ontario, Rock became a leading practitioner of "barnboard realism." In the 1970s his shows at the Walter Klinkhoff Gallery in Montreal and the Laing Galleries in Toronto were usually sold out. "Sometimes we couldn't even get into our own shows," Joan remarked with some amusement.

When the Rocks came west, they lived first in the Gulf Islands, but the coastal forest didn't reveal enough of "the hand of man and the passage of time" for Rock's needs. He spent a lot of time wandering in Vancouver's Chinatown.

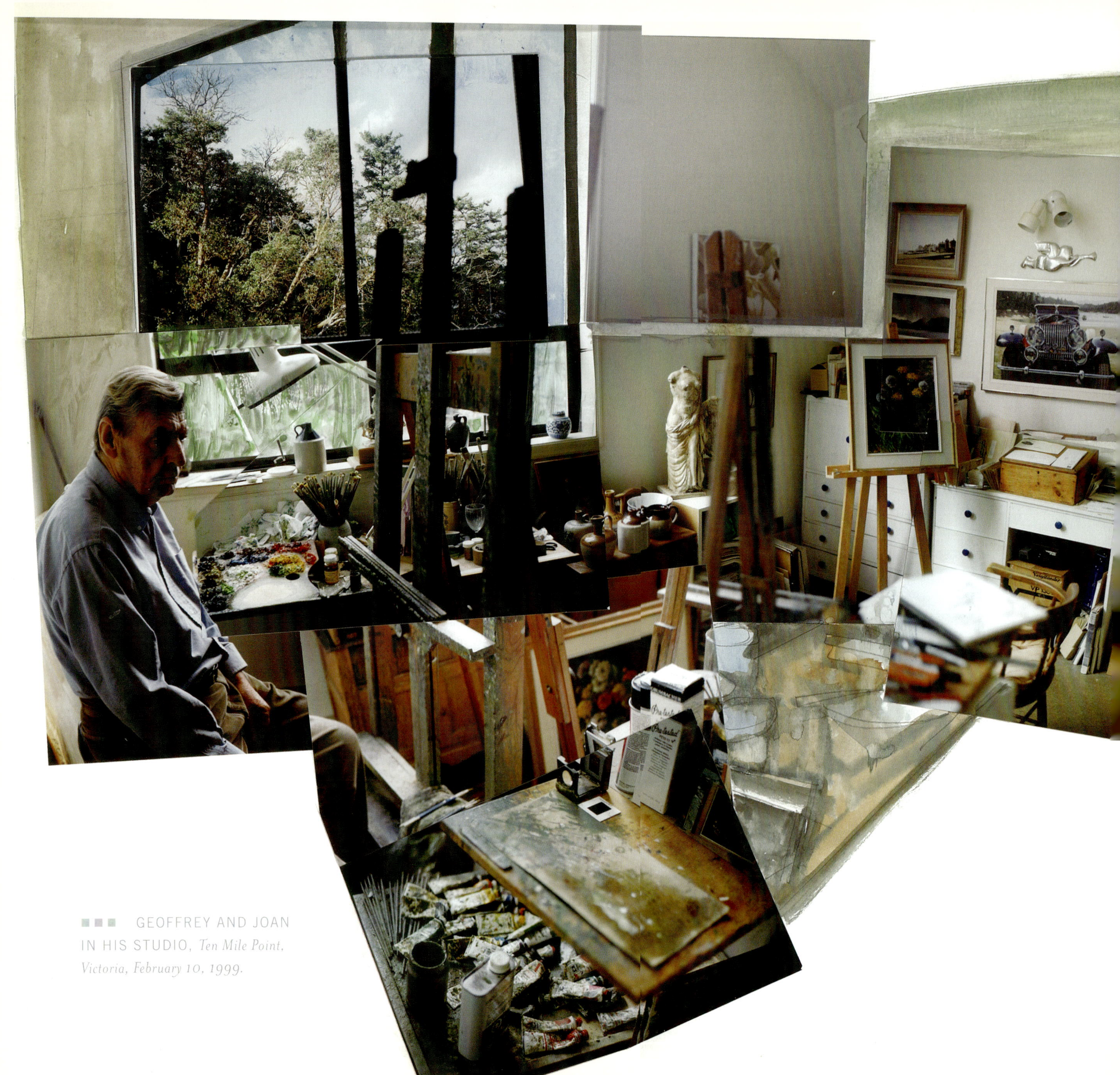

■■■ GEOFFREY AND JOAN IN HIS STUDIO, *Ten Mile Point, Victoria, February 10, 1999.*

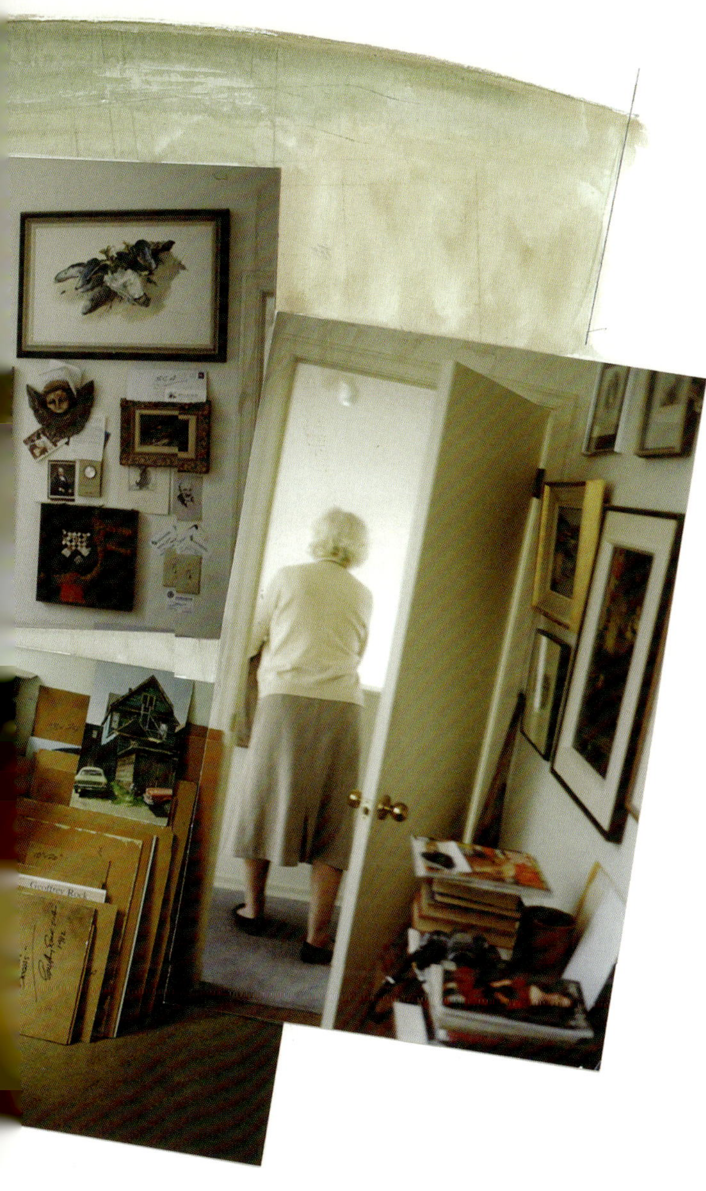

A new world opened up to him in the early 1970s. He was invited to C. N. "Chunky" Woodward's ranch, known as the Douglas Lake Cattle Company, northwest of Cache Creek, B.C. There, Rock found a rich vein of subject matter. On the range with working cowboys he set to work, eventually completing about 30 oils and a few pencil sketches. Rock's smoothly brushed oils confidently capture the pale, dusty light of summer rangeland and the menacing clouds of an advancing storm. Bustling cattle kick up the dust as they flee in all directions to escape the cowboys coming to brand them.

"I use reality as a starting point," he has said, "but project on the canvas my most intimate reaction to the subject... I enter a trance-like state and it is hard to come back to reality."

In my photocollage you can see Rock's slide viewer and his reference photo on the table to his right. Joan, whose form is echoed by the draped classical torso on the left, stands just outside the door to the studio.

In his later years Rock produced large, close-up renderings of flowers. And though he rarely showed them, he took pride in his skill as a sculptor of animals. He brought rare skill and excellent training to the challenges he set himself as an artist and, though he died in 2003, the results will stand the test of time.

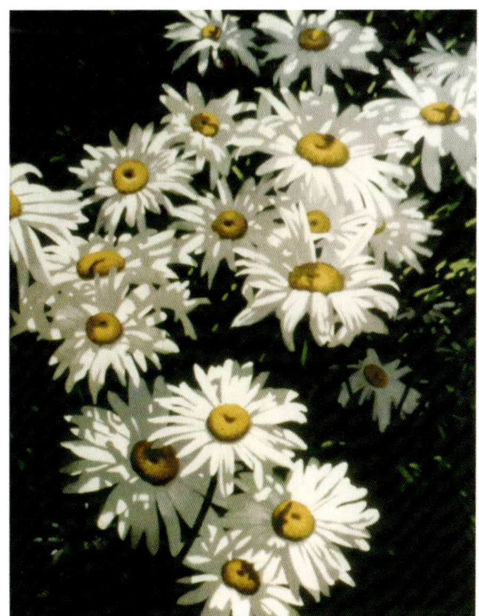

MICHAELMAS DAISIES,
Geoffrey Rock, oil on canvas, 24 x 18 inches, not dated.

CAROLE SABISTON

VICTORIA

WHEN I FIRST MET HER, CAROLE SABISTON WAS COMPLETING THE SETS AND COSTUMES FOR PACIFIC OPERA VICTORIA'S PRODUCTION OF MOZART'S *THE MAGIC FLUTE*.

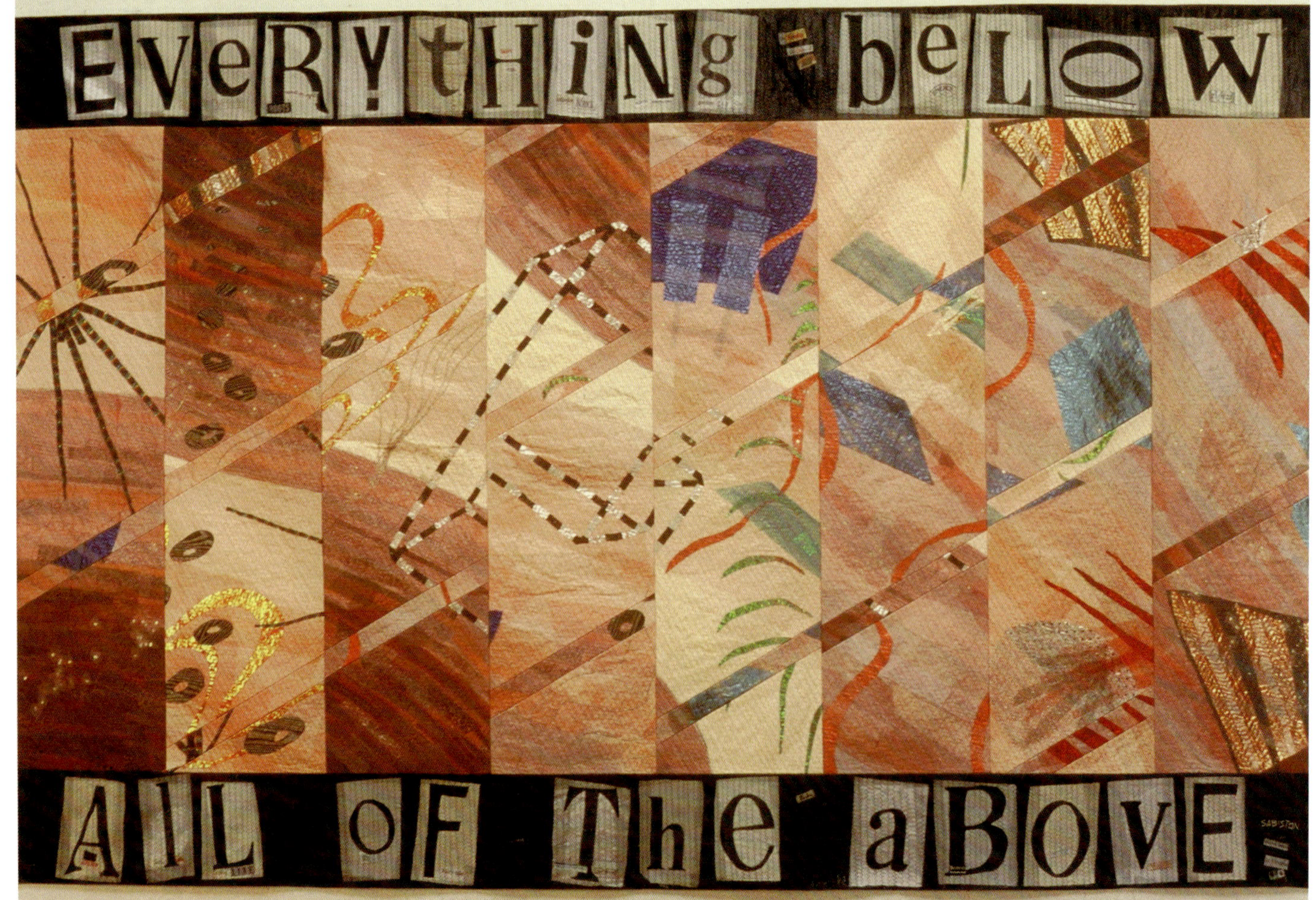

ALL OF THE ABOVE, *Carole Sabiston, textile assemblage, 6 x 8 feet, not dated.*

At that point she was working in a large space over a bookstore with her team of assistants. Later, she turned her hand to large and small folding screens and assemblages framed under glass.

Sabiston does not weave or embroider. She describes her justly famous medium as "textile assemblage." To accommodate her expanding repertoire, she built a comfortable studio adjoining her heritage home in Victoria's Rockland neighbourhood. Clerestory windows provide plenty of light without cutting down on wall space or letting in distracting views.

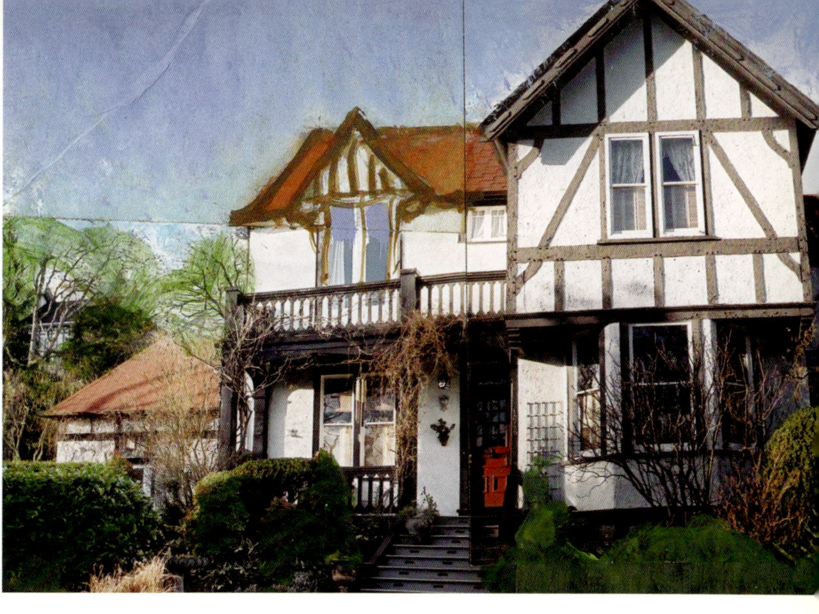

Sabiston's Victoria studio and home.

Sabiston was born in London, England, but has lived in Victoria, with a few breaks, since 1952. A student at both the University of Victoria and the University of British Columbia, she later taught art in Victoria and Vancouver. In those early days she had come from painting to a sort of collage, wherein appliqué and drawing with thread enhanced the surface of her canvases. In 1967 she had her first solo show at the Victoria Art Gallery (now the Art Gallery of Greater Victoria) and every piece sold. The complex little panels caught the attention of designer and artist Allan Edwards.

Edwards' encouragement and commissions liberated Sabiston. He gave her a free hand to produce whatever she thought appropriate to complement the interiors he was designing for hotels all over the world. And he asked her to work big. Her first project for him was almost two metres long. Subsequently, he asked for panels as much as seven by four metres for hotels in Toronto, Ottawa and London. Her unique technique began to evolve.

On a base of non-woven canvas interfacing, Sabiston layers strips of fabric, making up her "palette" from cloths of an incredible range of colour and sheen. She is likely to "draw" with pieces of pure brilliant colour pulled from her rainbow textile palette. She tears tinsel strips from silver fabric and hurls them onto a night sky of indigo watered silk. The ribbon-like strips are arranged like a painting, then pinned closely. This base design is overlaid with tulle or netting. Into the mix Sabiston places patterned materials or evocative objects—a glove or two, a bit of lace, a sailor's middy—which add a narrative engagement to the purely visual thrills. The entire assemblage is repeatedly run through her heavy-duty sewing machine.

Though Sabiston has travelled widely, studying sites and presenting projects, Victoria has been her home. And she has richly endowed this city. Appliquéd butterflies flitted about the Crystal Gardens Ballroom; the central atrium of the Pacific Forestry Centre is the setting for three enormous banners, 10 metres long, with the imagery of trees; the reception areas of Government House, the McPherson Playhouse, City Hall and the University of Victoria Library are all made more inviting by work from her studio. Almost all of Victoria's visitors have caught a glimpse of the extensive series of hangings that add colour and texture to the walls of Munro's Books.

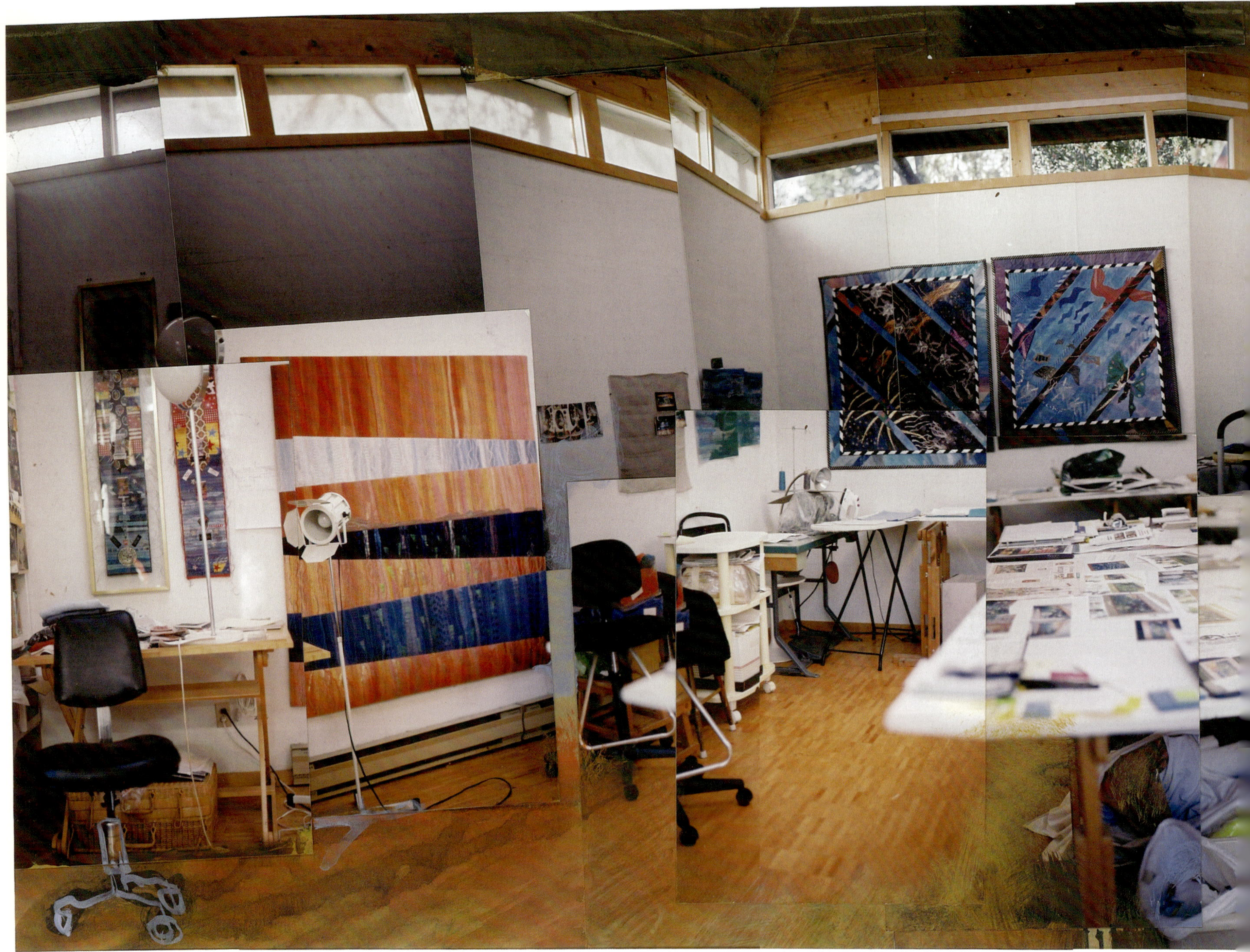

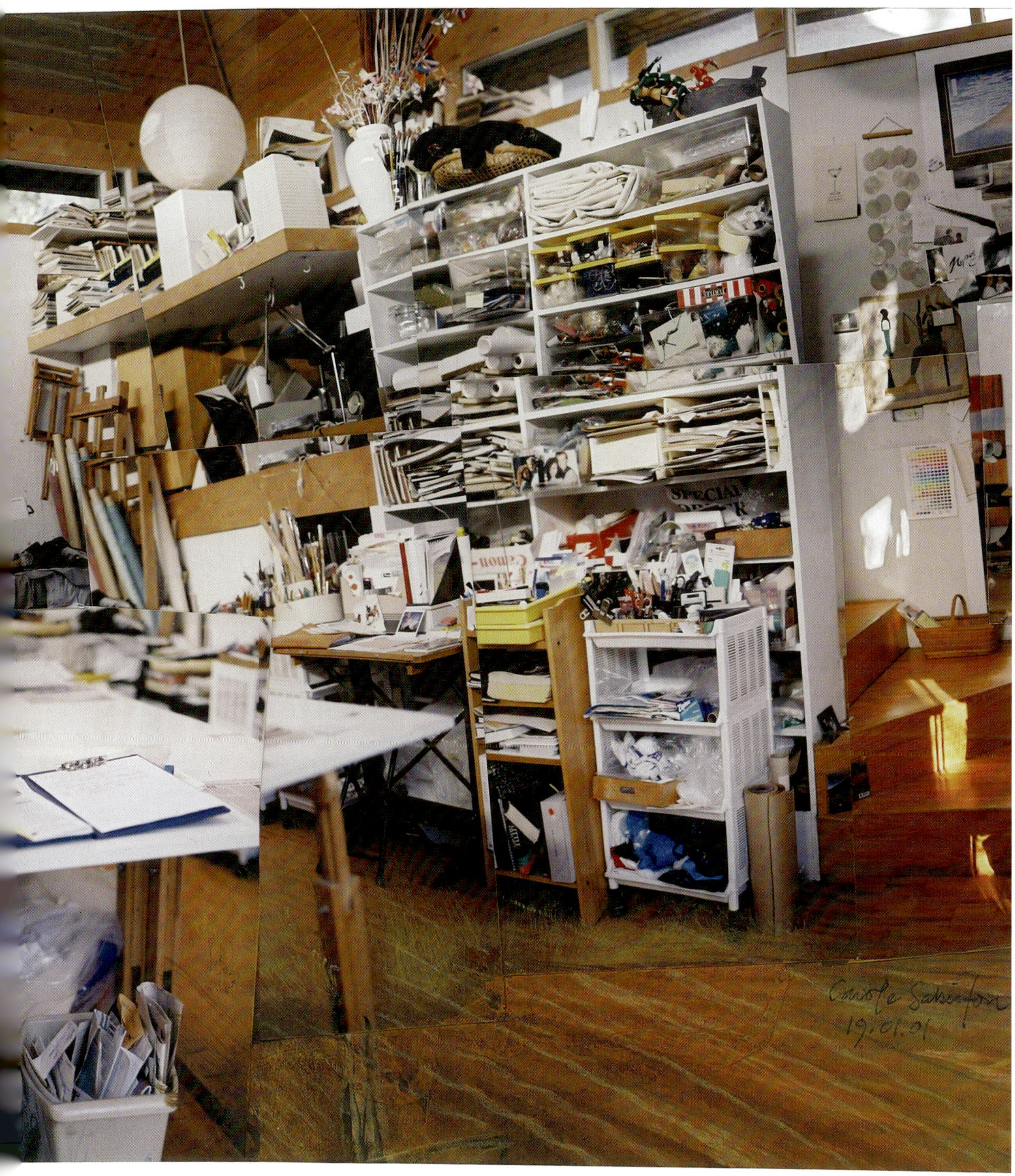

Sabiston created an altar cloth and reredos for Christ Church Cathedral and the curtain for UVic's theatre. She designed the massive backdrop for the opening of Expo '86 in Vancouver, a 50-metre sun derived from the British Columbia flag. Her designs were part of the closing ceremonies at Victoria's Commonwealth Games in 1994.

Sabiston was made a member of the Royal Canadian Academy of the Arts in 1987 and in the same year was given the Saidye Bronfman Award, Canada's highest honour in applied arts design. She received the Order of British Columbia in 1992 and an honorary doctorate from the University of Victoria in 1995.

Clerestory windows let in light without taking up wall space.

CAROLE SABISTON'S STUDIO,
Victoria, January 19, 2001.

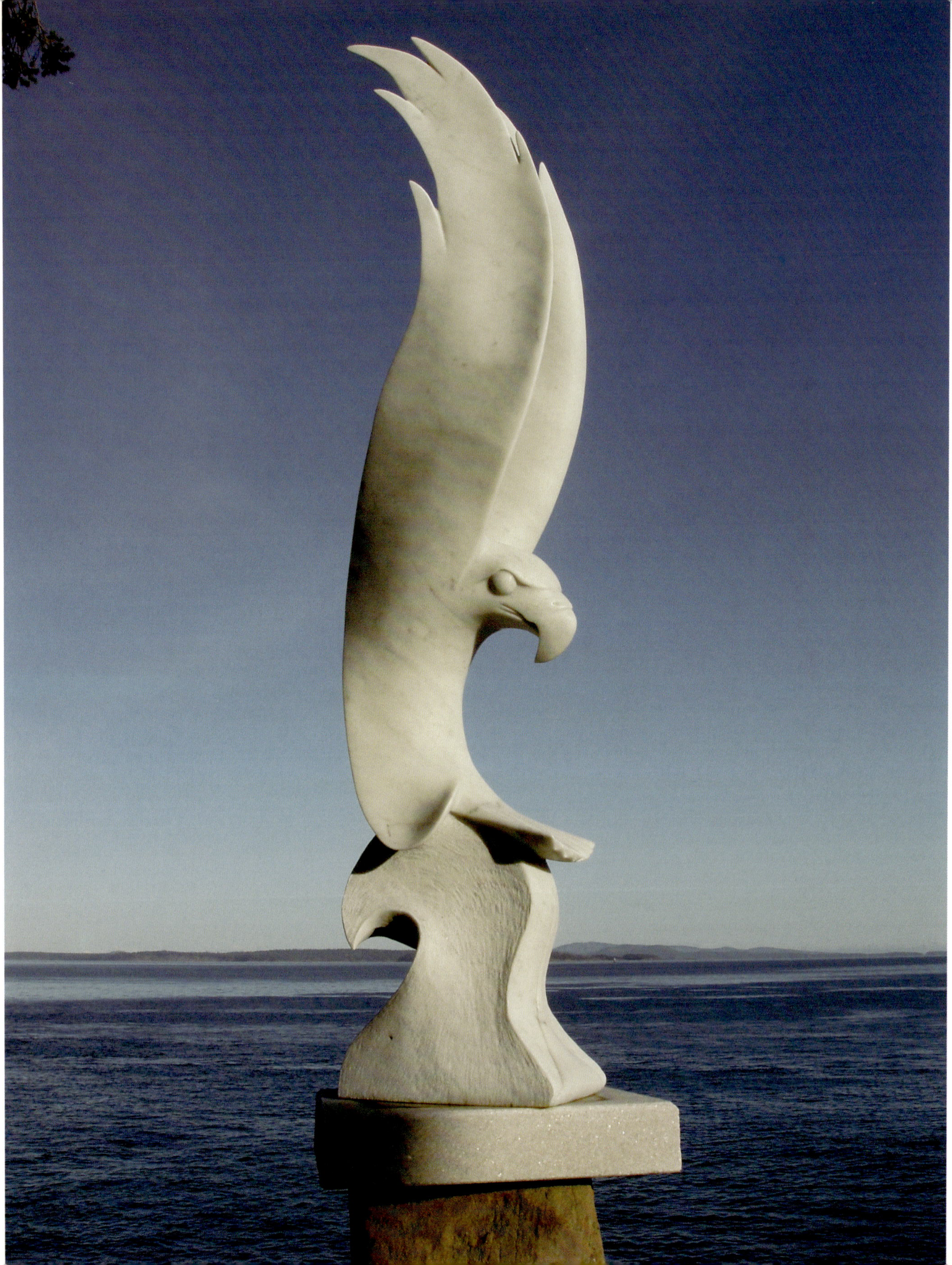

MAARTEN SCHADDELEE

SAANICH

THE WORK OF AN ARTIST IS NOT EASY. CARVING STONE IS PARTICULARLY DIFFICULT. MAARTEN SCHADDELEE UNDERTAKES HIS PROJECTS IN A GARDEN HOME HE SHARES WITH HIS DEVOTED WIFE, NADINE.

Their world is suffused with peace and serenity. On the outside, this waterfront domain is home to orcas and eagles. Within, it is well ordered, a show space for his sculpture and an inspiring place to live.

The approach to Schaddelee's studio takes one along a winding path where the forms—chunks of marble, huge cast-concrete leaves—are even more striking than the vegetation. The Schaddelees live on a wooded point overlooking Haro Strait at the south end of Victoria's Cordova Bay. Maarten's studio is in two parts and occupies the ground floor on the waterfront side of their home. Chunks of stone, already carved or awaiting his inspired touch, rest amid the greenery. A little forklift capable of hoisting 250 kilograms waits outside the massive doors of the stone-carving room.

When I arrived, Schaddelee was working on a three-metre-long block of local grey marble, in the process of revealing a whale's tail and an eagle in flight. The diamond-set chain saw and pneumatic grinders he works with, and his air-filtration hood, dispelled any notion of the romance of this artistry. When he's at work, "You can't see across the room," he told me. I didn't bother photographing that workshop.

Next to it, beneath the deck of the Schaddelee home where it faces the sea, is the wood-carving studio. Windows on three sides let in inspiration and lots of light. A patina of wood dust covers every surface, though there is a workmanlike orderliness to things. This deliberation mirrors the clear intentions of the sculptor. With

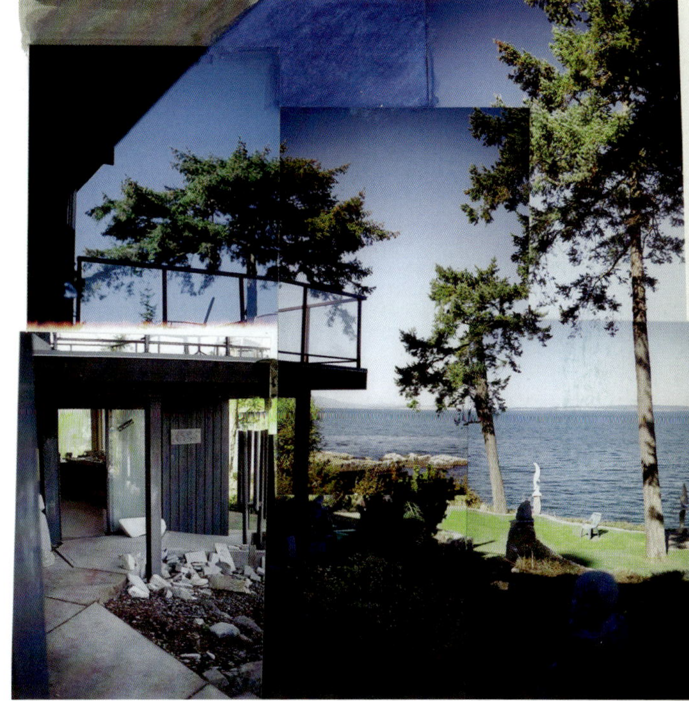

Schaddelee's waterfront studio.

■ ■ ■ AQUILLA, *Maarten Schaddelee, marble, 53 inches tall, 2006.*

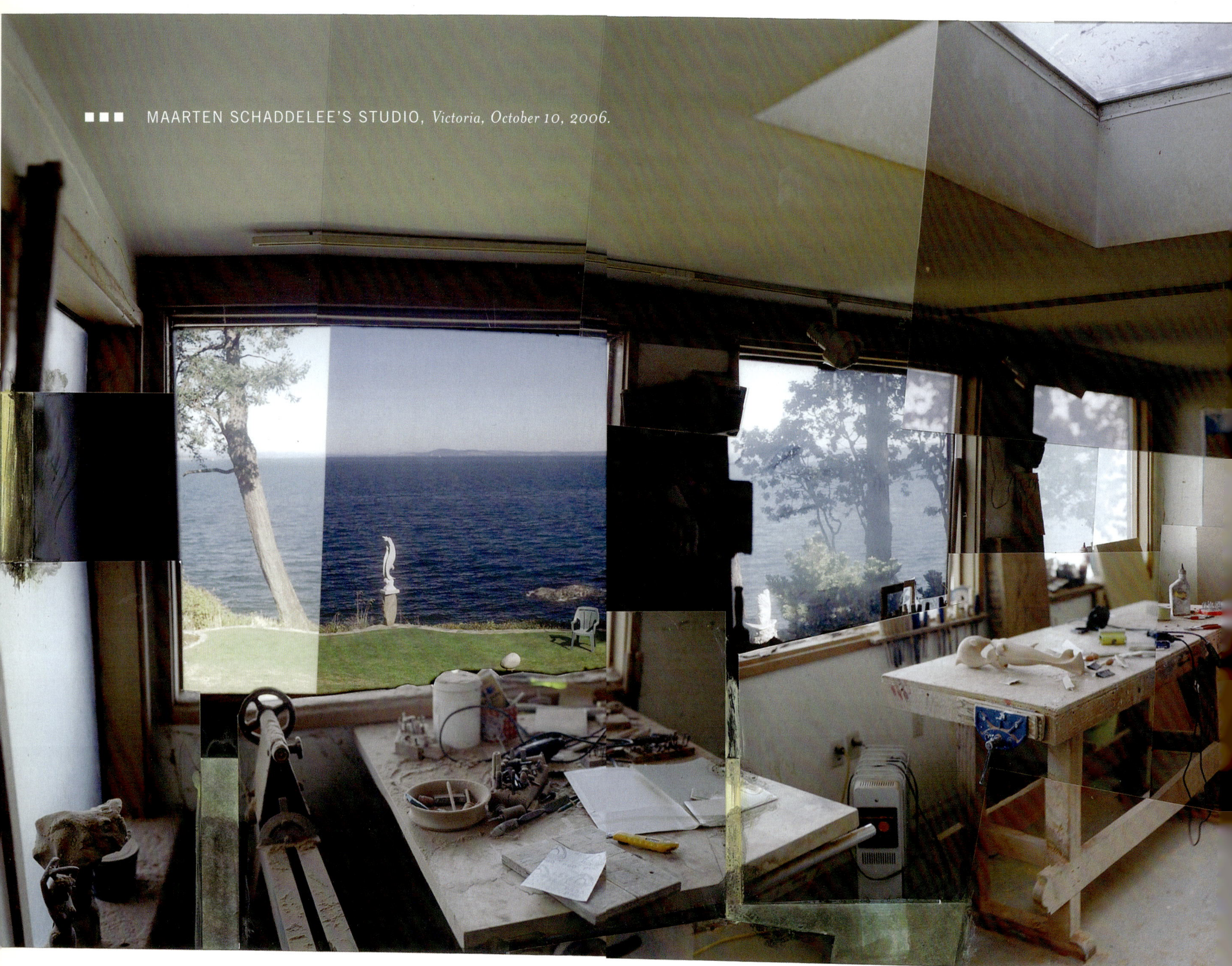
■■■ MAARTEN SCHADDELEE'S STUDIO, *Victoria, October 10, 2006.*

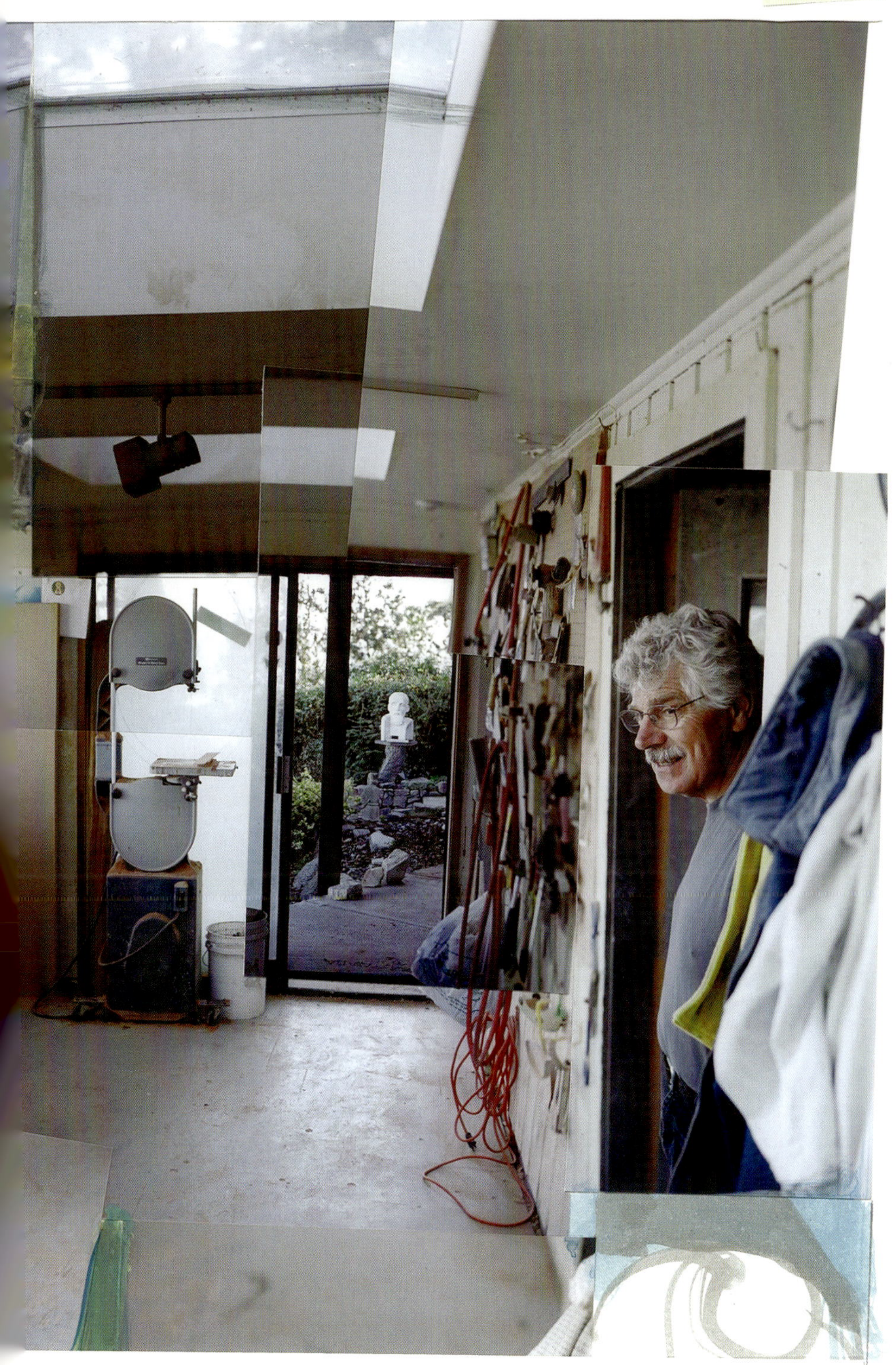

a methodical approach, Schaddelee tackles just one project at a time.

Maarten Schaddelee was born in Soest, Holland, in 1947 and immigrated with his family to Victoria in 1955. He told me he discovered sculpture at the age of 14, working with red clay he dug out of nearby Mount Douglas. After years of employment in the family's bakery he became a full-time artist in 1990.

The artist reminisced about his first piece. "I built the studio and bought a lathe to turn bowls. I made one. And with the next piece of wood, I saw a whale within it—so I carved that." He never turned another bowl.

Though he is known as a wood carver, his work is actually done with an air-powered disc grinder for the most part, driven by a compressor located outside the studio. This artist visualises his carving complete before he begins, and generally works without sketches or maquettes.

Fluid, graceful sculptures from his studio have been chosen as gifts for Victoria's sister cities—Suzhou, China, and Morioka, Japan—and for Government House in Victoria. In 1999 Schaddelee participated in a month-long sculpting symposium in Iqaluit, Nunavut.

Since April 2000, Maarten and Nadine have combined her talents as a wellness educator and storyteller with his sculpting, and they have made some inspiring public art together. Their collaborations are now part of the rooftop garden at Victoria Hospice. Their masterwork, *Millennium Peace*, is handsomely situated at Victoria's Clover Point. The 2,500-kilogram carving is made from a single piece of white Vancouver Island marble. The birds and flowers on the front are beautiful, but my favourite detail is the spiral seashell carved discreetly into the back—a tribute to the ancient animals whose life and death created the marble itself. ■

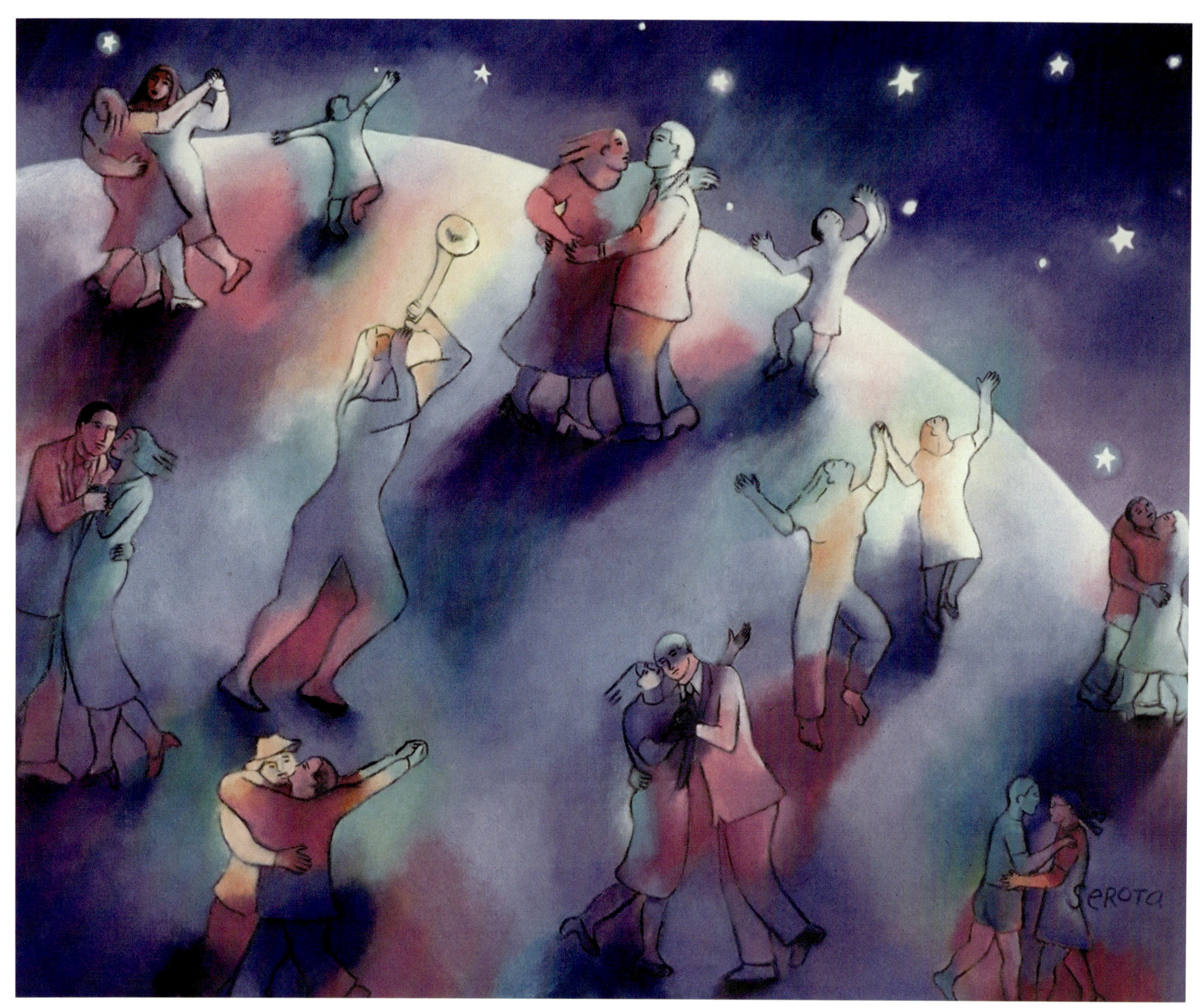

■■■ GABRIEL'S DREAM, *Phyllis Serota, oil on canvas, 54 x 66 inches, 1995.*

PHYLLIS SEROTA

VICTORIA

UPON ARRIVAL AT THE JAMES BAY HOME PHYLLIS SEROTA SHARES WITH HER PARTNER, ANNIE WEEKS, I WAS GREETED WITH A HUG. SEROTA THEN LED ME INTO THE COMFORTABLE SITTING ROOM WHERE WE ADMIRED HER LATEST PAINTINGS IN THE AFTERNOON SUNSHINE.

After catching up on mutual friends we made our way to the back of the house where she has constructed a two-storey addition as her studio. The studio is spacious and bright. In addition to the tools of her craft it also seems to be full of the life experiences that are the subject of her art.

Born into a Polish-Russian family in Chicago in 1938, Serota in childhood was surrounded by aunts and uncles whose fish market and wedding dances have provided the rich imagery from which she draws. In 1968, she was horrified by the riots surrounding the Democratic convention in Chicago and, with her husband, she immigrated to Maple Bay on Vancouver Island.

They raised a family in the new environment of village life on the west coast and their subsequent separation freed Serota to pursue a formal training in the arts in Victoria. Four years of art therapy put her in touch with her feelings in a visual way and brought her to the threshold of a career.

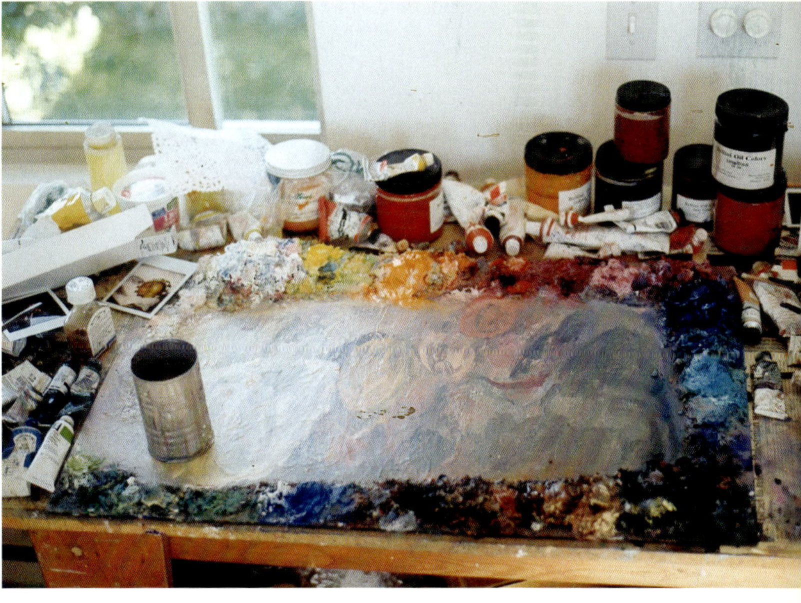

Phyllis Serota's palette is a sheet of plate glass heaped with bright colours. It used to be the back window of the Volkswagen Beetle that she drove out from Chicago years ago. A Polaroid photo of a baby joins the fun on her amiably cluttered work table.

Serota's willingness to show some emotion has drawn a strongly supportive community close around her. Her "memory pictures" have enriched many homes and, building on the confidence this gives her, she has been unafraid to expand her subject matter ever wider. Explorations of dreams, classical mythology and an extended meditation on the Holocaust have each pushed her beyond her technical "comfort zone." While success is never assured,

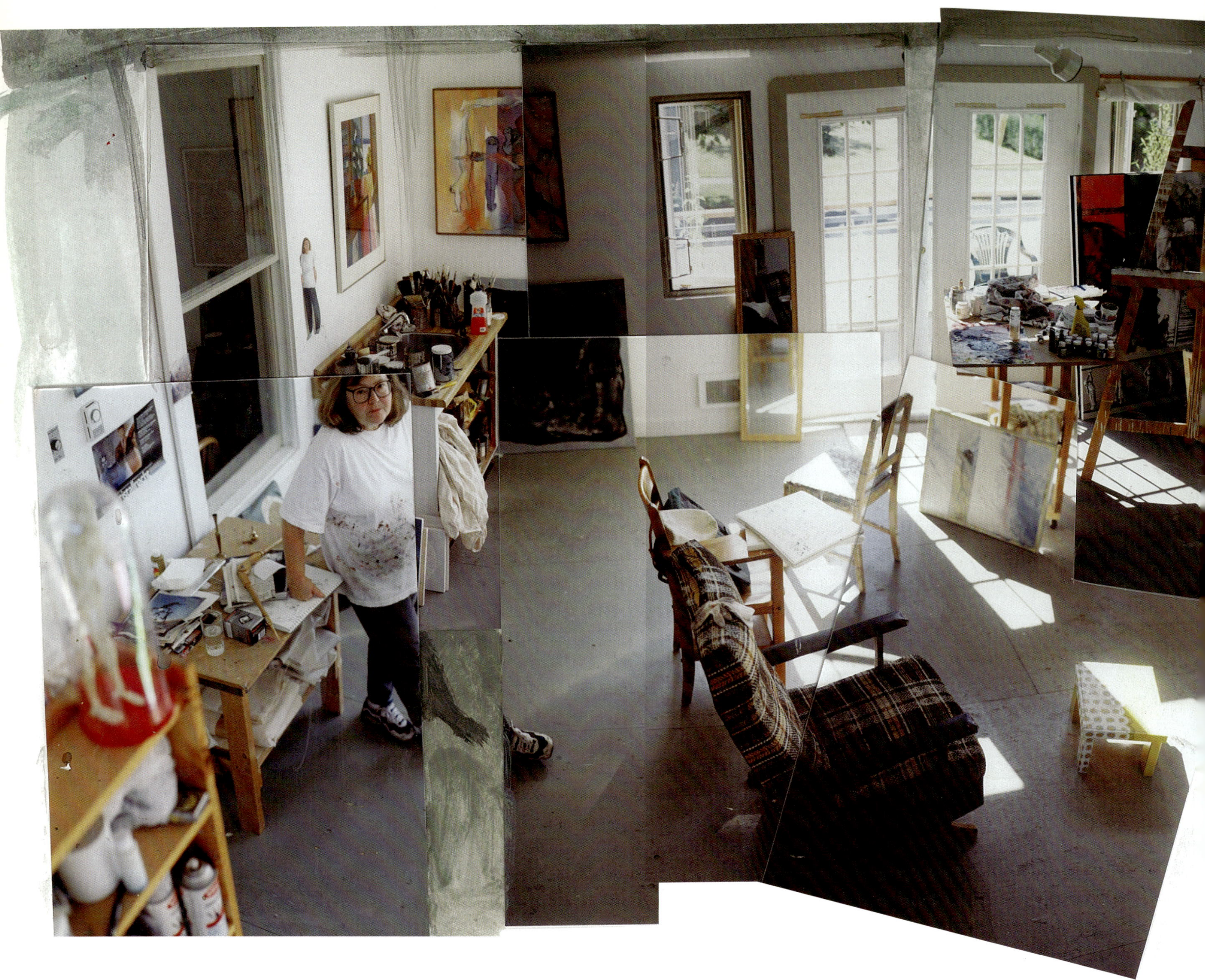

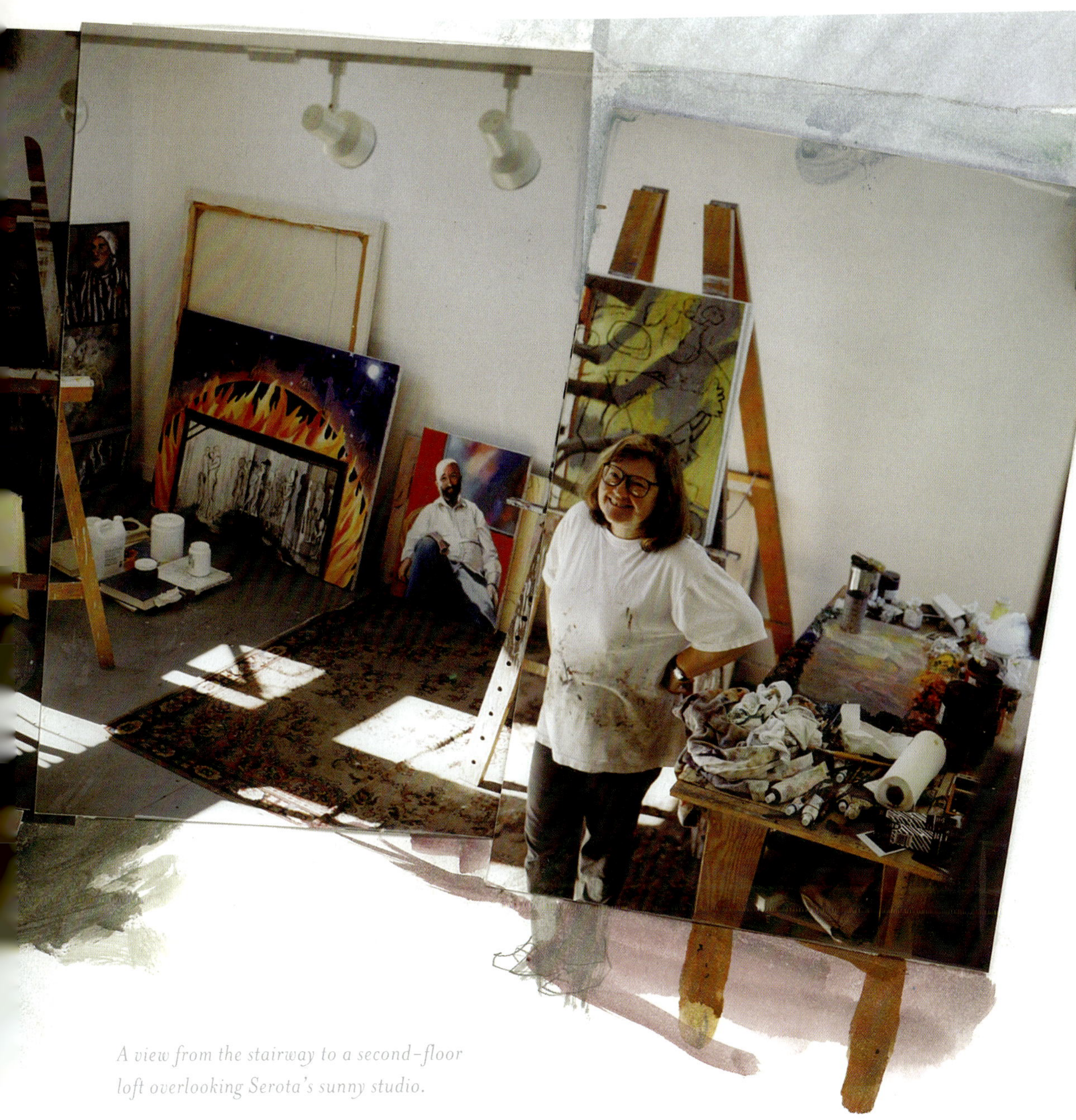

A view from the stairway to a second-floor loft overlooking Serota's sunny studio.

her fans love her all the more for her brave investigations.

With a paint-stained shirt and a ready smile Serota has come to terms with her Jewishness, feminism, lesbianism and the challenge of making a living through art. Somehow, the sunshine that plays across the floor gets into her pictures and enlightens us all. "I have always felt a strong need to communicate," Serota has written, "and have sometimes felt that I am a sort of conductor: ideas come through me and out into the world."

Recently a fellow artist jotted down her thoughts for Serota. "Throughout your years of working," she wrote, "you have shown us that the making of your art is not simply the production of a handmade commodity, neither a decoration, nor an anecdote. For you it is a deep human necessity." ■

■■■ PHYLLIS SEROTA'S STUDIO, *James Bay, Victoria, September 24, 1997.*

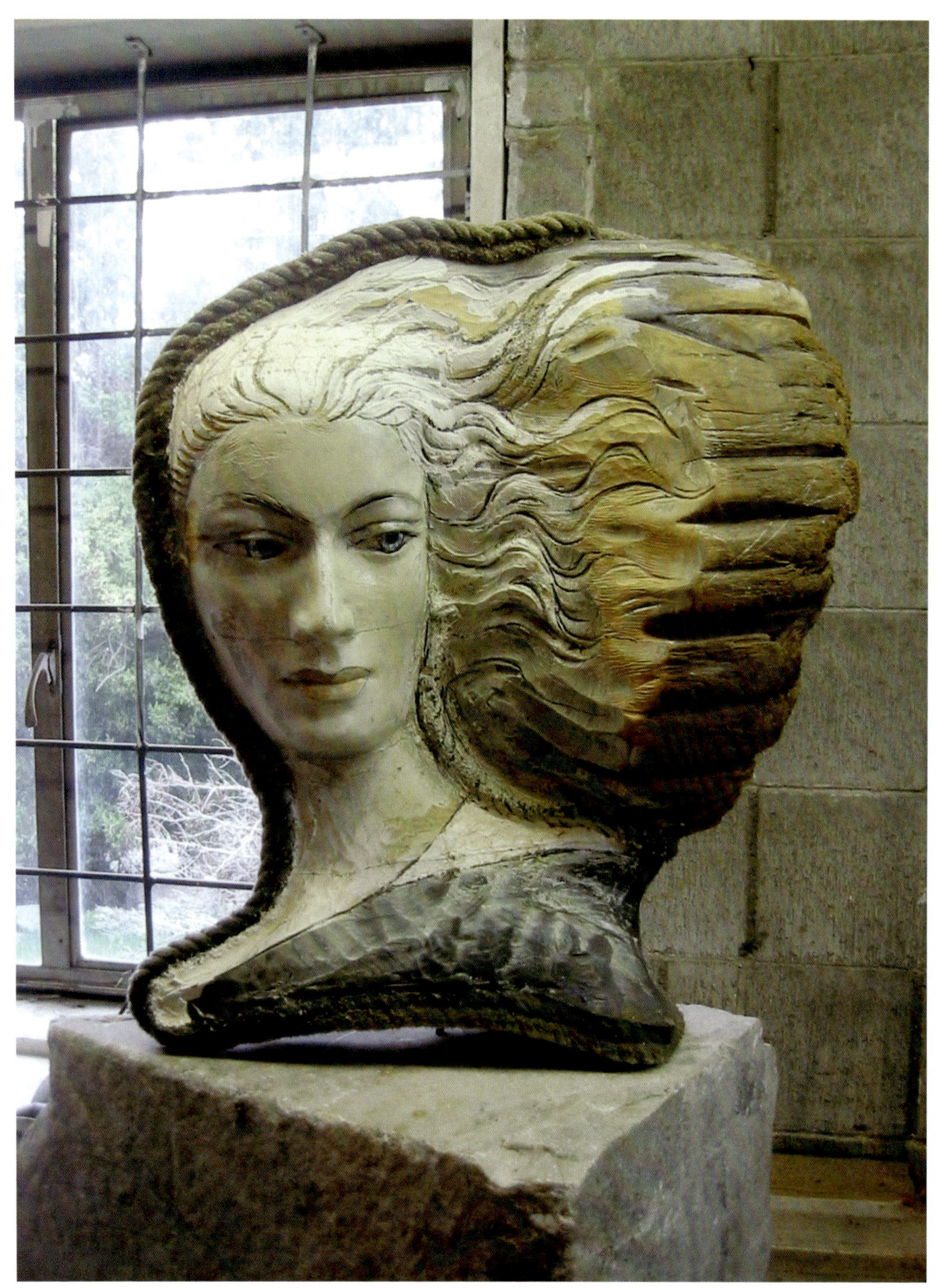

GODFREY STEPHENS

ESQUIMALT

GODFREY STEPHENS' STUDIO IS IN HIS BACKYARD, JUST A COUPLE OF BLOCKS FROM THE WATERFRONT. IT WAS FORMERLY A TWO-CAR GARAGE, AND YOU GET TO IT BY WALKING PAST A GROVE OF HIS LARGER SCULPTURES, INCLUDING THE WEEPING CEDAR WOMAN.

She's a sort of totem pole he carved to protest the imminent logging of Meares Island in 1986. The pole stood on Strawberry Island in Tofino Harbour for years.

His latest sculpture was a sweeping vertical column made of rifles and guns—real ones, which were turned in to the police department. They were subsequently rendered useless and offered to Stephens who took them away as scrap metal. He welded the firearms, along with helmets and swords, into an emphatic plea for peace. The whole thing swirls up into the air from a base made of a ploughshare.

Stephens, now in his later 60s, always lived the definitive alternative lifestyle. He never dropped out: he was out there from the beginning. His life has been one long romantic adventure, whether sailing his own boat to Mexico (where it sank) or living in driftwood palaces on Long Beach before it became a national park.

On a visit to his studio I took notes and offer this random sample of a true original. He was in motion when I arrived, darting among the piles of miscellaneous material that filled his studio. Stephens soon found the CD of old-time Greek music he was digging for.

"I haven't been to Greece since 1965." He continued to rummage about, looking for an axe amid the multitude of sharp blades he keeps at hand for all sorts of purposes. "Do you find this Greek music distasteful? A lot of people do." He began to lay into a chunk of yellow cedar with a hatchet. "It's such a shame to cut this wood. Here—smell it." He thrust the split stick under my nose. "Golden cypress—that's

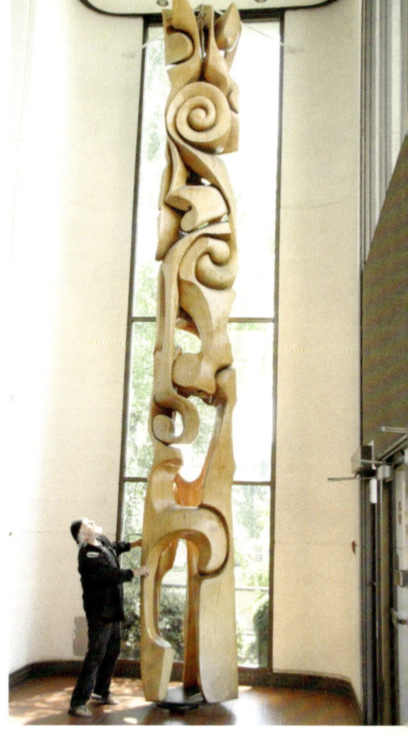

Stephens beside one of two poles he created for the Victoria Press building.

KUTTERSMUKETT, *Godfrey Stephens, wood carving with rope, 21 inches tall, 2006.*

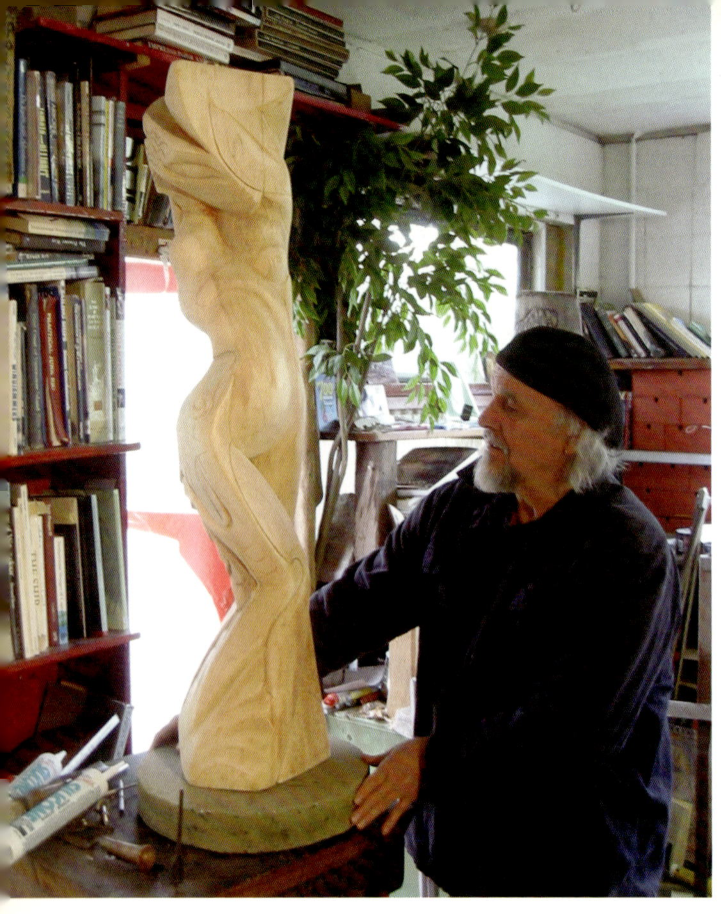

Stephens and a sculpture in his studio, March 2007.

what I call yellow cedar. That's what I used for one of my poles in the foyer of the Victoria Press Building." That pair of abstract totems is a landmark of public art.

"I was born in 1939," he went on. "In Duncan at the King's Daughters Hospital. A lot of my relatives are buried in the Quamichan Cemetery. My father was a farmer, a farmer-poet really." Stephens paused and quoted a stanza of his father's verse.

"He sold his farm in Goldstream and moved me and my brother to Hollywood, California." It was 1956 and Godfrey had the wrong haircut, the wrong clothes and the wrong accent. Even then he was the artistic type—not cool.

"I had always wanted a motorcycle and when I was 16 I told my dad it was what I needed to succeed at school. I talked him into buying me a 1952 Harley original Model K Sportster. He said I had to work to pay for the gas, so I did. It was the only time in my life I worked for someone else. After about two weeks, well, I wasn't going to let a lack of money stand in the way, so I quit."

The motorcycle didn't last long but Stephens' roaming days were well begun. "I hitchhiked my way through four passports, 60 countries at least. I had 138 stamps in one of the passports," he recalled with pride.

Stephens was soon flipping through a little logbook. "Here we are," he said, having found the right page. "Greece, 1961. I loved living in Greece. I landed in Greece with five drachmas in my pocket and I stayed for three years. I have total recollection of everything that happened in those years."

"This is music from Crete!" he interrupted himself. "Cretan music! I was there when they were filming *Zorba the Greek*. I wasn't on the set; I was preoccupied up at the other end of the island with 'the wild woman to walk the wind with.'" A twinkle from his eyes said the rest. "That was 1962."

With a huge mallet and a chisel the size of a baseball bat, Stephens shattered an enormous chunk of dark chocolate for us to eat. He loaded more wood into the stove. His studio is a convergence of maritime arts, ship signs and figureheads of his own making. His own boat, the

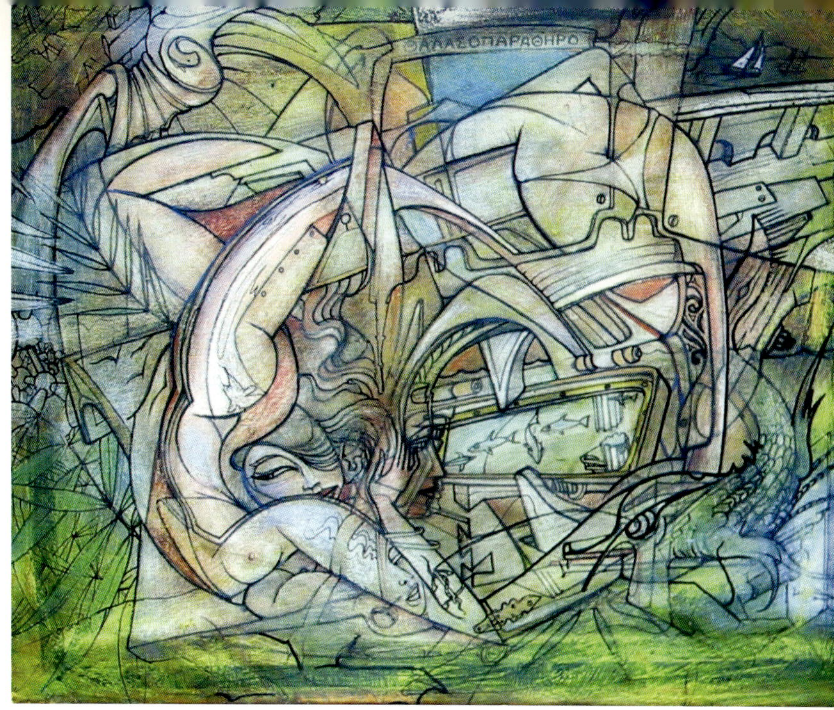

UNTITLED,
Godfrey Stephens,
mixed media on canvas,
18 x 24 inches, 2005.

latest, is moored nearby at West Bay. It's steel-hulled, junk-rigged and ready to go.

All around his studio was a collection of "guy stuff": pirate flags, swords and guns, native imagery and his own overwhelming glorification of the eternal feminine. He loves to paint and draw women. Our conversation roamed across the famous artists who have whiled away some hours in this man's workshops and ships: Mungo Martin, Chief Tony Hunt, Richard Ciccimarra, Kate Craig and her brother Jamie Craig were remembered. "Jamie Craig died in a plane crash. He was a really good friend of mine," Stephens said. "He was a poet. He was neat. Here's one of his poems: 'My spit hits a spot of snow/and the mountains tower above me.'" Stephens surprised me by the amount of poetry he could quote.

The rake and rambling man is also a proud father. "I have two daughters (that I know of). One's 31 and one's 35." He flashed the crest on his *Pirates of the Caribbean 3* T-shirt. The film stars Johnny Depp, and Stephens went to the "wrap" party. His younger daughter, Tilikum, was working on the set. He named her after the modified dugout canoe on display in the Maritime Museum of British Columbia. Captain John Voss sailed the *Tilikum* around the world, leaving from Oak Bay in 1901.

"The *Tilikum* is Victoria's finest artifact," Stephens said conclusively.

The Greek music had come back with a vengeance. "Oh, the dancing at that party," the artist mused. He thought back to the number of paintings he left in Greece—that was his currency in the days of yore.

Stephens paused for a moment. "I'm enjoying myself," he reflected, "because I'm still alive." ■

As I enjoyed an afternoon sitting by the stove, Stephens decided to paint my portrait. Like so much else in his world, the portrait is not yet finished.

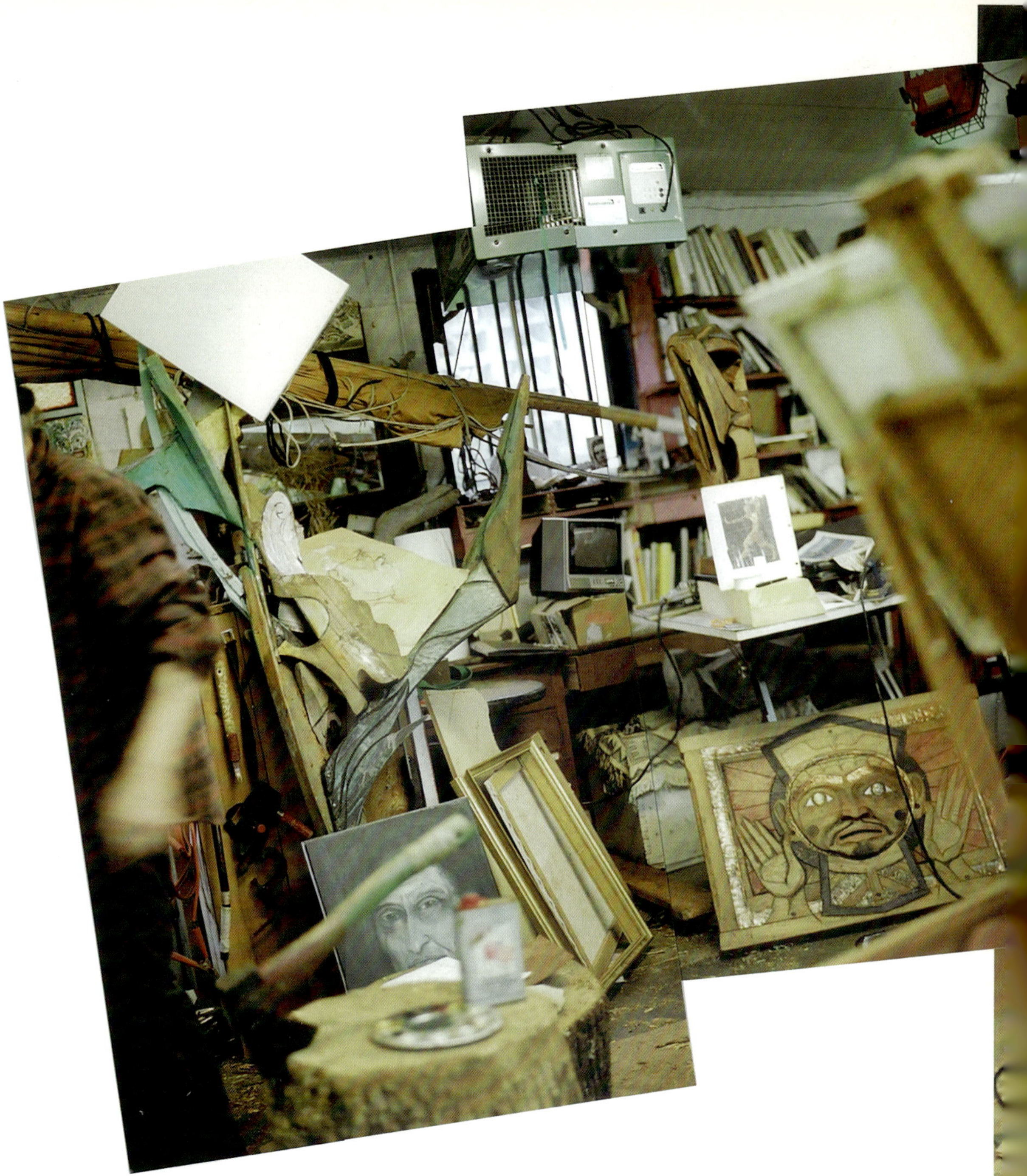

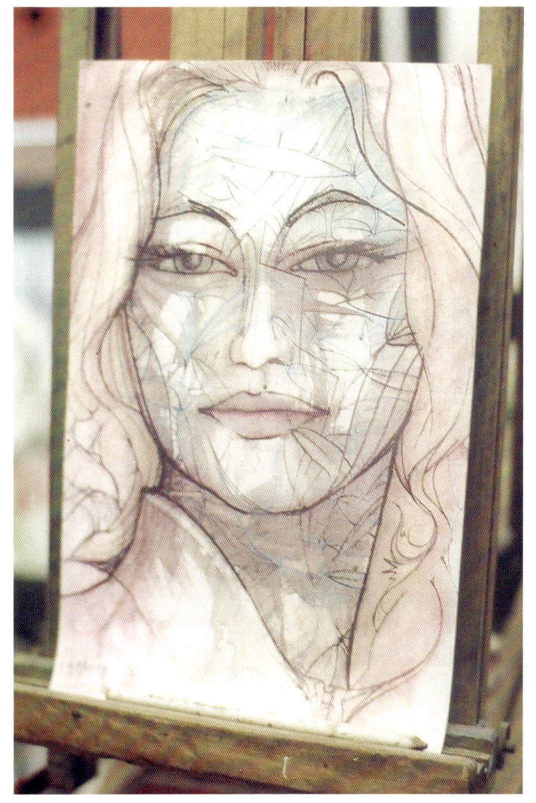

UNTITLED,
Godfrey Stephens, mixed media on card, 12 x 16 inches, 2005.

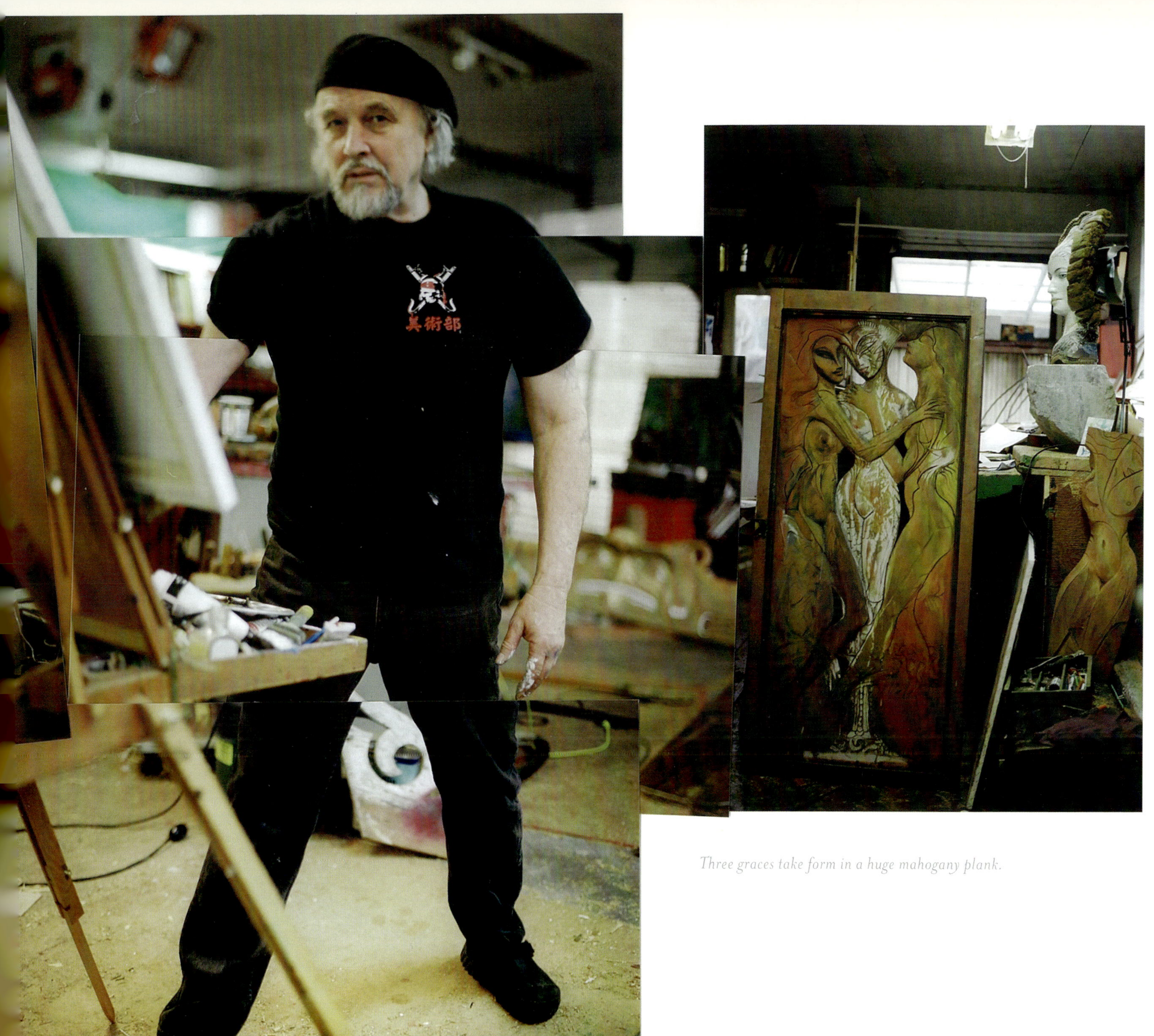

Three graces take form in a huge mahogany plank.

■ ■ ■

GODFREY STEPHENS' STUDIO, *Esquimalt, February 2007.*

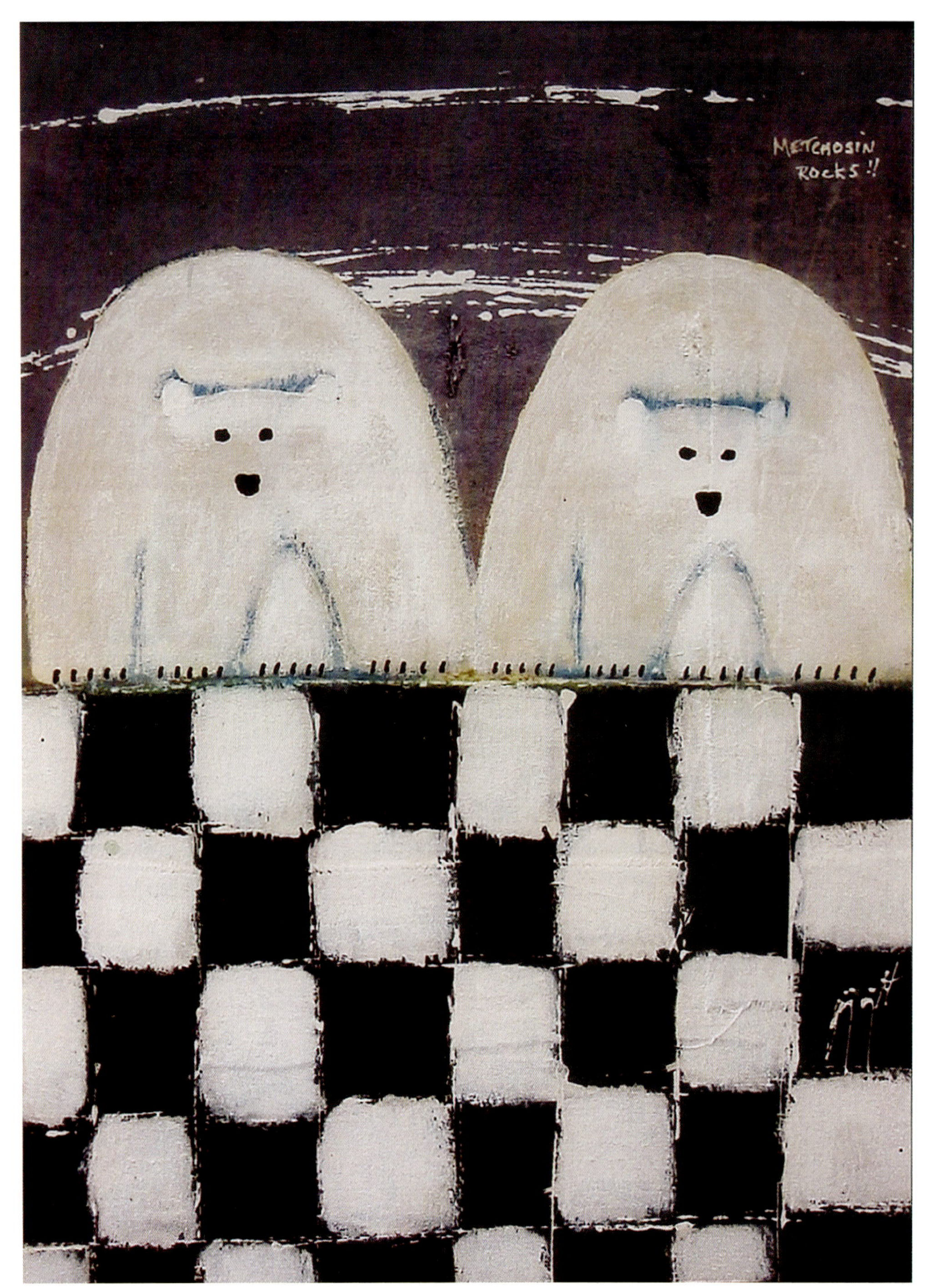

CHECKERBOARD BEARS, *Jimmy Wright, acrylic, 18 x 24 inches, 2006.*

JIMMY WRIGHT & PAT COOK

METCHOSIN

PAT COOK AND JIMMY WRIGHT DO JUST WHAT THEY LIKE TO DO—HE PAINTS, SHE MAKES PAPER. THEY HAVE CREATED A DRAMATIC, PURPOSE-BUILT STUDIO HOME ON 10 ACRES OF WOODS AND FIELDS LOOKING OUT TOWARD THE STRAIT OF JUAN DE FUCA IN METCHOSIN.

Jimmy Wright paced about his workspace. "This is my art factory," he said by way of introduction. "I'm an artist, but I'm more than that. My job is to paint stuff that people are gonna buy." But isn't an artist supposed to be some sort of divinely inspired genius, in touch with the cosmos? "We are not different from other workers," Wright insisted.

Earlier in his life, Wright was an economist and learned to relate to the world in a pragmatic way. Later, he became a fishing guide in northern British Columbia, and developed his vision working as a photographer. When I met him in 1986, he had just arrived in Victoria, and opened an art gallery. He was ready to make his living by creative expression. At that time I was dubious, but since then he has done very well with his art.

"I don't have any inventory," Wright smiled, looking around his spacious studio. On easels in front of him, a half dozen large canvases awaited shipment. These canvases were basically abstract, but each carried an "icon"—a polar bear motif, for instance.

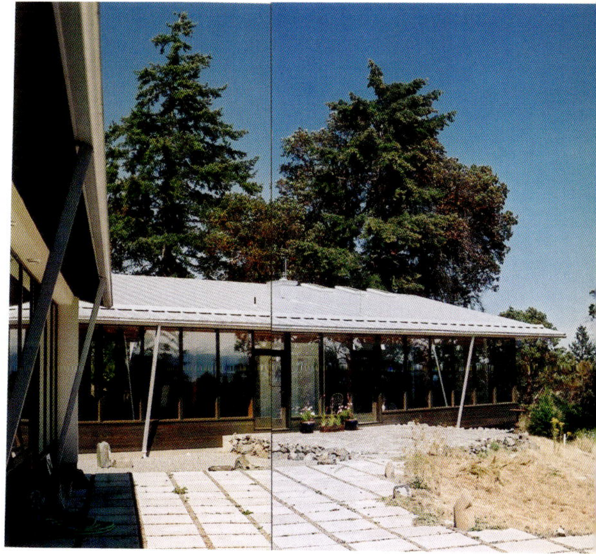

Outside Jimmy Wright's studio.

Wright's favourite painter is Mark Rothko, an American artist whose veils of colour are studiously devoid of any representational intent. One of Wright's own paintings, which hangs over the mantel in his home, is as simple as a Rothko.

Each of Wright's canvases begins with a lightly inflected texture, a scrim of colour that he scrubs on linen with acrylic paint. He calls this "The Cave Wall." He showed me his photos from a recent trip to Mexico, and each of them in fact was a close-up of a crumbling wall. This roughly brushed field of colour is enough for him.

But it's not enough for the buying public, and Wright is making art for them, not for himself. So he introduced a little bit of imagery. First he tried a dog, and then a profile of a standing buffalo. Surprised and delighted by the success of these introductions, he developed further icons, including his signature image, the polar bear. "When I designed that thing," he told me, "I no longer had to cope with anguish."

What anguish was that? "The anguish when you are looking at an empty canvas and saying 'What am I going to paint?' Once I painted that bear I never really had that issue anymore. A lot of people who start with abstract, they just keep pushing paint around, and finally the process becomes the product. I'm tired of chasing the process." Any horizontal line can read as a horizon, turning his paintings into landscapes. A tiny person, in silhouette, immediately implies a story. Over the years, Wright has painted many little figures walking on the horizon line: a naked fishermen, a parade of nuns and the black birds with red beaks which are called oystercatchers.

Inscribed onto his "cave walls," like anonymous graffiti, are Wright's discreet little messages. Near a buffalo icon are tally marks. You sense that the painter/economist has considered the value of these "kills" and is telling us these marks will never add up to what was lost when the buffalo were decimated. Abstruse mathematical formulae written nearby are actually the code by which our exploitation of natural resources is driving us into what he calls "well-upholstered poverty."

Happy in his studio, Wright finds painting a delightful way to spend time. "The more time you scratch at 'em, the more you build up the surface, you're just enhancing it," he said. "You're creating that wonderful textured wall that you're gonna drop your icon on."

"Art is just a product," Wright concluded. In his case, it's a product that is well made, and created with consideration for those who will buy it and live with it and love it. If that allows Jimmy Wright and Pat Cook to continue to enjoy their lives, it's a good thing.

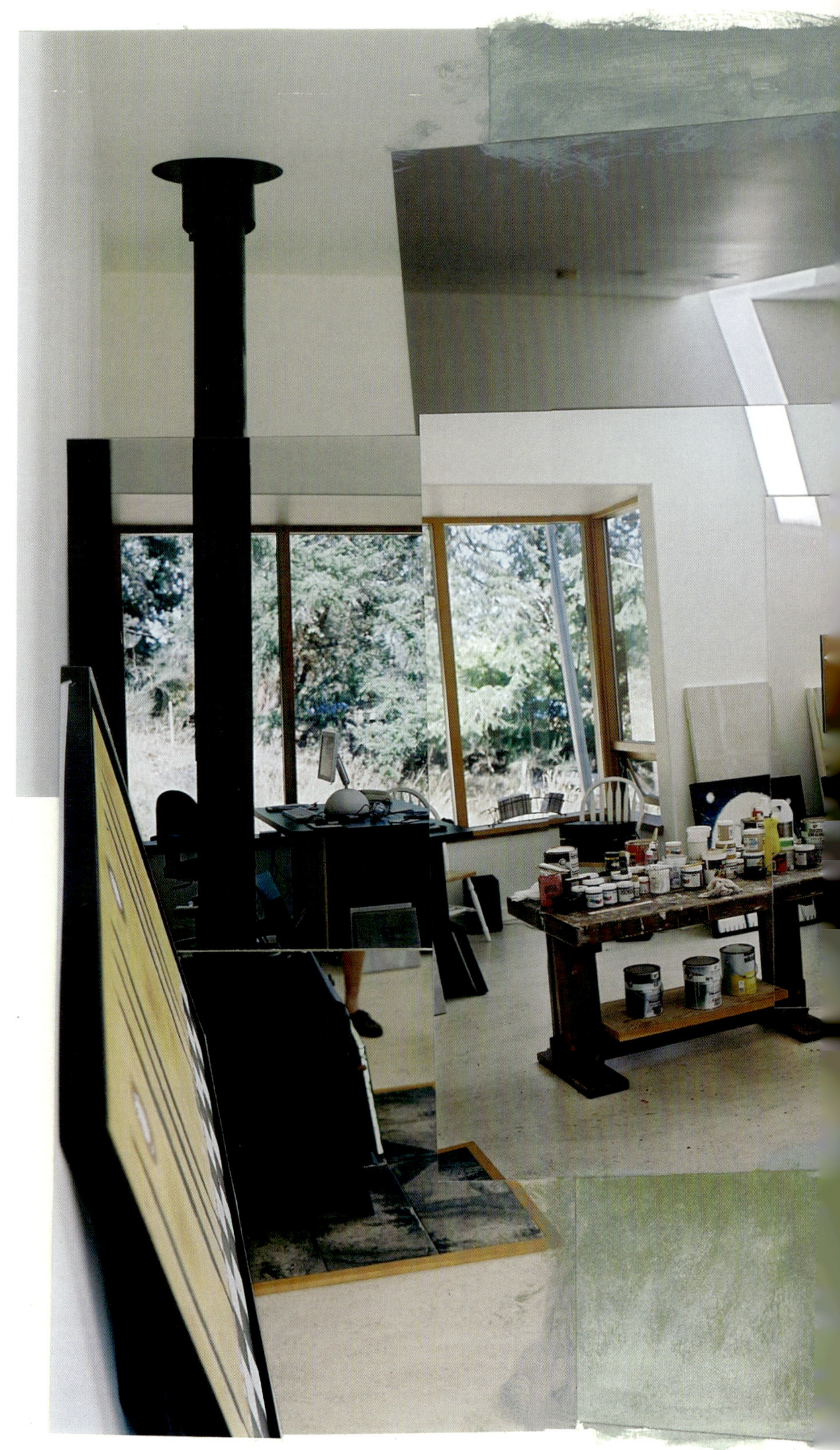

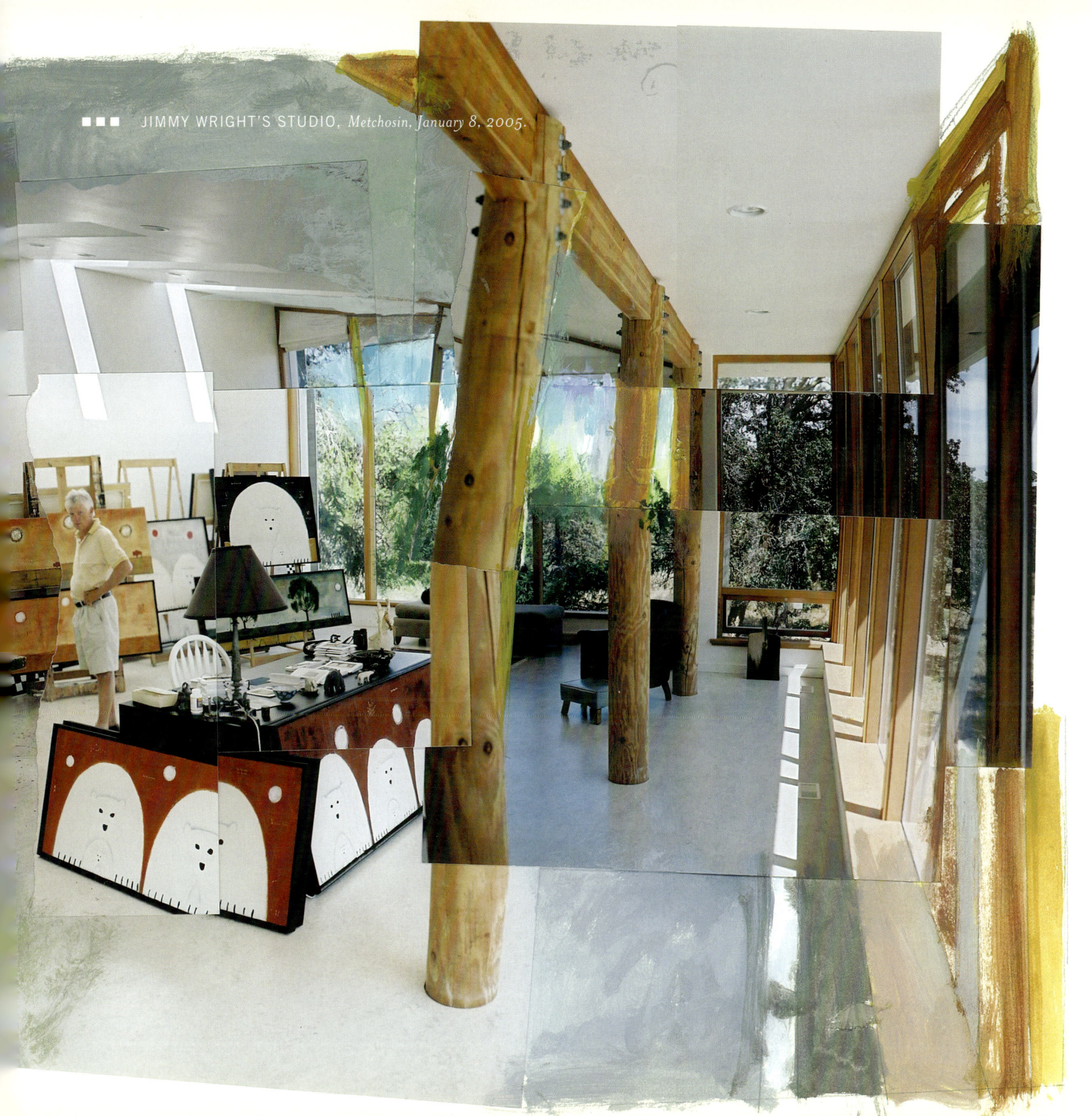

■■■ JIMMY WRIGHT'S STUDIO, *Metchosin, January 8, 2005.*

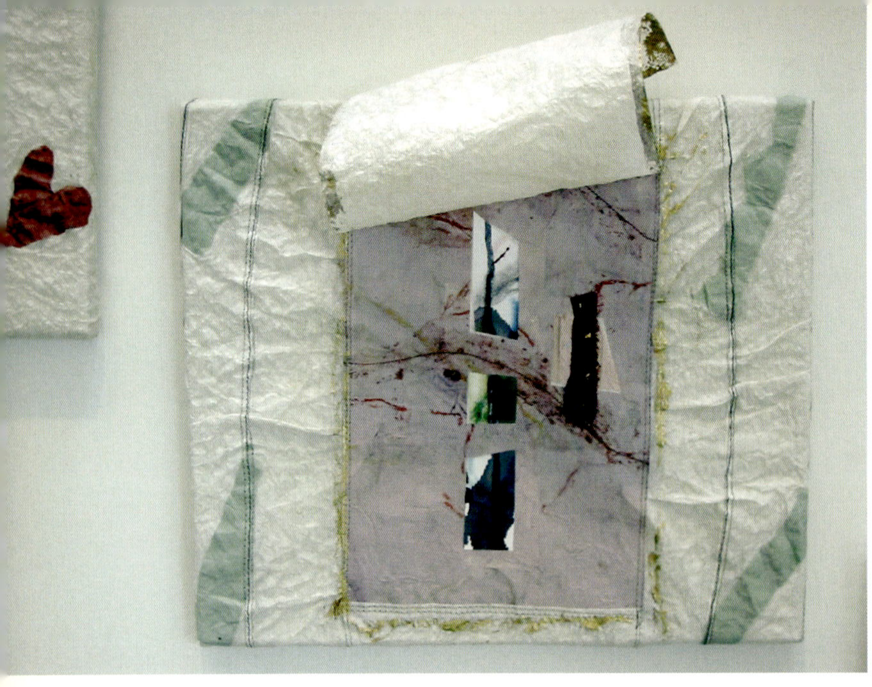

PAPER PROJECT,
Pat Cook.

PAT COOK'S STUDIO IS SPACIOUS AND WELL-EQUIPPED, WITH EVERYTHING NEEDED TO TEACH PAPERMAKING. THIS INCLUDES WATER AND DRAINS, REFRIGERATORS, TABLES, PRESSES AND PLENTY OF BIG, FLAT SHELVES. SHE OFTEN HOSTS CLASSES WITH TEACHERS FROM AROUND THE WORLD.

"I was a professional figure skater for many years, with the Ice Follies," Cook told me. "I travelled in five countries, away on tour for a year at a time." Now she cherishes her home base. After she retired from skating, Cook came to Victoria. One day, in Munro's Books, she saw a poster for the Metchosin International Summer School of the Arts. That summer, MISSA offered a one-week course with Sharon Yuen of Vancouver's Kakali Papers.

"As soon as I read it, I thought, 'Oh, that looks like fun!'" Cook said. And the thrill continued: "The first time I put my hands in a vat of pulp, I fell in love with it. It's a great joy." Following the MISSA course and other training locally, Cook travelled extensively in Japan, visiting papermakers. Paper became her fascination.

In the modern world we think of paper as a thoroughly commercial commodity, the ultimate throwaway. Yet the Japanese word for paper is *kami*, which is also the word for "god" in the Shinto religion. "There is a sacredness, a spirit in paper," Cook said quietly.

She begins her work by collecting plant matter with which to make her papers. Much of this matter is imported; her favourite recipe uses fibres from inside the bark of a variety of the

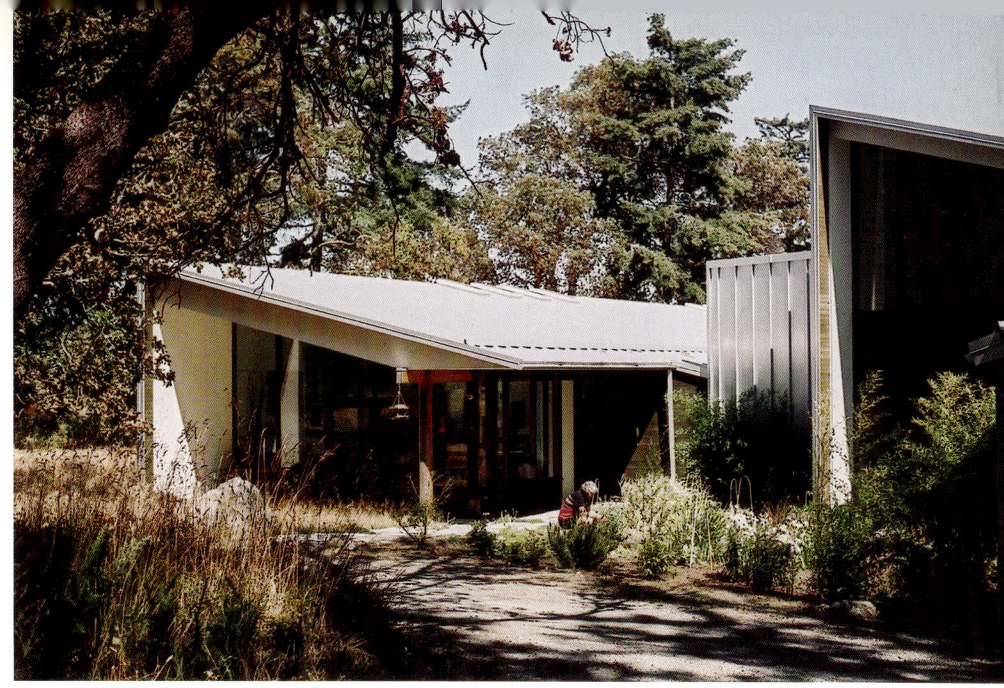

Front entrance to Pat Cook's papermaking and teaching studio, Metchosin.

paper mulberry bush called *kozo*. Though *kozo* is identified with Japanese paper, she imports it from Thailand. Cook also uses fibres indigenous to Metchosin. She gathers them in nearby fields and roadsides, then she soaks them, cooks them and beats them to a fibrous broth. To this raw material are added both colouring and sizing; the latter determines the surface finish and absorbency.

"I might make 50 sheets of paper at a time," she said. A common size is about 9 by 14 inches. "It's a three-day process. On the first day I make a post of paper and then I put it in a press so the water can run out slowly."(A post is a pile of paper fresh from the mould, laid with alternate sheets of felt.) "I leave it there overnight. On the following day I lay it out on a Formica surface to dry." On the third day it comes off the drying board with a satisfying snap.

All around us were her original paper creations. Two plaques that looked like slabs of jade were set on little stands. A book of many colours, bound like a burst accordion, flew across the high wall like a kite. Free-standing lamps, scrolls and little cast paper fish are part of her environment.

Up to this point her work has been somewhat literary, involving poetry, inscriptions, bus tickets and the shredded pay stubs from her years of employment. She also has a penchant for including Chinese texts in fragmentary form. Cook likes to make wall coverings, screens and things that come out into the room.

Pat Cook is capable of making gossamer sheets of immaculate Japanese *kozo* paper, but more often adds kelp, arbutus bark or papyrus into the blend. Thus the paper object becomes much more than a "substrate upon which things are inscribed." ■

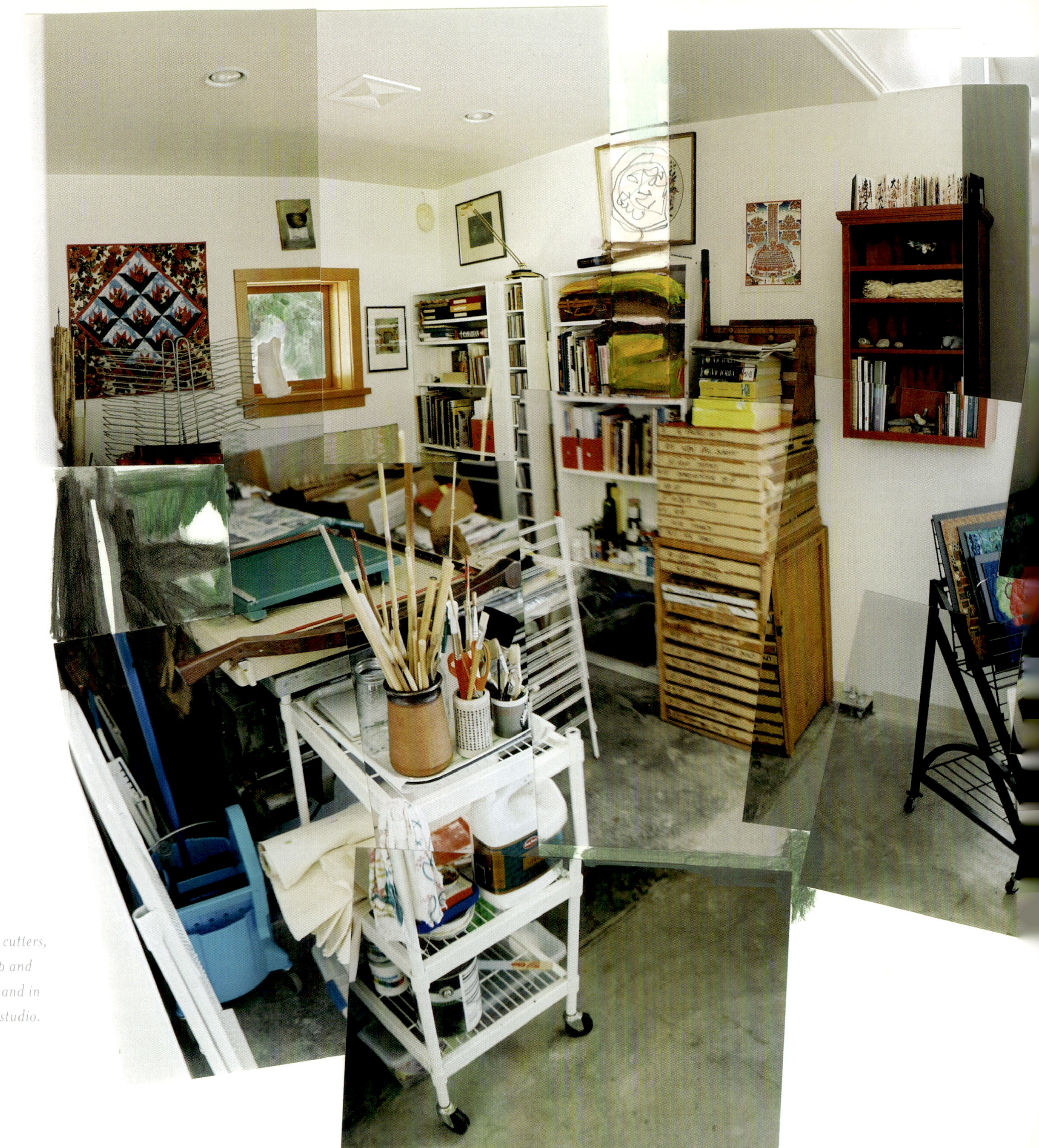

Drying racks, paper cutters, type cases and a mop and bucket are close at hand in the cement-floored studio.

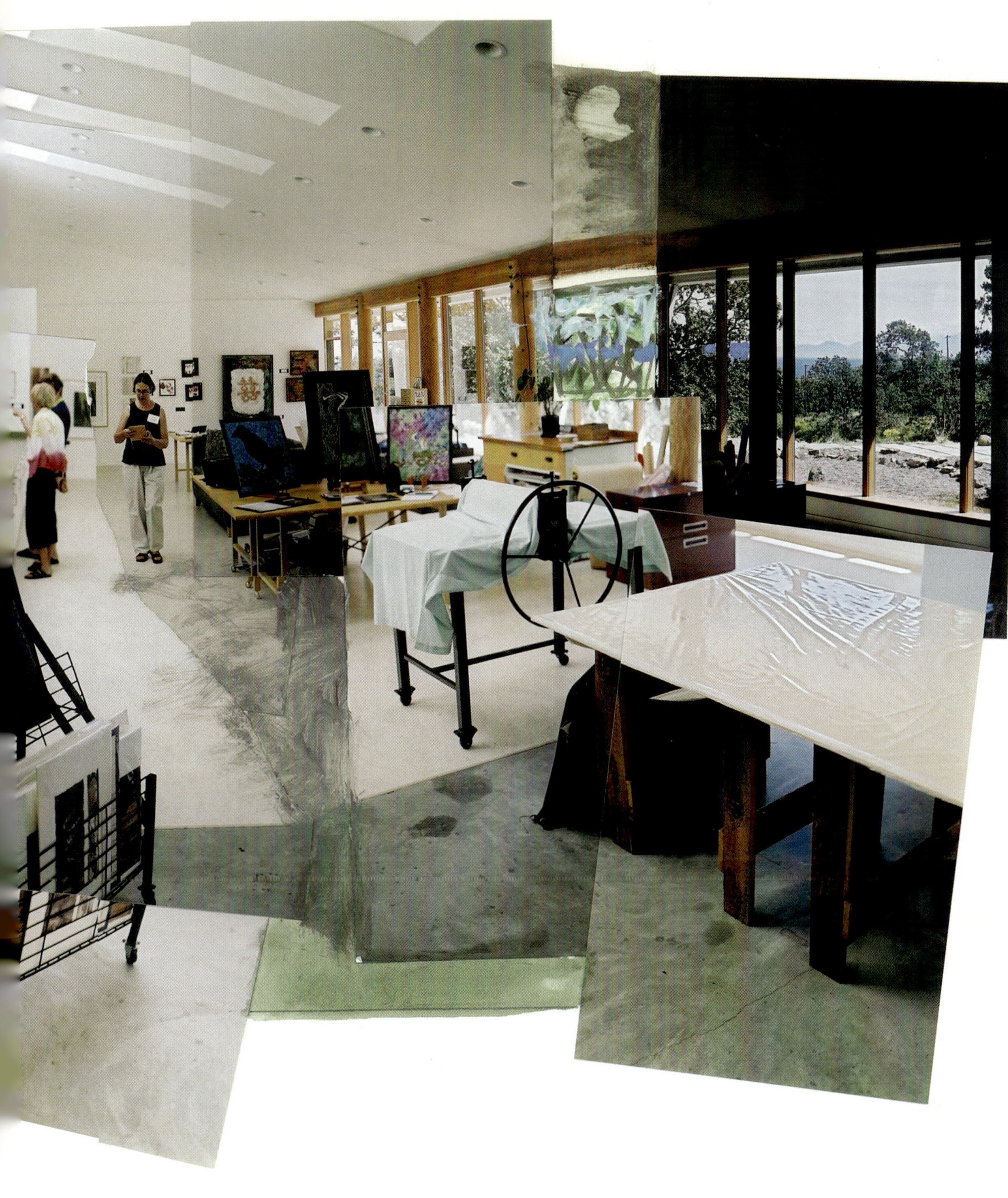

PAT COOK'S STUDIO, *Metchosin, January 5, 2005.*

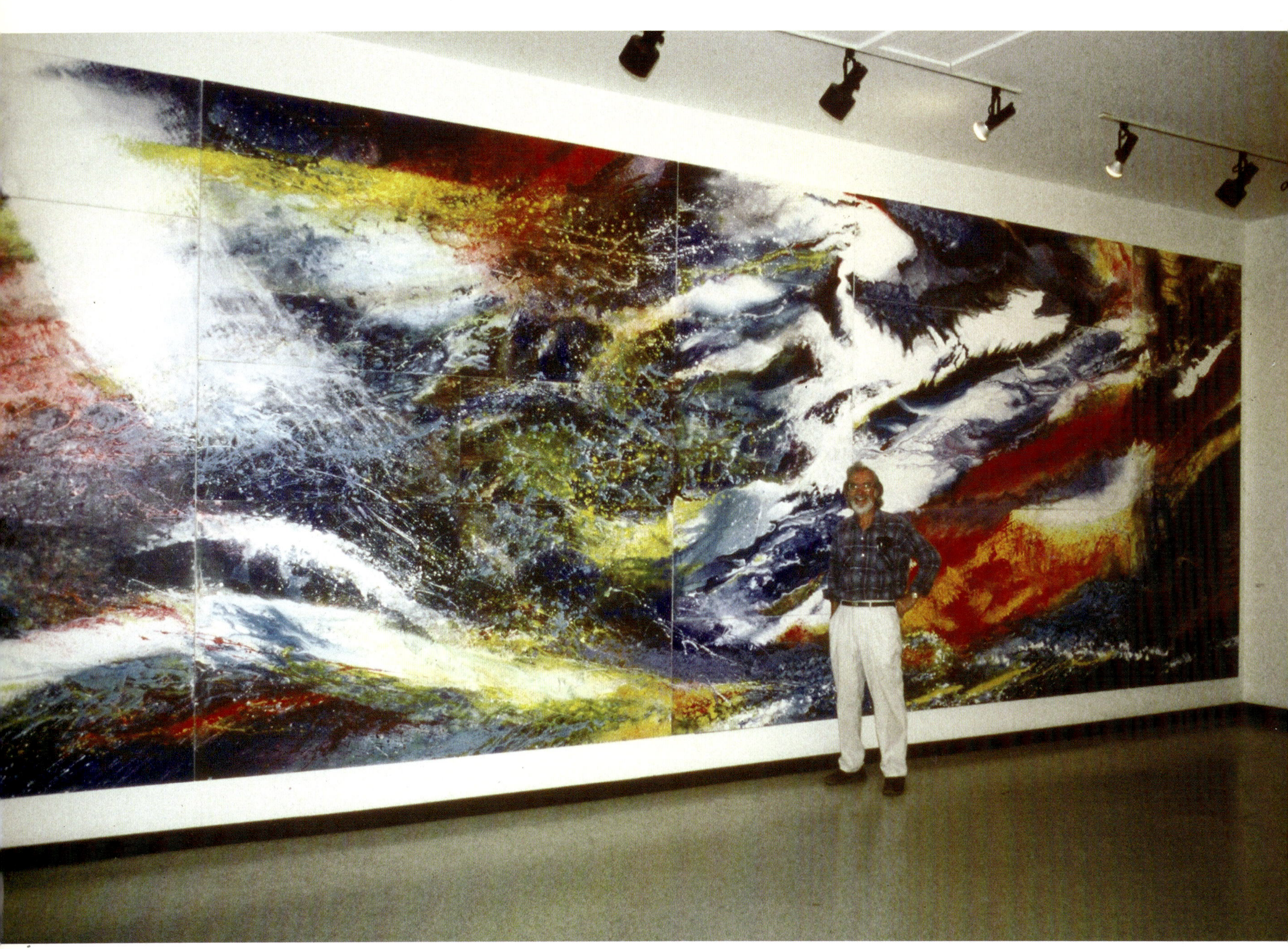

■■■ *Norman Yates in front of his painting* LANDSPACE 160—THE CARIBOO, *acrylic on 14 panels, 304 x 851 centimetres, 2000.*

NORMAN YATES

VICTORIA

"SOMETIMES I FEEL LIKE I'M JUST SOMEONE WHO'S HOLDING THE POT OF PAINT AND THE WHOLE THING IS HAPPENING AROUND ME, A DISINTERESTED OBSERVER," NORMAN YATES EXPLAINED TO ME.

On the occasion of the opening of an exhibition of work by Yates at Victoria's Fran Willis Gallery, I called the artist and asked if I could come over and photograph his studio. "Why would you want to do that?" he queried. "There's nothing here at the moment." I suggested he let me be the judge.

The exhibition was called, fittingly, The Big Picture, and it centred on one huge painting, three by eight-and-a-half metres. He had created it with acrylic paints, thinned down to a fluid consistency, on a series of foam-core panels of a manageable size. The picture grew and grew under his hands: he added one panel above or beside another as he went along.

Working on the floor of his sky-lit, two-car garage, which he long ago converted to a studio, Yates lets the paint speak for itself. He pours it, he lets it run, he sweeps inspirations onto the panels using wide brushes. When he has a good start on one panel he lays another down next to it and continues. The composition evolves in front of him, as he dances over the surface and burrows out beyond the margins of his previous expression.

Born in Regina in 1923, Norman Yates made a major contribution through his 30 years of teaching at the University of Alberta in Edmonton. Throughout his life he has painted constantly.

Yates lived in Ontario for a number of years, and when he left in 1954, it occurred to him that the Group of Seven was completely concerned with the "surface" of things. Their light was reflecting off facets of rock and the shapes of leaves. Even the clouds were presented in this way. He became determined to find a way to paint from *within* their landscape.

One day he found himself on a quarter section he owned near Tomahawk, Alberta, looking out at the land, which had been cleared for hay. "I had put a big canvas down in the field and splashed away, cans of paint all around," he recalled. At that point Yates realized he had been seeing the world as if through a window. "Suddenly I felt a little rising of the hairs on the back of my neck and I realized there was as much space behind me as in front."

To recreate the boundless space he sensed, he had to get rid of the "window frame" through which most of us view the world. Eventually, this practice took him into a realm of freedom that is almost transcendental.

What was previously a limiting framework could be ignored as the picture grew in all directions. Yates was free to build his image as he went along, expanding and expanding. The horizon around him was now seen as endless, not cut off by the edge of the canvas. He was at the centre of the landscape. His world had turned inside out.

As he added to his series of panels, Yates made the paint surge and flow, overlaying huge veils as he built up a homemade universe from skeins of transparent colour. The paint surface before him was evolving as it dripped and dried; gravity pulled it, colours merged in their own way. The accidental dynamic quality of the paint provided a road to discovery.

In the gallery, one can stand back and take in the total composition created by this play of energy, something Yates can't do in his smaller studio. Truly, he works from inside the painting. Yates is a creature of this universe, not separate from it. It is a giddy sensation, to be participating in nature's creation. What pleasure it must be for this artist to confront the thundering wall of cosmic surf as it collapses into a shimmering tideflat of exquisite serenity before him.

At the mention of the great English artist J. M. W. Turner, Yates lit up. Turner began as a superb draftsman, he told me, and later painted snowstorms, burning ships and the most dazzling lighting effects conceivable.

"When he painted the Houses of Parliament on fire, the burning buildings were just an opportunity," Yates explained. "As subject matter became more and more incidental, he was painting space, change, movement and colour. Let the paint speak for itself." ■

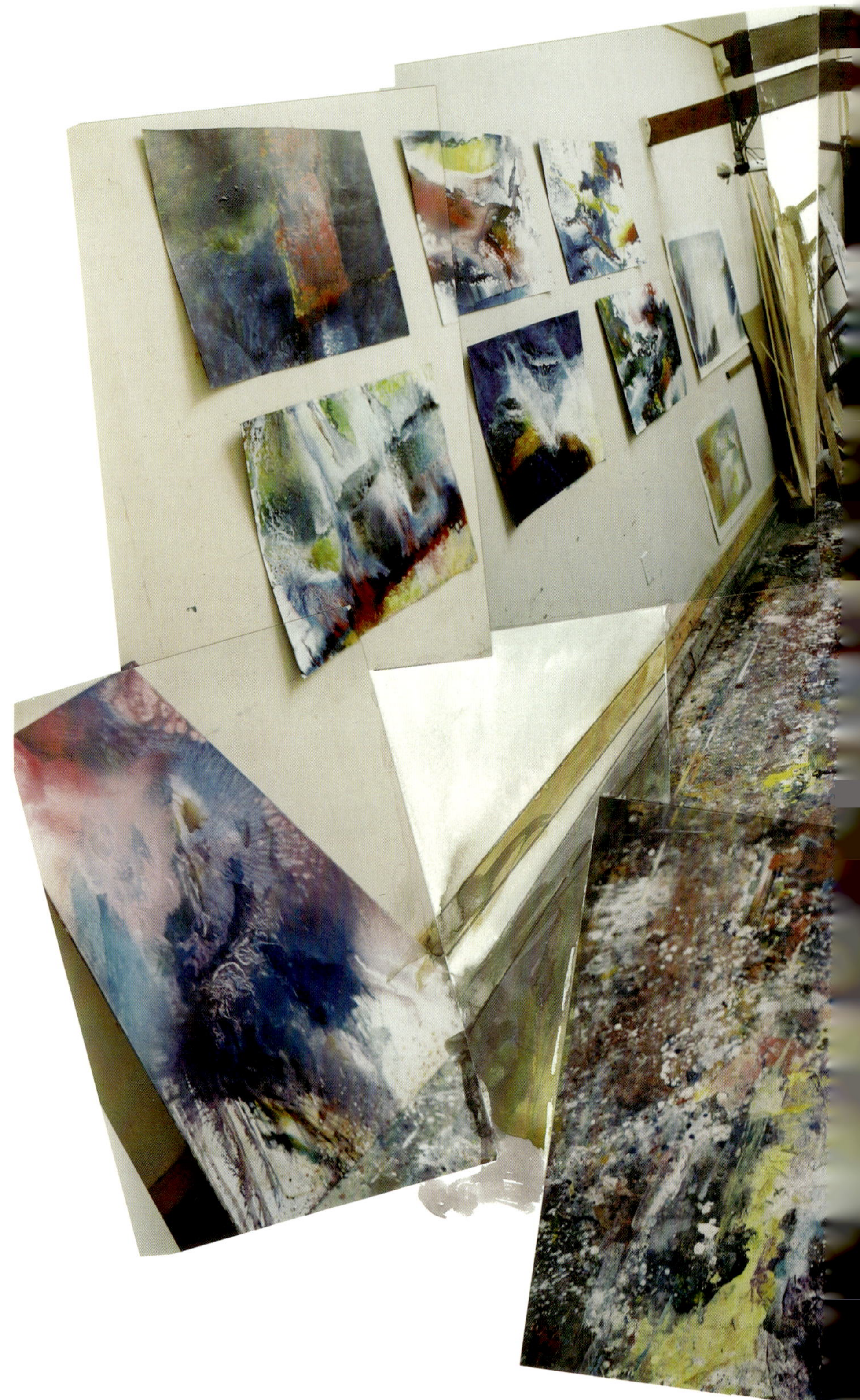

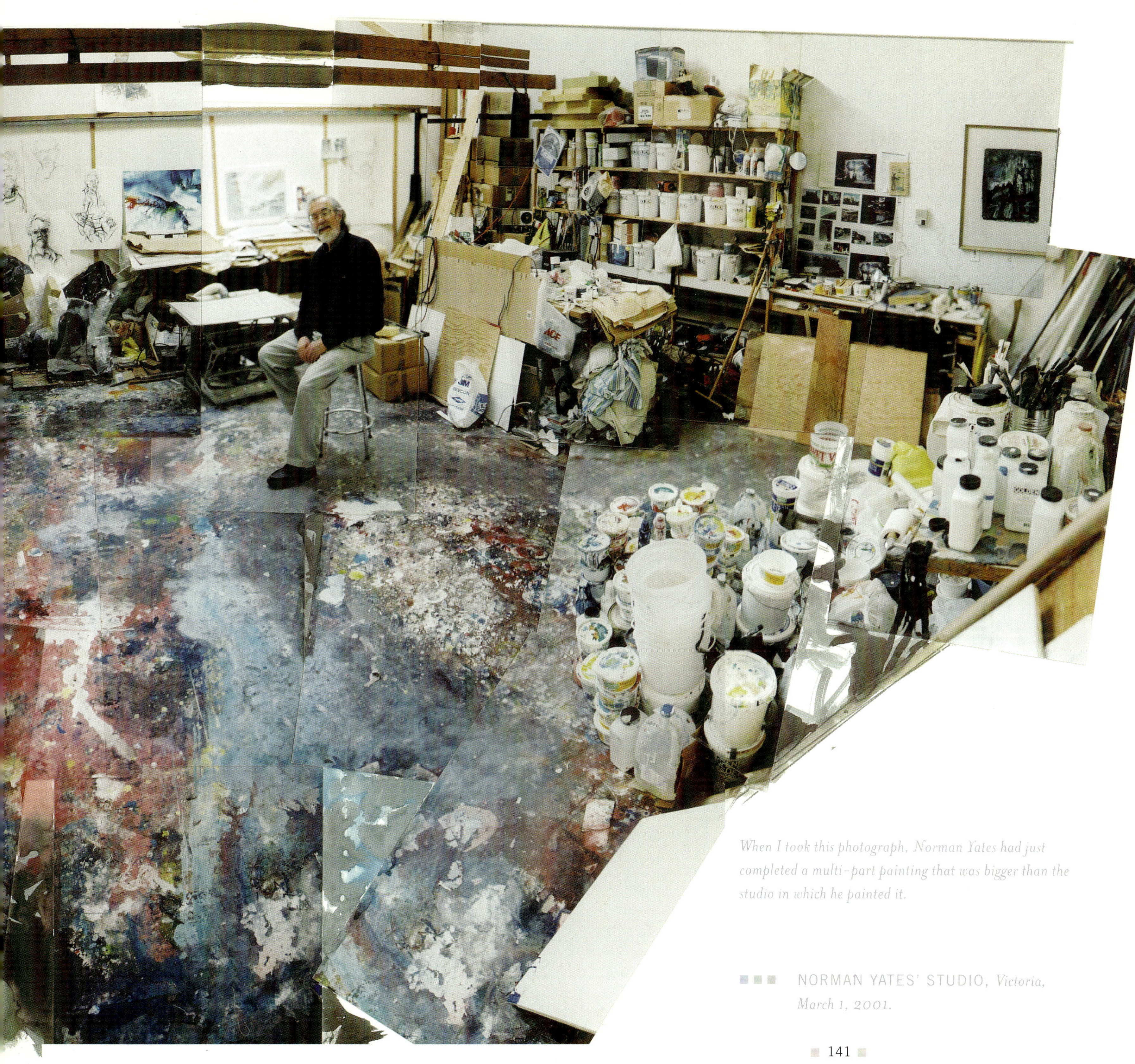

When I took this photograph, Norman Yates had just completed a multi-part painting that was bigger than the studio in which he painted it.

NORMAN YATES' STUDIO, *Victoria, March 1, 2001.*

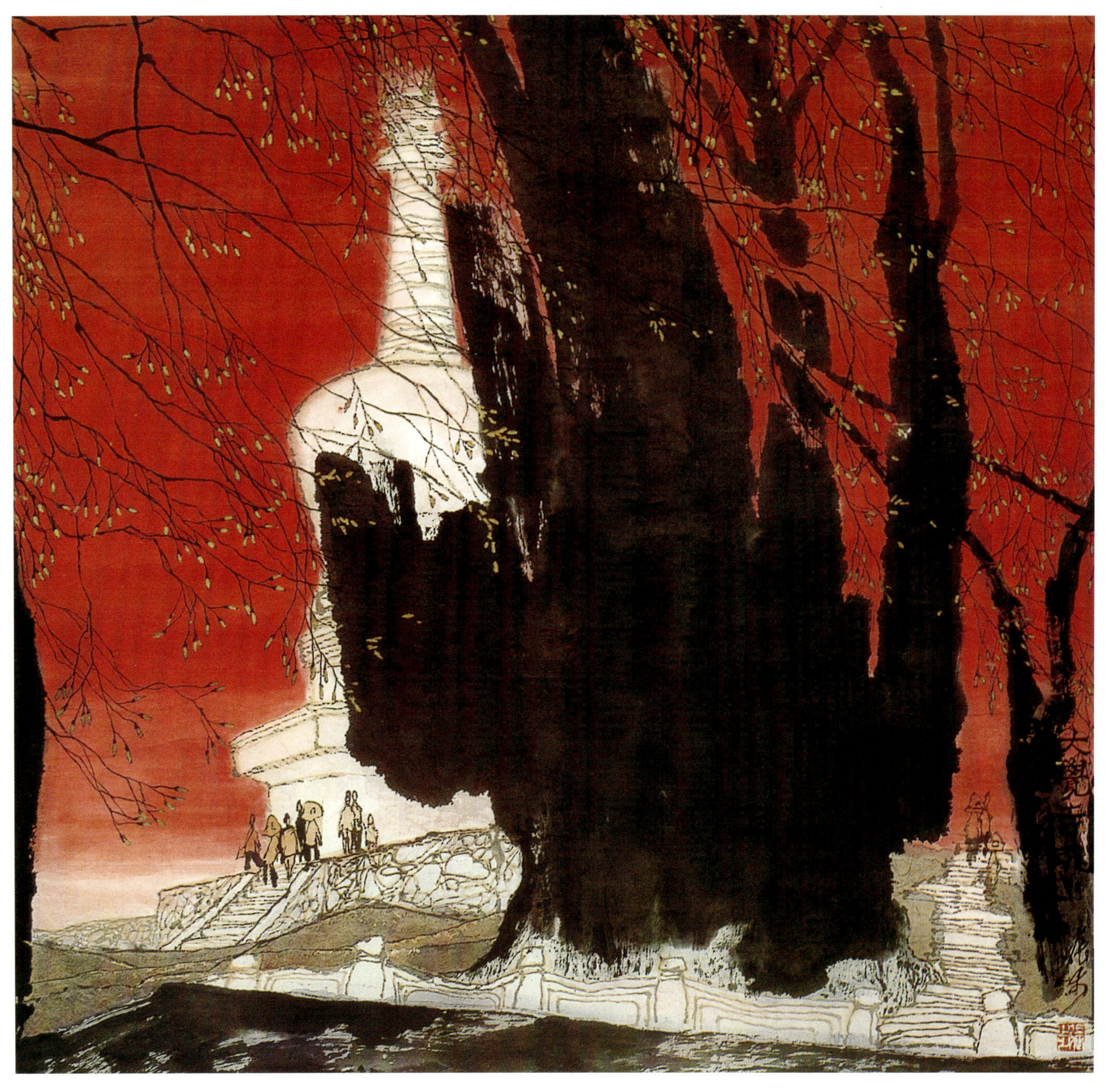

■ ■ ■ WATER VILLAGE UNDER THE ROSY COLOR, *Zhang Bu, ink and tempera colours on paper, 56 x 63 cm, 1988.*

ZHANG BU

VICTORIA

WHEN ZHANG BU MOVED TO VICTORIA FROM BEIJING IN 1992 HE BOUGHT A BIG, RANCH-STYLE HOUSE IN THE UPLANDS, THE FINEST RESIDENTIAL AREA IN THE CITY.

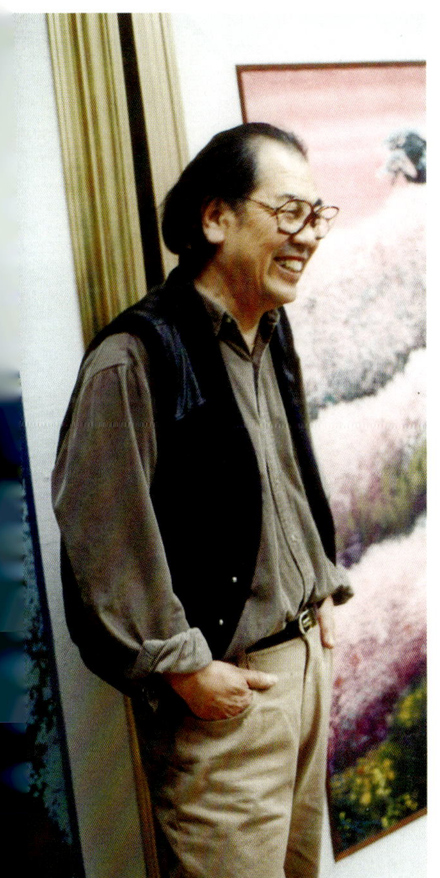

Zhang Bu.

It had white walls, white broadloom and modern white furnishings—everything in it was white except the five-piece black bathroom that was set, open-plan, in his white bedroom.

On a tour of his home he took me to the dining room, which had a dramatic fieldstone wall. He then opened some louvred doors, which I had taken to be a cupboard, and revealed to my amazement a room beyond—there, a few steps down, was a studio big enough for a full basketball game.

In the studio was an abundance of new paintings, each about two by three metres, painted on silk-like polyester stretched on wooden frames. They were stacked one in front of another all around the room. On the floor was a crop of smaller works and an eight-metre-long landscape in bright yellow. All of this work had been prepared for an exhibit at the Art Gallery of Greater Victoria, after which it was sent to a gallery in Japan where it was immediately sold.

Zhang Bu is hugely productive and stunningly creative. For a decade he lived and worked in Victoria, diligently developing his art and creating paintings to be shown in China, Hong Kong, Japan, the United States and Canada. Everywhere, he is acknowledged to be a modern master.

Zhang Bu was born in 1934 in the dirt-poor countryside of Hebei province, outside Beijing. He is the son of a carpenter, and was encouraged in his skill at decorating the furniture his family made. The times of his upbringing were, as they say, "interesting"—the embattled government of Chiang Kai-shek, the Japanese occupation, World War II and Chairman Mao.

From 1950 Zhang Bu trained as an electrician, rising by 1958 to a professional level. Then, at a crossroads in his life, he took an outrageous chance and applied to China's leading art school, the Central Institute of Fine Arts in Beijing. In a scene out of Dickens, the electrician presented himself at the school's front door and was asked to state his case.

"I love art. I do not want to do anything else and I must have the best teachers in the world," he told the person who answered the door. He was brought in and seated at a table, and paper, ink and colours were brought to him. "Paint whatever you like. You have 45 minutes," he was told. Upon completion of this impromptu exam, he was accepted on the spot.

After five years he graduated at the top of his class, specializing in landscape. His teacher, Li Keran, took a special interest in him and helped to forge this powerful talent that had developed within a fortuitous conjunction: Zhang Bu had a politically correct peasant background, was taught by teachers who still nurtured the immense tradition of Chinese culture and was exposed to the new, progressive Western art.

Upon graduation he was appointed editor of fine arts for the Beijing *Worker's Daily*, but the paper was soon forced to close by the actions of the Cultural Revolution. Eventually, the Red Guards caught up with Zhang Bu at an art exhibit. His paintings were said to be too black, apparently an implied criticism of the Communist government. Ironically, he was sent to be re-educated as a peasant, "working as a beast in the field, between the shafts of a plough," he recalled.

He survived six years of this, and in 1975 was rehabilitated to become art editor of the new *Shining Sun Daily*, a newspaper with a daily press run of more than two million. All this time he was expanding his art practice and by 1980 he was selected for the Beijing Art Academy. This meant that he became one of 80 official state artists and was provided with a studio, materials, an apartment and food, travel expenses, a salary and the chance to exhibit at home and abroad.

Since then Zhang Bu has had exhibits in Japan, throughout China and in prestigious galleries in Hawaii. He has published seven large picture books of his work. A fellow artist has called Zhang Bu "a Herculean figure on the art scene."

As Zhang Bu has written, "My energy has all been spent on searching for a synthesis of Western and Chinese art, ancient and contemporary. During the past few years, I have also been studying the organic integration of traditional ink and wash of Chinese painting and the colouring of Western painting, in order to generate the momentum for the continuous progress of Chinese painting, as well as the formation of a new artistic style." This is a large program for a painter to undertake. But have a look. You will find Zhang Bu is accomplishing this enormous goal, and much of the work was done in Victoria.

Zhang Bu later battled a serious bout of cancer and then, in 2004, returned to live and work in China, a nation that during his absence had transformed itself politically. In April 2006 he was given a solo show at the China Art Gallery in Beijing, an honour as profound as any living painter in China can aspire to.

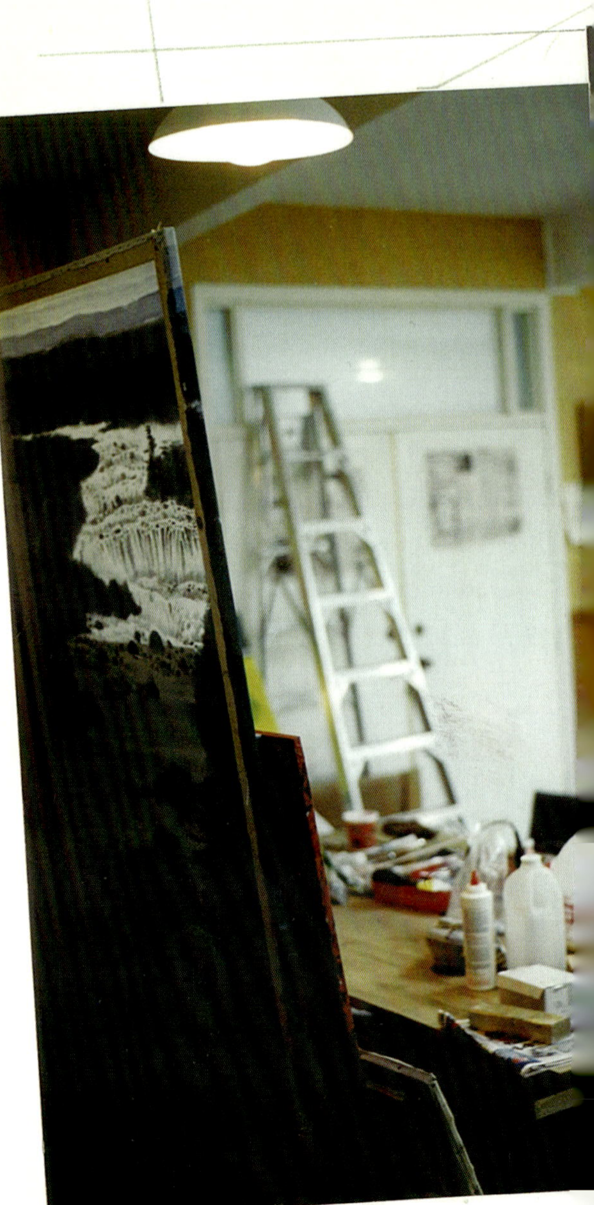

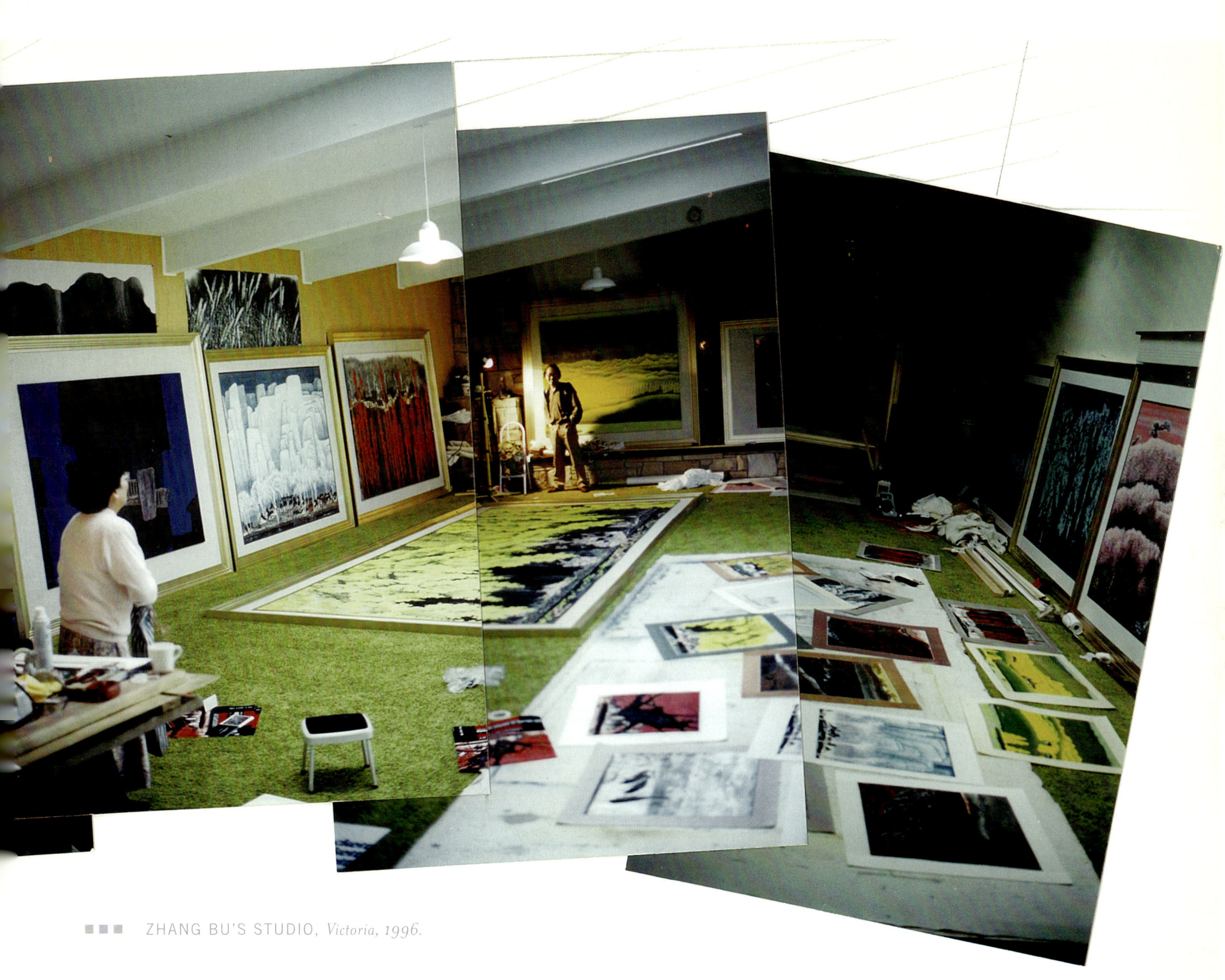

■■■ ZHANG BU'S STUDIO, *Victoria, 1996.*

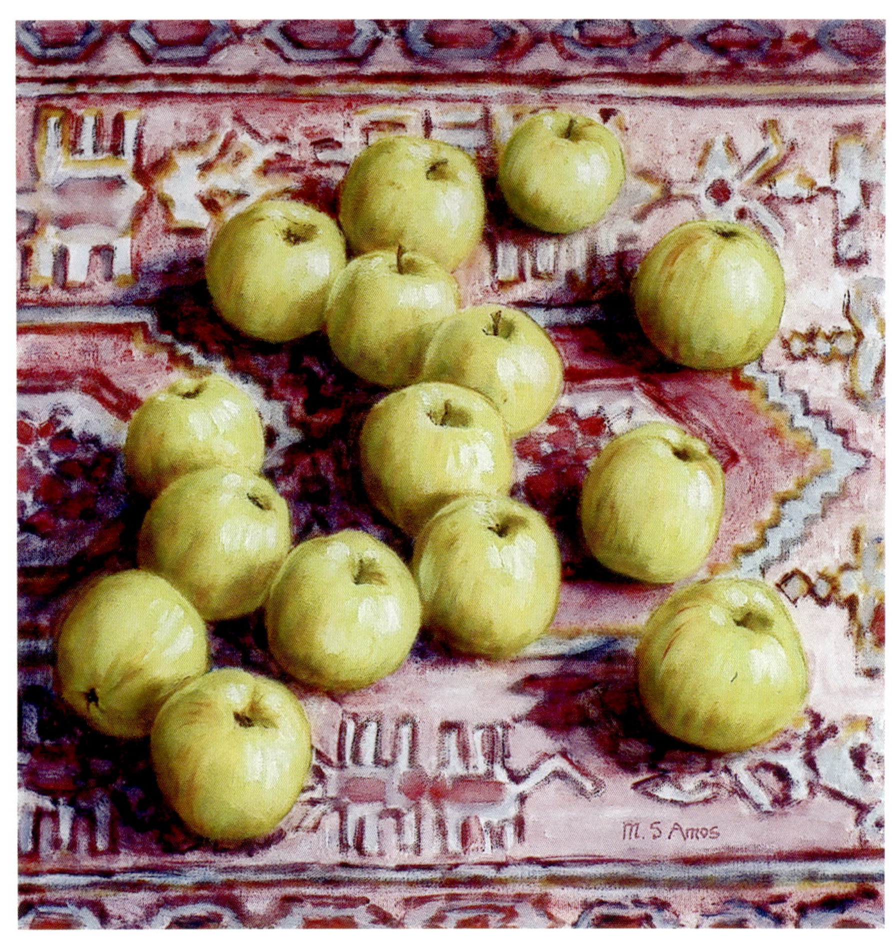

■■■ APPLES ON A PERSIAN CARPET, *Sarah Amos, oil on canvas, 16 x 16 inches, 2007.*

SARAH & ROBERT AMOS

VICTORIA

THIS CHAPTER IS PERHAPS THE MOST DIFFICULT OF ALL TO WRITE. MY OWN STUDIO SEEMS TO ME TO BE THE EPITOME OF ORDINARINESS. IS IT MORE INTERESTING ON ONE DAY THAN ANOTHER? INEVITABLY, WHAT YOU SEE AT ANY PARTICULAR MOMENT IS WHAT YOU GET.

Fifteen years ago my wife, Sarah, and I built a new house for ourselves and our two daughters in Victoria's Fairfield neighbourhood. The large room at the front (which most people would use as a living room) was intended as our studio. It has that cool, even north light artists prefer. Across the front hall from it is a smaller room that was intended as a storage room.

That's not how things turned out. The larger room became a gallery where I show my creations to visitors and prepare for exhibitions elsewhere. It was the smaller room that became my painting studio. Having worked out of a knapsack or on the kitchen table for years, I found this cozy space felt just right. Though it may appear spacious in the photocollage, in fact it's about 10 by 12 feet in total.

The small sofa on the left was formerly the removable double seat from a minivan we owned. Weeks after we sold the van I realized I still had the seat in my studio. It is compact and comfortable. Farther along the west wall an untidy bookshelf acts as my filing system—I try to throw away all my notes when I am done with them. My desk, a tall, rugged, homemade model, is flanked by a pair of our former kitchen cupboards. The handsome easel on the right is used more for holding things than for painting.

Careful observers will notice various paintings spread around the room, awaiting consideration. The needlepoint cushion of Carr House on the sofa is my work, as is the large calligraphic piece on the easel. This wooden panel was destined for Victoria's James Joyce Bistro at Peacock Billiards. Shoes, signboard, a copy of Joyce Cary's *The Horse's Mouth*—it's all here in this cluttered workspace that is always in transition.

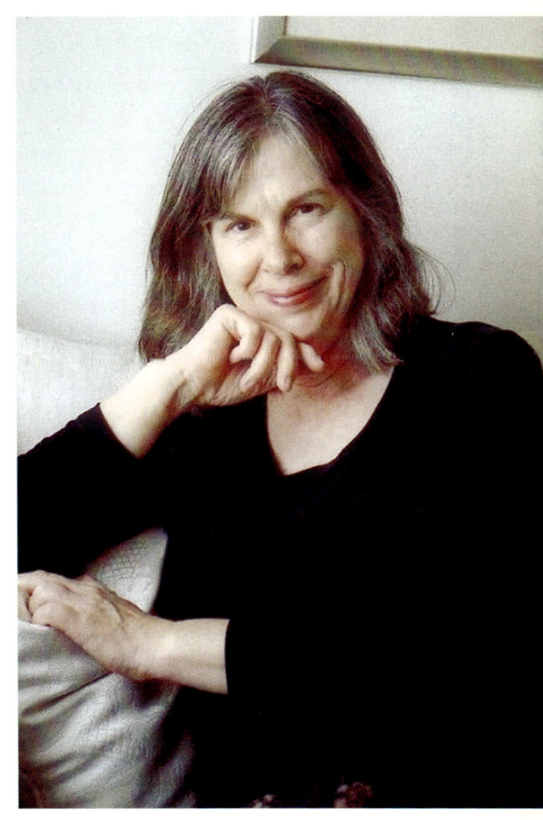

Sarah Amos.

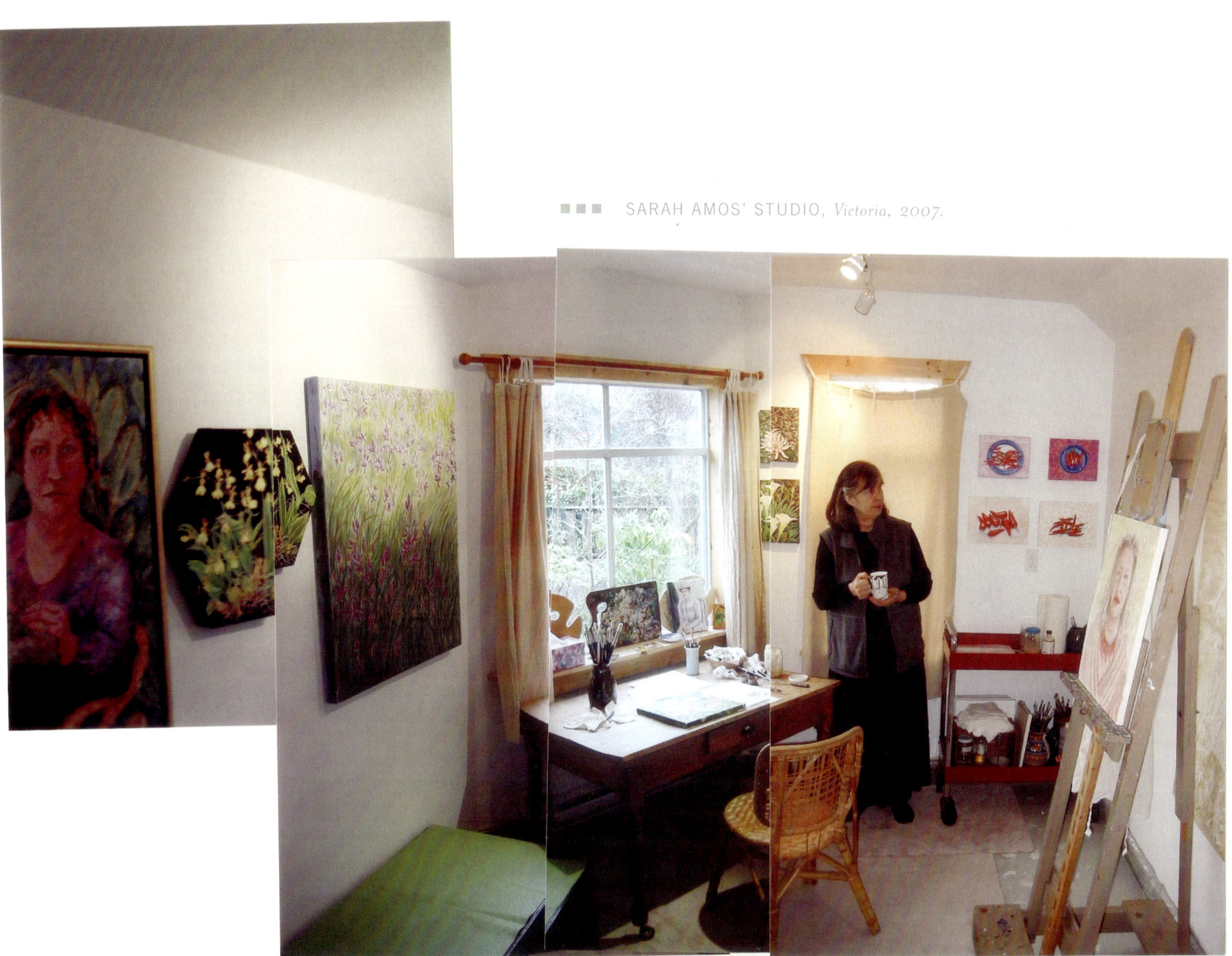

■ ■ ■ SARAH AMOS' STUDIO, *Victoria, 2007.*

Until recently, Sarah didn't have a studio, but did all her painting in the midst of our family's social space or in the kitchen. Certainly this was not an altogether satisfactory arrangement but it is one that is all too common among women who are wives and mothers as well as artists.

Sarah Amos has had a wide experience in the art world. She participated in performance art pieces at Portopia in Kobe, Japan, and at the Western Front in Vancouver. Her paintings have been shown in Calgary at the Stephen Lowe Gallery, on Gabriola Island at the Sandstone Studio and in Shawnigan Lake at the Auld Kirk Gallery, as well as at numerous locations in Victoria. She initiated and directed the Fairfield Artists' Studio Tour from its inception in 2001 until 2005.

With a healthy respect for tradition, and building on her years of study with Eric Metcalfe in Vancouver, she creates oil paintings and watercolours based on careful drawing. Her pictures bloom with a love of colour. She paints the things she knows best—flowers from her garden and food from her kitchen. Best of all, she likes to paint portraits created "from life" during extensive sittings with women she admires.

Sometimes when I return from photographing the glamour and creative wonderfulness of other artists' studios, I wish my dear wife had just such a place of her own. Last year she built a tiny oil-painting studio for herself in our garden. It's not grand but it is private—"a room of one's own." There, no telephones ring, no accounts beckon to be attended to and she can get away for

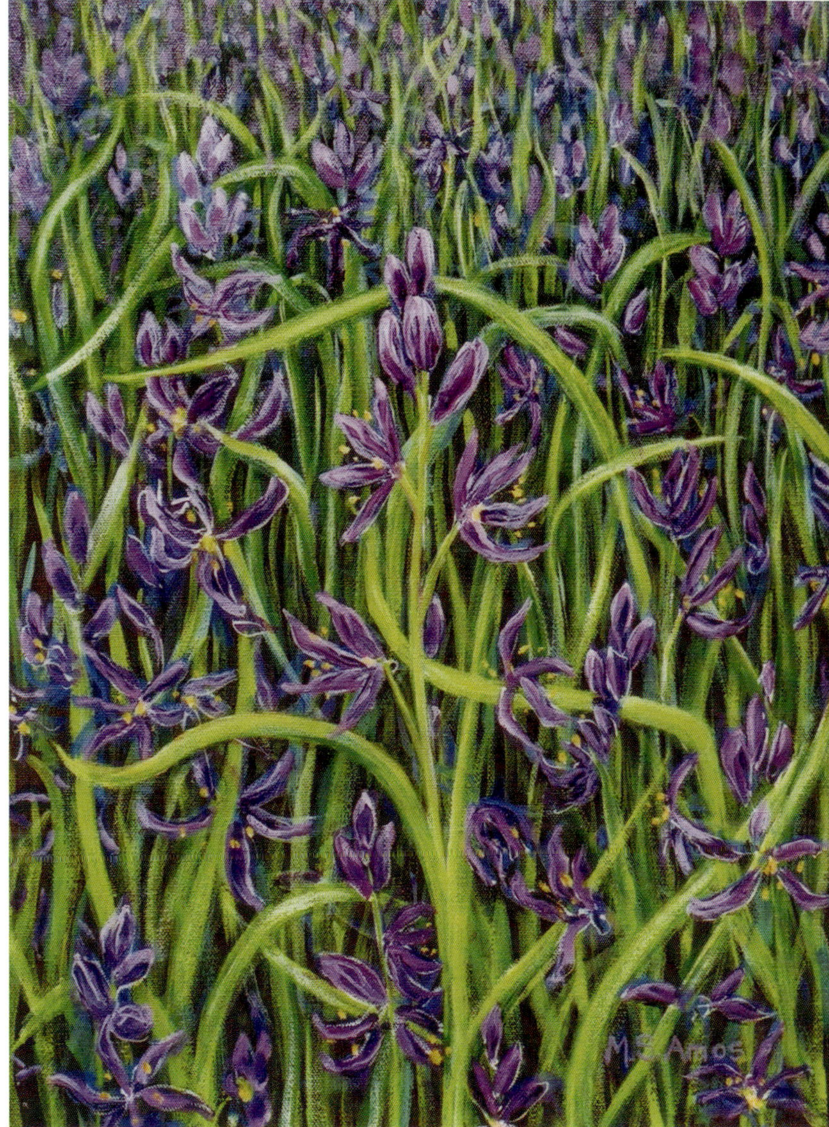

CAMAS, *Sarah Amos, oil on canvas, 20 x 30 inches, 2004.*

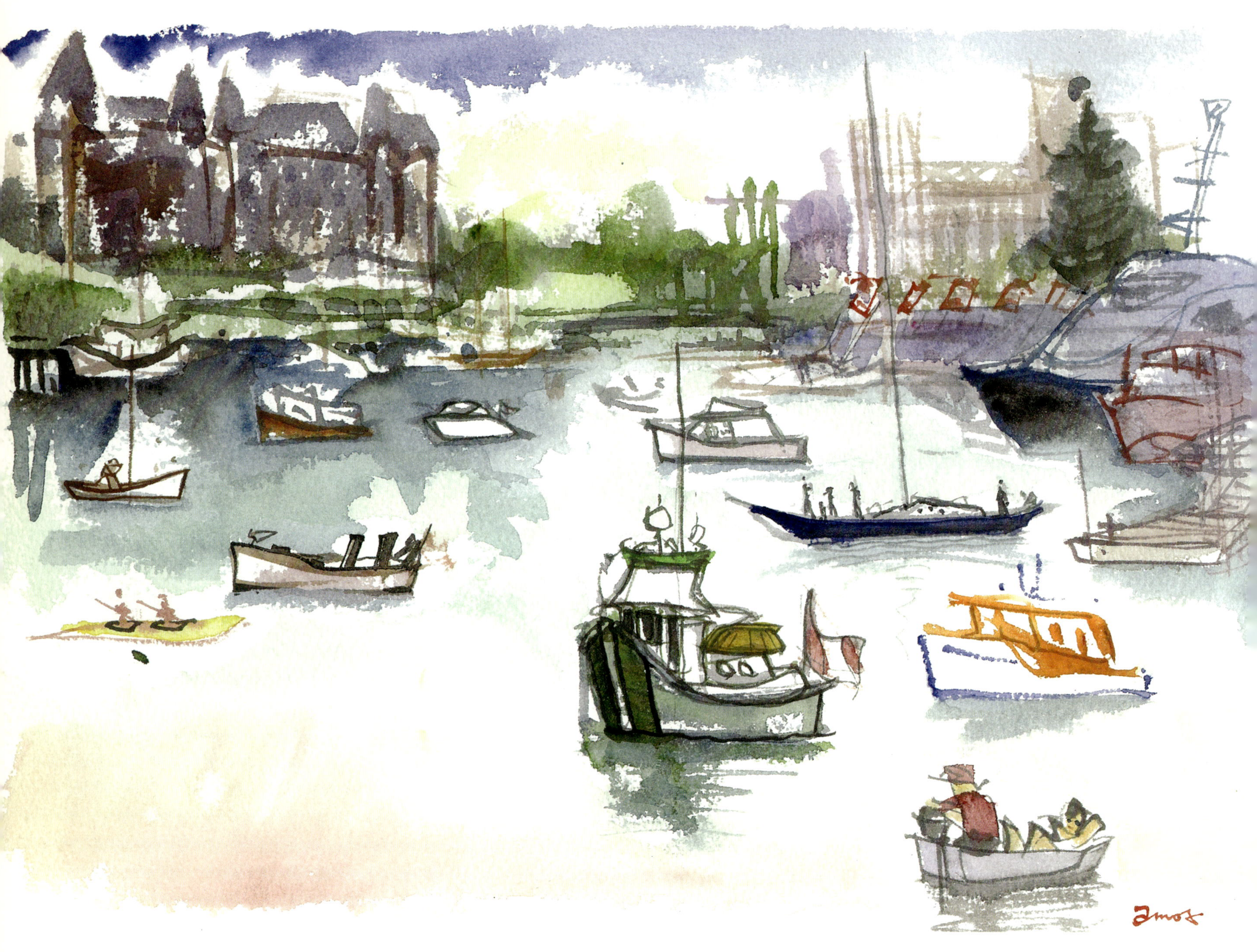

■■■ CLASSIC BOAT FESTIVAL, *Robert Amos, watercolour, 11 x 15 inches, 2006.*

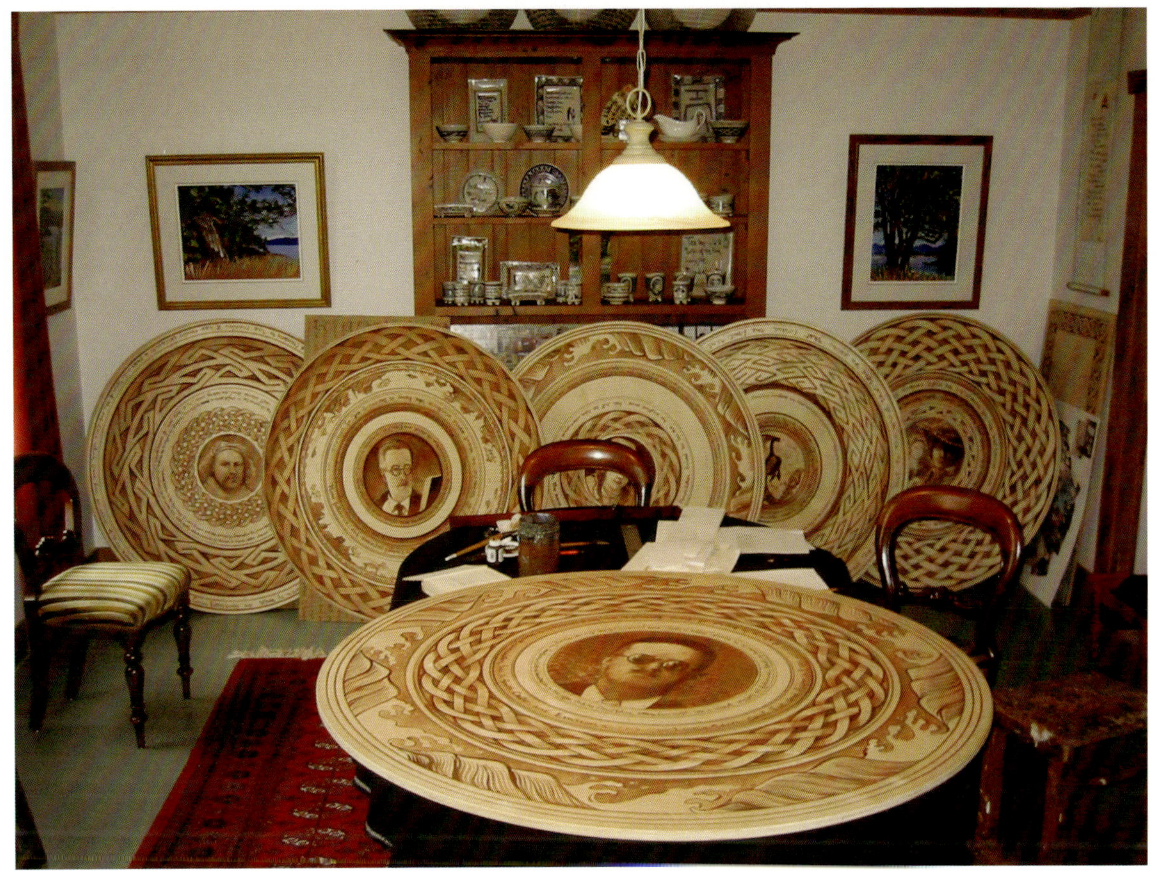

Robert Amos' gallery, Victoria, December 2006.

a time from a demanding husband whose appetite for dinner and art projects never seems to be satisfied. Her small room has heat and light, a view of the garden and no distractions at all.

In appreciation of the efforts she constantly makes to enable my creative expression, I dedicate this book to Sarah.

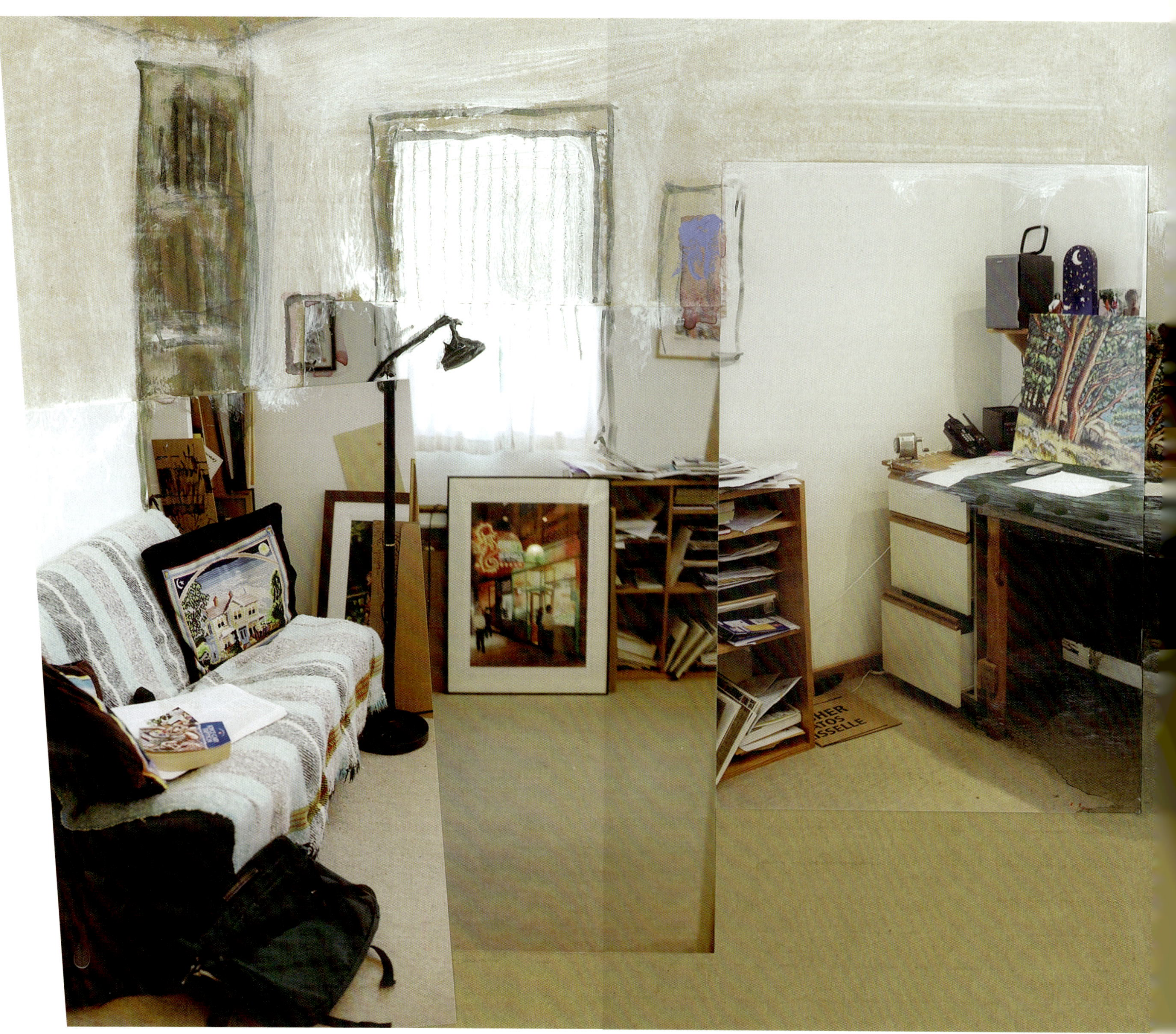

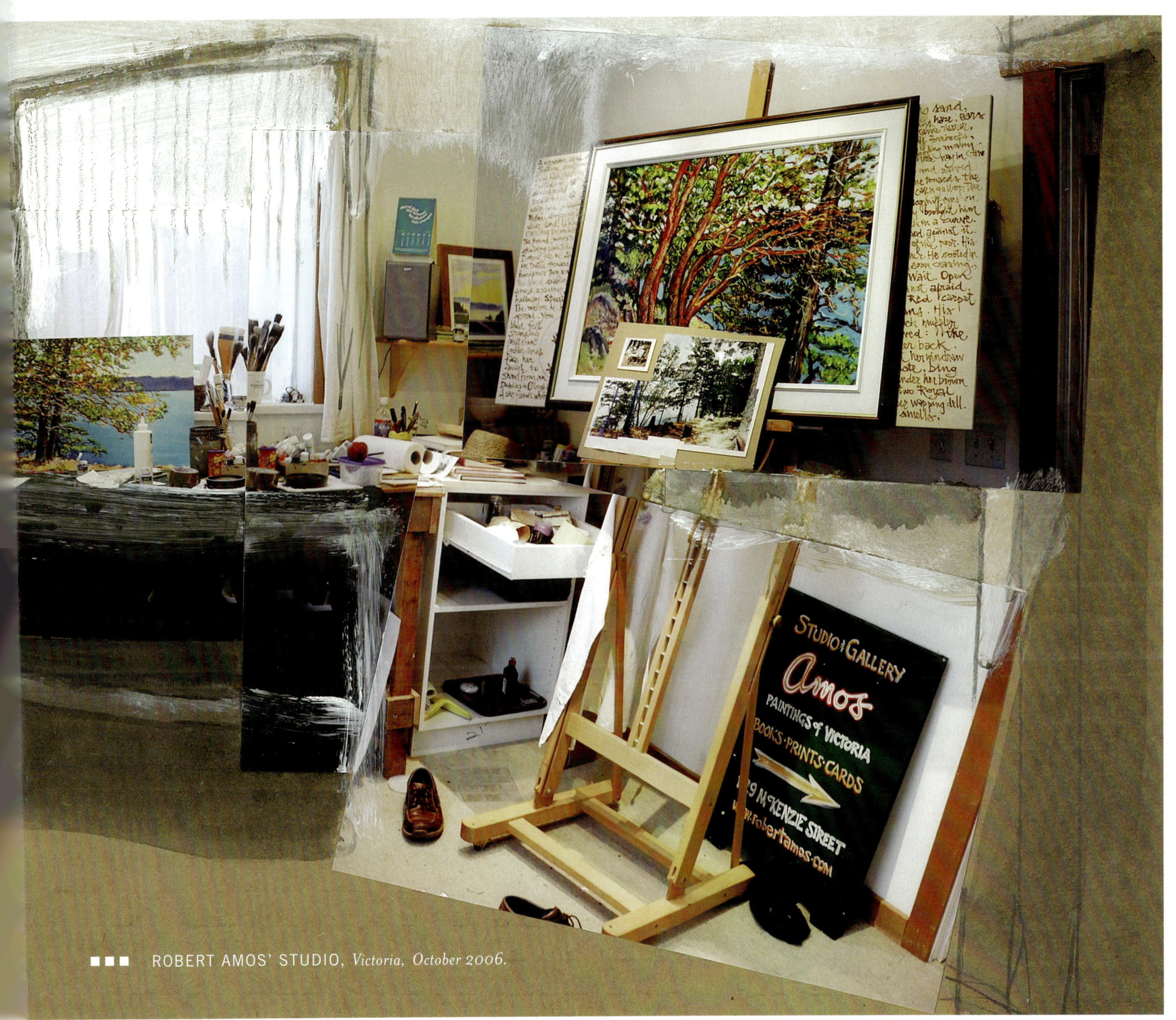

■■■ ROBERT AMOS' STUDIO, *Victoria, October 2006.*

ACKNOWLEDGMENTS

Unless otherwise noted, all photographs in this book were created by the author. The exception to this is the reproduction of some of the artworks; those images were provided by the artists for this publication.

For a project this complex, I owe thanks to many people. The artists and their families have been generous to my many requests. Others I would like to thank include:

Vicky Husband
Birgit Freybe Bateman and Alex Fischer
Murray and Leslie Glazier
Marguerite Chantreau
Irene Davies
Jacques Barbeau
Pat Salmon
Gunter Heinrich and Anthony Sam, Winchester Galleries
Dan Hudon, West End Gallery
Ian Copus
Lloyd Kahl
Kileasa Wong
Cindy Wang and Pou Yung
Bob Wright
Barbara at Copy Plus
Lucinda Chodan and Caroline Heiman at the *Times Colonist*
Martin Segger, Kerry Mason and Caroline Riedel at the Maltwood Museum, University of Victoria
and the people at TouchWood Editions, in particular Pat Touchie, Vivian Sinclair, Marlyn Horsdal, Susan Adamson and Jacqui Thomas.